A Dynamic Reading of the Holy Spirit in Revelation

A Dynamic Reading of the Holy Spirit in Revelation

A Theological Reflection on the Functional Role of the Holy Spirit in the Narrative

HEE YOUL LEE

WIPF & STOCK · Eugene, Oregon

A DYNAMIC READING OF THE HOLY SPIRIT IN REVELATION
A Theological Reflection on the Functional Role of the Holy Spirit in the Narrative

Copyright © 2014 Hee Youl Lee. All rights reserved. Except for brief quotations in critical publications or reviews, no part of this book may be reproduced in any manner without prior written permission from the publisher. Write: Permissions, Wipf and Stock Publishers, 199 W. 8th Ave., Suite 3, Eugene, OR 97401.

Wipf & Stock
An Imprint of Wipf and Stock Publishers
199 W. 8th Ave., Suite 3
Eugene, OR 97401

www.wipfandstock.com

ISBN 13: 978-1-62032-882-8

Manufactured in the U.S.A.

Unless otherwise stated, Scripture quotations are from the New Revised Standard Version Bible, copyright © 1989, Division of Christian Education of the National Council of the Churches of Christ in the United States of America. Used by permission. All rights reserved.

Contents

Foreword by Grant Macaskill　　vii

Foreword by Paul S. Kang　　ix

Preface　xiii

Acknowledgments　　xv

Summary　　xvii

1. Introduction　1
2. Narrator, Point of View of the Narrator, and the Holy Spirit in Revelation　32
3. Character Presentation of the Holy Spirit in Revelation　68
4. Plot and the Holy Spirit in Revelation　130
5. Structure and the Holy Spirit in Revelation　176
6. Concluding Remarks　239

Appendix: Tables for the Divine Frame of Reference in Revelation　255

Afterword by Gary G. Cohen　　267

Bibliography　269

Foreword

Although the situation is beginning to change, historically, New Testament scholarship has either neglected or minimized the pneumatology of John's Apocalypse. While the Christology of the book has been robustly and extensively treated, in relation to the representation of God, the portrayal of the Spirit has received little attention. John is widely considered to have a basic pneumatology, saying little about the Spirit by comparison to other parts of the New Testament corpus, with much of his use of "spirit" language understood to refer to angelic figures.

Hee Youl Lee's examination of the Holy Spirit in Revelation is, therefore, a welcome addition to scholarship on the book. Although not the only study to appear in recent years focused on this theme, it makes a distinctive and valuable contribution by taking seriously the narratival dimension of the Apocalypse. Revelation is a *story* and, as such, requires to be taken in its entirety, with the recognition that it may communicate ideas (and engage its audience) on more levels than just the surface meaning of its words. At the same time, that story interlocks a series of micro-stories and cycles, each with its own distinct patterns of reference, yet determined by the patterns occurring within the others. Taking this into account, Lee approaches the material using an appropriately complex methodology, utilizing various specific methods of literary analysis in order to identify the ways in which the Spirit is represented, even when not explicitly named. Crucially, too, the necessity of the readers' collective response to the Spirit, as part of the actualization of the narrative, is developed throughout the analysis.

As a result of this properly complex approach, Lee is able to develop a theological account of John's pneumatology. That is to say, his study is not simply a historically careful examination of John's pneumatology or an analysis of the text of Revelation: it is a reading of one part of the

Foreword by Grant Macaskill

New Testament that must speak to any attempt to develop Christian pneumatology, a doctrine inseparable from Christology and, of course, from the life of the church.

Grant Macaskill
Senior Lecturer, University of St. Andrews

Foreword

The author, Hee Youl Lee, sheds a new perspective on the book of Revelation. He portrays the book of Revelation as a mission oriented book of how the kingdom of God will be built in this world through spiritual warfare, rather than as a book of eschatology. He focuses exclusively on the Holy Spirit, while drawing from his experience, the spiritual revival occurring in the most densely Muslim populated country in the world. I'd like to recommend this book because I believe that this book will serve as a wake-up call to the modern Church and the people of God by reviving them from their spiritual recession through an accurate portrayal of the Holy Spirit and a vivid description of spiritual warfare.

Lee takes an unconventional method of approaching the book of Revelation. In fact, he utilizes *a dynamic reading* of the Holy Spirit. This book employs recent literary methods to uncover the plot and structure of Revelation while illuminating the characters in the narrative as well as the narrator perspective. He succeeds in overcoming the repeated failure of historical-critical scholars to define both the real author and the real readers of the book of Revelation by offering new insight on both the implicit author and implicit readers. Lee guides readers through the book of Revelation, scrutinizing its text rather than its contextual and historical background and discovering the story of Revelation and both its narrator and its narratee. Thus, I recommend this book to readers who want to gain new insight about the book of Revelation, as the author does a fantastic job of seamlessly incorporating the storyline as well as offering insight as to who the intended audience is as well as going in depth about the narrator.

Taking into consideration his background in secular study such as Economics and Business Administration, he efficiently converges the secular literary theories into the theological study of the book of

Foreword by Paul S. Kang

Revelation. Lee manages to overcome the limitations of adopting literary theory. Instead of viewing Scripture as an ancient passive literary work without Divine impact, Lee recognizes the book of Revelation as definitely God's work as well as the book inspired by the Holy Spirit. Lee succeeds in unveiling the role of the Holy Spirit in the book of Revelation. Particularly, his illumination of the Holy Spirit as a divine frame of reference for the first person character and narrator, John, who is in the Spirit, shows a fresh and unique perspective that helps us understand the role of the Holy Spirit in the whole narrative of the book of Revelation. According to Lee, we cannot avoid noticing the significant impact of the Holy Spirit on John, as evident in his activities in the narrative.

By carefully observing the direct expressions of the Holy Spirit, Lee discovers that these expressions are recorded nineteen times in the book of Revelation whereas the traditional consensus claims that it is eighteen times. Moreover, the characters of the Book are well researched according to the characterization theory, with which we will be able to get the information of how we can analyze the characters in the biblical narratives. This book contains the tools of characterization that serve to explain how to study the characters in the narrative as a whole. The author focuses on the characterization of the Holy Spirit according to the title of his book. However it can be applied to the other characters in the narrative of Revelation such as Jesus, God, angels, etc. I believe Lee's innovative methods and fresh perspective offer us a new way of studying the different characters not only in the book of Revelation, but also in the whole Bible!

This book depicts a new way of studying the Bible by applying many literary elements such as the plot, point of view, narrator, story, and various structures, as well as the characters. The narrative approach mentioned in this book may be also applied to the study of the apocalyptic books in the Old Testaments as well as the Gospels and Acts in the New Testament. This is why I strongly recommend this book to those who are interested in finding new ways to study the Bible, as well as to pastors and theological students.

This book will also contribute to broaden the systematic understanding of the Holy Spirit in the Bible. Thus, I want to recommend

Foreword by Paul S. Kang

this book to anyone who wants to understand the more wholesome systematical picture of the Holy Spirit in the Bible. The author reads the book of Revelation as a "reflective practitioner" in the missiological perspective just as he was a pioneer to open our view in both biblical theology and systematic theology.

I believe that Lee was under guidance of the Holy Spirit as he was researching, analyzing, and writing this book, because the Holy Spirit wants to reveal Himself to the saints more clearly, and is making Himself known through Lee and this book. I consider this book to be guided by the Holy Spirit because of the difficulty for a hardworking missionary to finish such a creative book while serving in the mission field.

Finally I would like to deeply recommend this book with my whole heart to everyone because all who read this book will be able to enjoy a deeper fellowship with the Holy Spirit; more intimate and closer than ever felt before.

Dr. Rev. Paul S. Kang, ThD, PhD
Founder and Former President of Cohen University and
Theological Seminary (CUTS)

Preface

My research began in the remote villages of Indonesia. I was working in the field as a missionary whilst donning the cloak of a researcher. The words of John Stott echoed in my head. He stated during his lecture at Oxford University, "It must be the most difficult job in the world to be a research student in the United Kingdom." Not only was I learning a new language but also adapting to a new culture. I also served as a professor in a local Indonesian university teaching Accounting and Economics. Thus, conducting my research on the book of Revelation took a backseat to all the other activities, a spare-time and after-hours activity at best. I attempted to stop my research several times but each time I was encouraged by the Holy Spirit to continue.

Another motive in continuing my research comes from recognizing that the book of Revelation has been widely misunderstood as an eschatological book that serves to explain the time of when Jesus will come again. This conveyed message negatively impacted the churches. Believers were focusing on waiting for the last day to arrive, neglecting their duties to preach the gospel to nonbelievers. The churches were also threatened by the dispensationalism, which was based on a misunderstanding of the book of Revelation as well as the terrorism of the Muslim extremists. These reasons are why I believed that the "true" main theme of the book of Revelation had not been uncovered yet. Moreover, I recognized the importance of the role of the Holy Spirit among the churches. The conservative churches tended to altogether disregard the role of the Holy Spirit, while the charismatic churches depicted the Holy Spirit solely as a producer of miracles. That is why I focused on the overall role of the Holy Spirit throughout the book of Revelation.

My method of adopting the literary approach, that is, the narrative approach, to read the book of Revelation in a new way was due to the failure of scholars in coming to a consensus about the book of Revelation

Preface

using their traditional hermeneutics. I believe that this narrative approach opens a new window of understanding for the main theme of the story in the book of Revelation. I utilize the characterization theory to scrutinize the plot and structure of the book of Revelation that helps guide readers in understanding the book of Revelation as a whole.

The messianic war and the conversion of all nations can be considered the main theme of the book of Revelation. The role of the Holy Spirit is vital in the messianic war and the conversion of all nations. It means that churches must participate in the messianic war in their daily lives. The churches must take part in actively converting all nations under the guidance of the Holy Spirit. If readers correctly interpret the book of Revelation, they will be alert, and with the guidance of the Holy Spirit, will be aware of the messianic war and actively involved in the conversion of all nations.

I discovered that the Holy Spirit plays a significant role as a divine frame of reference in the narrative of the book of Revelation, especially since the main character, John, was in the Spirit when he experienced all the visions and events. The identity of the Holy Spirit is clearly displayed through direct and indirect characterization. The works of the Holy Spirit can be traced along the four levels and six stages plot as well as the five types of the structure of the book of Revelation.

I hope this book is helpful for those who are striving to understand the book of Revelation as well as the Holy Spirit in it. I pray that the churches will be blessed by uncovering the true meaning behind the book of Revelation in such a way that they will go and make disciples of all nations and live in accordance with the Holy Spirit.

Rev. Hee Youl Lee, PhD
President, CUTSI (Cohen University and
Theological Seminary Indonesia)

Acknowledgments

I want to dedicate this study to the Holy Spirit who has guided me in the whole process of writing. I really appreciate Robert Forrest, my first supervisor, for his encouragement and patience. He motivated a missionary to decide to start this study and helped a non-native speaker overcome many barriers to become a research student. I would also like to acknowledge the kind supervision of John Nolland as my second supervisor. None of this would have been possible without the sacrifices that my lovely wife, Wonsun Park, and my dear children, Jaisung, Jairyung, and Jaemin made for me. I wholeheartedly give thanks to them for their support through prayer and for encouraging me through the hard times. I also appreciate my sister Bongsoon Lee, Bundang Jungang Church for choosing me as a scholarship recipient, Rev. Munsoo Hong of Shinbanpo Church, and The First Presbyterian Korean Church in Hartford, Connecticut, for their dedication in supporting me financially. I appreciate my Indonesian friends, including Jamli Barus, Augus Sinaga, and Yakub Santoya, who have encouraged and prayed for me. I also appreciate my missionary colleagues Jaekyo Jung and Eben Park for their help. I thank Rev. Oh Abraham and other pastors in Global Ministry Development for their sincere prayers in the Holy Spirit. I also cannot forget all of my prayer supporters, especially my mother for unceasing prayer for her son. Finally I appreciate Grant Macaskill who recommended that I publish my dissertation as a book in VIVA as an external examiner. My thanks to Dr. Paul S. Kang, who appointed me as president of Cohen University and Theological Seminary, Indonesian Campus. I dedicate my book to all of the aforementioned people.

Dr. Paul Bagio Hee Youl Lee
From the hillside on Mt. Merbabu, Indonesia

Summary

Thematically, this study focuses on the Holy Spirit. Methodologically it employs the literary approach. More specifically, it is called a "dynamic biblical narrative approach." In view of this approach, I read the text of Revelation as "a final and unified form of ancient and canonical narrative" in which the Holy Spirit is rhetorically presented as a "divine character" and a "divine frame of reference." The dynamic interaction among the implied author or the narrator, the text, and the implied reader has been considered. It presupposes that the book of Revelation is not only an apocalyptic and prophetic letter, but also a narrative since apocalyptic literature usually has a story. The narrative approach presupposes that the implied author and the implied audience can be traced from the narrative.

This study attempts to prove how the Holy Spirit affects the narrative of Revelation through the narrator. The literary theories of the narrator and the divine frame of reference applied in this study illuminate that the Holy Spirit plays a significant role in the whole narrative by generating the viewpoint of the narrator as a divine frame of reference. This study also proves that the direct character-presentation theory presents the Divine Spirit as the Holy, Divine, Complete (or perfect), Life-giving and Prophetic Spirit of God and Jesus. The theory of characterization along the indirect character-presentation shows that the Divine Spirit is an enigmatic character with both person-likeness and person-unlikeness.

This study has examined the characterization of the Holy Spirit along the plot as well as the structure of Revelation. The Holy Spirit is characterized to be multi-functional: God-like, Angel-like, and Person-like. Above all, a new definition in the plot of Revelation is proposed in this study: a sixfold and four-level scheme plot. A new definition of the five types of structures within Revelation is also proposed: narrative-syntactic structure, fundamental-syntactic structure, narrative-semantic structure, fundamental-semantic structure, and pragmatic structure.

Summary

With a dynamic reading of the Holy Spirit, readers may more concretely than ever before understand who the Holy Spirit is and what functions the Holy Spirit carries out in Revelation. The intention is that this study will become a steppingstone for future studies in the book of Revelation.

1

Introduction

During the approach of the new millennium, Revelation[1] received significant attention from both New Testament scholars and Christian groups.[2] Some of this attention produced new insights while some simply registered current social anxiety.[3] Amongst many issues relating to Revelation, the topic of the Holy Spirit has been one of the least discussed. This is surprising since the Holy Spirit has been extensively discussed in relation to other New Testament books. The first reason for this scholarly neglect has been terminology. The phrases, "the Holy Spirit" or "the Spirit of God" are missing from Revelation.[4] Nonetheless, there are three categories of parallel references to the Holy Spirit: *the Seven Spirits* (τῶν ἑπτὰ πνευμάτων), *in the spirit* (ἐν πνεύματι), and *the Spirit* (τὸ πνεῦμα).[5] But although these three phrases are assumed to stand in place

---

1. In this study, Revelation means the book of Revelation in most cases. Rev also represents Revelation, meaning the book of Revelation in the whole text. Where the term "revelation" is intended to mean "disclosures by God," a lowercase "r" is used.

2. The use and abuse of the book of Revelation has been quite remarkable in times of great danger and periods leading to a change of eras. The third millennium has fed a renewed desire to decipher the message that lies at the heart of Revelation. Desrosiers, *Introduction to Revelation*, 2.

3. In the period leading up to and following the turn of the millennium (the year AD 2000) there has been much interest in apocalyptic ideas and thus also in the eschatology of Revelation. For the history of the interpretations of Revelation in AD 1550–1900, see Newport's *Apocalypse and Millennium*.

4. Aune, *Revelation 1–5*, 36.

5. Bauckham, *Climax of Prophecy*, 150.

of "the Holy Spirit," there remains wide disagreement about the use of the terms.[6] The second reason is the "comparative rarity of references" to the Spirit in Revelation—only eighteen occurrences, compared with many references to and ways of referring to both God and Christ.[7] Bauckham, however, notes that despite this comparative rarity of explicit references "it would be a mistake to conclude that in the theology of Revelation the Spirit is unimportant."[8] Indeed, Bauckham argues rightly that the central role of the Spirit in Revelation has been disregarded in theological studies. The third reason is related to methodology. The majority of studies in the last two decades have been dominated either by the historical-critical approach or the socio-rhetorical approach.[9] But, as Du Rand has argued, the *narratological* literary approach may better highlight the function of the Holy Spirit in Revelation since "each viewpoint sees the message of Revelation from a different angle."[10] Now while the narratological approach is gaining in favor, there has correspondingly been a renewed interest in the *function* of the Spirit in Revelation.

Given the narrative critical approach's potential fruitfulness in disclosing the role of the Holy Spirit in Revelation, this will—with certain adaptations—be the chosen method of study in this book.

Firstly, however, I will briefly review several recent scholars' analyses of the Holy Spirit in Revelation: those of F. F. Bruce, D. E. Aune, R. Bauckham, R. L. Jeske, and J. C. de Smidt, since they have observed the Holy Spirit in Revelation by adopting their own approaches. Then, I will offer my own methodological approach, namely, *a dynamic narrative approach* of the Holy Spirit in Revelation. Afterwards I will provide a theological reflection on the function of the Holy Spirit in the messianic war and the messianic feast in Revelation, both of whose themes I will later argue are central to the book.

---

6. The wide disagreement over interpretation of *the Seven Spirits, the spirit*, and *in the spirit* will be shown later in this chapter.

7. Bauckham, *Theology of the Book*, 109. According to Bauckham, The Alpha and the Omega, The One who is and was and is to come, The Lord God The Almighty, and The One who sits in the throne are used seven times each (66). God the mighty is used two times (30). Other designations of God, like "Creator," are used many times in Revelation. Jesus' name is used fourteen times, Christ is used seven times, and The Lamb is used twenty-eight times in Revelation (66–67).

8. Ibid., 109.

9. Various interpretational approaches to Revelation will be elucidated in the following paragraphs.

10. Du Rand, "Your Kingdom Come," 75.

Introduction

I hope, by means of the *dynamic narrative-critical approach* both to offer new viewpoints on the function of the Holy Spirit in Revelation and also thereby to offer resolutions to some of the existing scholarly controversies.

Previous Studies of the Holy Spirit in Revelation

F. F. Bruce

F. F. Bruce's *The Spirit in the Apocalypse* attempts to classify the Holy Spirit in Revelation using four categories of reference: (1) the *Seven Spirits*, (2) the *Spirit of prophecy*, (3) what *the Spirit says to the Churches*, and (4) the *responsive Spirit*.[11] We will consider each of these phrases in turn. [NL 1–4]

1. As for the *Seven Spirits* (Rev 1:4; 3:1; 4:5; 5:6), Bruce criticizes R. H. Charles's view as speculative that "the Seven Spirits" in 1:4 were "an early interpolation."[12] Indeed, remarks Bruce, Charles follows "a precarious course in default of textual support."[13] Bruce also dismisses as speculative Victorinus of Pettau's interpretation of the Seven Spirits "in the context of Trinitarian orthodoxy."[14] Thus, Victorinus read Isaiah 11:2 as "a reference to the personal Spirit of God in his sevenfold plenitude of grace" and then used this interpretation as a key to Rev 1:4.[15] Instead, Bruce argues that the Seven Spirits in Revelation are to be treated as "the one Holy Spirit" sent out into all the earth for the prophetic ministry of Christian prophets in the world.[16] Thus, Bruce firstly draws attention to the location of the Seven Spirits "before the throne of God" (1:4b), which he notes is God's heavenly dwelling place according to 4:5.

Secondly, Bruce points out that the Seven Spirits are depicted as "attributes or accessories of the risen Christ" in 3:1 and 5:6. They are thus integrally linked to both Christ and God. In this respect, Bruce notes

---

11. Bruce, *The Spirit in the Apocalypse*, 333–44.
12. Charles, *Critical and Exegetical Commentary*, 9, 11. Charles argues that "the Seven Spirits are to be identified with the seven archangels" (11) since it is "a redactional addition of the Seer" (12). He seeks to verify this claim from 1 Enoch (13).
13. Bruce, *The Spirit in the Apocalypse*, 334.
14. Ibid.
15. Ibid.
16. Ibid., 334–37.

Revelation's allusion by means of the Seven Spirits to Zechariah 4:2, 10b where the seven lamps are described as "the eyes of Yahweh, which range throughout the whole earth."[17] These seven eyes are associated in Zechariah with the prophetic ministry of the two olive trees, who are also alluded to in Rev 11:4.

2. As to Rev 19:10, Bruce insists that "the Spirit of prophecy" is the Spirit who "bears his testimony in the witnesses of Jesus," that is, through Christian prophets.[18] Bruce also identifies parallel usages of this phrase in the Targum of Jonathan, which in commenting on Isaiah 61:1, says, "The Spirit of prophecy from before the Lord God is upon me." Bruce also notes a similarity to the phrase, "the Spirit of prophecy" (19:10) in 1 Peter 1:11, which speaks of "the Spirit of the Messiah." The Spirit of the Messiah may, Bruce argues, be *the Spirit of messianic prophecy*. Thus, according to Bruce, in the phrase μαρτυρία Ἰησοῦ in Rev 19:10, the genitive form of "Jesus" is "most probably objective."[19] That is, the testimony *of* Jesus is the testimony *about* Jesus.

Bruce then connects the phrase "the Spirit of prophecy" to the phrase "in the Spirit," which represents that "the Spirit of prophecy comes upon John" (1:10; 4:2) and that he is carried away to an "appropriate vantage-point"[20] (17:3; 21:10). To explain these two concepts, Bruce finds "the nearest approach to this phraseology"[21] from Ezekiel 37:1: "The hand of Yahweh was upon me and carried me out in the Spirit of Yahweh."

3. With respect to what "the Spirit says to the churches" (Rev 2–3), Bruce concludes, "it is not that the Spirit is identical with the exalted Lord, but that the exalted Lord speaks to the churches by the Spirit and the Spirit can scarcely be other than the Spirit of prophecy."[22] He also detects parallel supportive usages from Rev 3:3; 16:15; Matt 24:43; Luke 12:39; and the Odes of Solomon 42:4, 6.[23]

---

17. Ibid., 335.
18. Ibid., 339, 337.
19. Ibid., 338.
20. Ibid., 340.
21. Ibid.
22. Ibid.
23. Ibid., 342.

4. Bruce also writes of what he calls "the responsive Spirit" (Rev 14:13; 22:17a), which he understands to be the same as the Spirit of prophecy. Although the words, "the responsive Spirit" do not appear in the Bible, Bruce uses this term to classify Scriptures in Revelation in which the spirit responds. He suggests that the responsive Spirit in 22:17a can be interpreted as the Spirit "indwelling the beloved community."[24]

To summarize, F. F. Bruce employs mostly a historical-critical approach.[25] By this means, he argues that the Holy Spirit in Revelation is primarily represented as *the Spirit of prophecy*, which highlights the Spirit's function as communicating truths about the Messiah, Jesus, through the prophetic community.

D. E. Aune

In commentaries on the book of Revelation, studies of the Holy Spirit tend to be woven into exegesis rather than treated as specific topics. Such an approach is found in Aune whose three-volume commentary on Revelation presents "wide-ranging surveys of scholarship throughout, much more inclusive than those found in other works on Revelation."[26]

Aune insists that the concept of the Spirit in Revelation has been changed through the compositional history of Revelation.[27] In the earlier stage of redaction, the role and function of the Spirit is concerned with the inspiration process of Revelation itself, as indicated by the phrase, "in the spirit."[28] Aune thus explains that the spirit mediates the apocalyptic vision through the experience of the seer.[29] However, he contends that

24. Ibid., 343.

25. Actually, Bruce adopted various kinds of interpretational methodology in his study. However, I found that the historical-critical approach is used dominantly in his study of the Holy Spirit. In this study, the historical-critical approach is understood to focus on the historical background of the text with a view to discovering the meaning of the text. It may include redaction criticism, form criticism, sociological criticism, etc. It is used to be compared with the new literary criticism which focuses on the text itself to find the meaning of the text, including narrative criticism.

26. Duff, *Who Rides the Beast?*, 218.

27. Aune, *Revelation 1–5*, 36. Bruce recognizes the words "the Spirit" as the Holy Spirit and therefore capitalizes "the Spirit." Aune, on the other hand, does not agree that "the spirit" is the Holy Spirit, and therefore does not capitalize the words. Out of respect for the various scholars and their views, this and other terms have been capitalized or lowercased accordingly.

28. Ibid.

29. Ibid.

the phrase "in the spirit" does not mean that the seer is "in the Holy Spirit," but rather that the seer is not "in his mind,"[30] that is, he is caught up in an ecstatic trance. In short, Aune altogether denies that "in the spirit" refers to the Holy Spirit in the accepted sense.

Aune's conclusion about in the spirit arises from his use of a historico-grammatical interpretation method. Thus, he examines parallel usages of these phrases from the Old Testament (Micah 3:8) and the Apostolic Fathers (the Didache and Barnabas).[31] He also finds similar usages within the New Testament itself, especially the letters of Paul, and offers grammatical studies of the usage of "ἐν πνεύματι" in the New Testament.[32] From his survey, Aune concludes that in the spirit is usually used as an *instrumental* sense to refer to the spiritual experience of the recipient of a revelation. For Aune, this study illuminates the particular meaning John gives to pneumatological terminology, namely, "John's revelatory experiences took place not 'in the body,' but rather 'in the spirit.'"[33]

Aune then argues that the emphasis shifts in the last stage of Revelation's redaction with the advent of the phrase, "the spirit of prophecy." Now, the function of the Spirit in Revelation is to speak to the churches, since the "Spirit" is used as a subject of the verb, "speaks" (λέγει). As mentioned above, Aune maintains that this usage is a late interpolation in Revelation's compositional history.[34] Indeed, Aune similarly claims (though with minimal evidence) that chapters 2 and 3 were inserted into the text at the same compositional stage. Thus, Aune presupposes, in the traditional mode of historical criticism, that the biblical literature had been edited in several identifiable sequences or layers. Despite these clear, if speculative assertions, Aune is unclear whether "the spirit of prophecy" in Rev 19:10a represents the Holy Spirit or not. Through his investigation of the church fathers of the second and third centuries, Aune concludes that the spirit of prophecy represents the *power* that allows someone to have visionary experiences and to bear witness to Jesus.[35] In Rev 22:6, Aune argues that "the spirits of prophets" does not refer to the Holy Spirit, but rather to the human spirits of those who are called to

30. Ibid., 83.
31. Ibid., 82.
32. Ibid., 83.
33. Ibid.
34. Ibid., 36.
35. Aune, *Revelation 17–22*, 1034–38.

be prophetic tools of the Holy Spirit.[36] He regards 1 Cor 14:32, "and the spirits of prophets are subject to the prophets," as supporting evidence for this interpretation.[37]

As for the Seven Spirits in Rev 1:4d; 3:1; 4:5; 5:6, Aune argues that these are identifiable with the seven (arch) angels in Rev 8:2.[38] His evidence comes from early Jewish literature, including the Old Testament and the Qumran scrolls.[39] Similarly, Aune cites Hebrews 1:14, which also describes angels as spirits. Following through his analysis, Aune insists that the "seven stars" in Rev 3:1, which represents the Seven Spirits of God, are angels. On the basis of this evidence, Aune concludes that Rev 1:4; 3:1; 4:5; 5:6 identify the Seven Spirits of God with the seven archangels in a way that is typical of contemporary Jewish angelology.

In short, Aune concludes that the use of language about the spirit in Revelation does not denote the Holy Spirit, but ranges in meaning from ecstatic trances to angelic presences. Aune's interpretation of Revelation assumes an identifiable redactional history, during which ideas have been introduced and developed. He also attempts to interpret the meaning of the spirit from the background usage of the spirit in Jewish literature. Thus, Aune's study of the spirit suggests that the earlier and later stages of revelation show no interest in any ontological "Holy Spirit" but rather in phenomenological descriptions of states of mind—of what is happening to prophets.

However, I find that Aune is sometimes unclear about the role of the Holy Spirit in his writing. He seems to accept that the Holy Spirit has a role in mediating the apocalyptic vision of John in Revelation when

36. Ibid., 1182.

37. Ibid.

38. Aune, *Revelation 1–5*, 219. Aune summarizes that there have been three interpretations of the Seven Spirits: seven astral deities, the Holy Spirit, and the seven archangels. He disagrees with the first two interpretations. According to him, the first interpretation is based on the emphasis on the situation in East Asia where worship of seven astral deities was common. The second interpretation is based on two pre-conceptions: the misunderstanding of the seven gifts of the Holy Spirit in Isaiah 11:2–3 as the Seven Spirits; and the assumption that the Seven Spirits are the fullness of the Holy Spirit which arises from an anachronistic preconception of the Holy Trinity. However, he argues for the third interpretation, that is, that the Seven Spirits are the seven archangels, based on his investigation from Jewish literature.

39. Aune argues that in early Jewish literature spirits usually mean demonic spirits. For example, *T. Reu.* 2:1–9 speaks of the Seven Spirits of deceit given to man by Beliar. He also argues that in Qumran Scroll 4Q405 23 I 8–9 the host of angels parallels the host of the spirit. Aune, *Revelation 1–5*, 34.

John was in the spirit with this description: "the Holy Spirit mediates the vision of apocalypse through the experience of the seer."[40] But this seems illogical since he does not accept that "in the spirit" means "in the Holy Spirit" in Revelation, but rather refers to ecstatic trances (that is, "in the spirit" is a psychological designation).

R. J. Bauckham

Both Bruce and Aune share a common methodology, that is, the historical-critical approach, to interpret the same subject, the spirit in Revelation.[41] However, their results were quite different. One argues that the spirit in Revelation represents the Holy Spirit. The other insists that there is no ontological description of the Holy Spirit in Revelation. This result in the study of the spirit in Revelation might be caused by the traditional historical-critical approach, even if not totally, but partially. In this situation, Bauckham attempted to use a sort of brand new methodology to break through the difficulty in interpreting the spirit in Revelation.[42] He employed not only the historical-critical approach, but also a new literary critical approach and a canonical approach to study the spirit in Revelation. It seems to shine a light to interpret the spirit in Revelation.[43]

Bauckham wrote two articles on the theme of the Holy Spirit in Revelation: one in each of his two books about Revelation.[44] These two articles register Bauckham's special theological interest in the theme of the Holy Spirit in Revelation. First of all, in search of the theological significance of the spirit in Revelation, Bauckham reviews the statistical frequency of the terms *the spirit* or *the Seven Spirits* and applies numerological principles

---

40. Ibid., 36.

41. As mentioned above, the historical-critical approach is understood in this study to focus on the historical background of the text with a view to discovering the meaning of the text. It may include redaction criticism, form criticism, sociological criticism, etc. It is used to be compared with the new literary criticism which focuses on the text itself to find the meaning of the text, including narrative criticism.

42. Chronologically Aune's commentaries were published later than Bauckham's books. However, in the perspective of interpretative methodology of the spirit in Revelation, Bauckham used more synthetic methodology than Aune.

43. Actually Bauckham opened the interpretive window of not just the study of the spirit in Revelation, but also the whole book of Revelation.

44. Bauckham wrote two books on Revelation in 1993: *The Theology of the Book of Revelation* and *The Climax of Prophecy*. The first includes a chapter called "The Spirit of Prophecy" and the second a chapter titled, "The Role of the Spirit."

Introduction

to the patterns he finds. Thus, in the apocalyptic tradition, four represents "the number of the world" (the four winds, the four corners of the earth, and so on), whereas seven (four plus the divine threefold) is "the number of completeness."[45] It is significant, therefore, that the phrase, "the Seven Spirits" appears four times in Revelation. Bauckham also suggests that there is a numerological link between the victorious Lamb and the Seven Spirits (5:6) since there are twenty-eight references to the Lamb (that is, four times seven). In short, the four references to the Seven Spirits "indicate that the Lamb's victory is implemented throughout the world by the fullness of divine power."[46] In addition, there are fourteen references to the spirit. These, Bauckham classifies into four groups: (1) the seven repeated phrases that the Spirit speaks to the seven churches (Rev 2:7, 11, 17, 29; 3:6, 13, 22); (2) the four usages of the phrase, "in the spirit" (1:10; 4:2; 17:3; 21:10), which he regards as chiastic signposts by which to read Revelation[47]; (3) the "two citing words of the spirit" (14:13; 22:17), and (4) only one usage of "the spirit of prophecy" (19:10), whereas the term "prophecy" itself appears seven times in Revelation (1:3; 11:6; 19:10; 22:7, 10, 18, 19). These identifiable patterns reflect, for Bauckham, deliberately crafted theological messages embedded in the text of Revelation that readers are intended to notice. In short, this represents Bauckham's attempt to employ a literary approach that examines the final text itself, not the background of the text, to study the Holy Spirit in Revelation.

Secondly, Bauckham tries to analyze the relationship between Revelation and early Jewish apocalyptic literature (including that in the Old Testament) in order to identify the meaning of the spirit and the Seven Spirits in Revelation. Thus, by using the historical-critical approach, he

---

45. Bauckham, *Theology of the Book*, 109. Bauckham argues that "the Seven Spirits are the fullness of God's power 'sent out into all the earth'" (Rev 5:6). Similarly, he suggests that the fourfold phrase "every tribe and language and people and nation," which represents the whole people of God, is used seven times (5:9; 7:9; 10:11; 11:9; 13:7; 14:6; 17:15).

46. Bauckham, *Theology of the Book*, 109.

47. Bauckham attempts to identify the structural signposts of Revelation in accordance with it being a book to be read aloud as a literary performance before a congregation (Rev 1:3). In this context, he asserts that "in the spirit" is a literary cue for the reader. That is why Bauckham divides the structure of Revelation into four sections: chapters 1–3 (the vision of risen Christ), 4–16 (the vision of the heavenly throne), 17–20 (the vision of the destruction of the evil ones), and 21–22 (the vision of New Jerusalem) according to "in the spirit" in chapter 1 of his *Climax of Prophecy*. Bauckham, *Theology of the Book*, 1–37.

seeks to decode several problematic phrases related to the Holy Spirit in Revelation.

As for "the Seven Spirits" before God's throne (Rev 1:4), Bauckham argues that these "should be understood as a symbol for the Divine Spirit," not as just another way of speaking of the seven archangels.[48] He suggests two reasons for his argument. The first is that Rev 1:4 refers to the Seven Spirits in a "quite different" way from how Rev 8:2 and Tob 12:15 refer to the seven angels.[49] The second reason is that the term spirit is "never" used for the angels in Revelation, and "very rarely" in early Christian literature, even though it "could certainly be used of angels frequently in the Dead Sea Scrolls."[50] Further, Bauckham finds support for his case from Zechariah 4:1–14. He argues that John uses the vision of "seven lamps" that are described as "the eyes of the Lord" in Zech 4:2, 10 to depict the Divine Spirit in Revelation.[51] Just as the seven *lamps*, that is, the *eyes* of the Lord in Zechariah are before God, so *the Seven Spirits* in Rev 1:4 are also before God.[52] In consequence, Bauckham is able to draw an important parallel between two passages in Revelation itself: the Seven Spirits are attributed to God in Rev 1:4, and 5:6 speaks of "the eyes of the Lamb."[53] Therefore Bauckham concludes that the Seven Spirits in Revelation are identifiable with the Divine Spirit.

In explaining the relationship between seven horns and seven eyes in Rev 5:6, Bauckham appeals to the message of the prophet Hanani in 2 Chr 16:7–9. He insists that Hanani not only makes "verbal allusion to Zech 4:10b," that is, "the eyes of the Lord range throughout the entire earth," but also links the eyes of the Lord to *the strength of the Lord to perform deeds through his servants*.[54] He argues that John makes this link to show that the Seven Spirits are linked to the seven horns, which represent the conquering power of the victorious Lamb. According to Bauckham, therefore, "the Seven Spirits are sent out into all the earth to make" the Lamb's victory "effective throughout the world."[55]

---

48. Ibid., 110.
49. Ibid.
50. Bauckham, *Theology of the Book*, 110; Bauckham, *Climax of Prophecy*, 163.
51. Bauckham, *Climax of Prophecy*, 162.
52. Bauckham, *Theology of the Book*, 110.
53. Ibid., 111.
54. See Bauckham, *Theology of the Book*, 112; and *Climax of Prophecy*, 164.
55. See Bauckham, *Theology of the Book*, 112; and *Climax of Prophecy*, 164–65.

Introduction

Bauckham notes the way in which John recasts Zech 4:14 in Rev 3:1 and 11:3–13. John derives his "the two witnesses" (11:3–13) from Zechariah's two olive trees and two lampstands (4:2–3, 14). For John, the seven lamps, which represent the Seven Spirits,[56] empower the two lampstands, which represent the two witnesses who testify the truth to the world. As to the *two* witnesses themselves, Bauckham regards them representatively as the true testimony of the church to Jesus Christ in every city on earth. This interpretation rests on the Law in Deuteronomy, that states: "A single witness shall not suffice to convict a person of any crime or wrongdoing . . . Only on the evidence of two or three witnesses shall a charge be sustained" (Deut 19:15). Since the church's witness to Jesus Christ is *true*, it is best represented by *the two witnesses*. Thus, the Seven Spirits are related to the two witnesses as the Spirit's voice of prophecy is related to the church's witness to the world.

In short, Bauckham argues that the Seven Spirits are the power of the truth sent by the conquering Lamb so that the churches may be faithful witnesses to his victory of the whole earth.[57] Bauckham also holds that John has been influenced in his reading of Zechariah, by Zechariah's declaration of the power of the Spirit in Zech 4:6b, "'Not by might, not by power, but by my Spirit' says the Lord of hosts."[58] Indeed, Bauckham believes John has given a comprehensive doctrine of the Holy Spirit in Revelation: "The Seven Spirits in Revelation represent the fullness of the Divine Spirit in relation to God, to Christ and to the church's mission to the whole world," whereas the spirit stands for "the activity of the Spirit through the Christian prophets within the churches."[59]

As for the phrase "in the spirit," Bauckham identifies two groups of four usages in Revelation. The first of the two pairs of usages is Rev 1:10; 4:2 in which John says, "I was in the spirit." The other is Rev 17:3; 21:10 in which the angel carries John away "in the spirit." To discover John's understanding of in the spirit, Bauckham emphasizes that "we must first enquire into the precedents in Jewish literature."[60] From the analysis of

---

56. See Bauckham, *Theology of the Book*, 111; *Climax of Prophecy*, 163; and Zech 4:10b, "these seven (lamps) are the eyes of the Lord." Bauckham understands that the seven lamps can be understood as the Seven Spirits through Rev 5:6, which says that the Seven Spirits are the seven eyes and seven horns of the Lamb.

57. Bauckham, *Theology of the Book*, 113–15.

58. Bauckham, *Climax of Prophecy*, 164.

59. Bauckham, *Theology of the Book*, 115. The term "the spirit," which is singular, is used fourteen times in Revelation.

60. Bauckham, *Climax of Prophecy*, 154.

parallel usages of "in the spirit" in Jewish literature such as Num 24:2, 4, 16–17; 11:24–29; 1 Sam 10:6, 10; Ezek 3:12, 14; 8:3; 11:1, 24; 37:1; 43:5; 1 Chr 18:12; 2 Chr 2:16; Joel 2:28 in the Old Testament and 1 Enoch 70:2; 91:1; Jub 25:14; 31:12; Pseudo-Philo; L.A.B. 9:10; 18:11; 32:14; 4 Ezra 14:22; Sir 48:24; T. Ab. A 4:8–9; 2 *Bar.* 6:3, Bauckham suggests that "I was in the spirit" in Rev 1:10 means "I fell into a trance" through the agency of the Spirit. On the other hand, "I was in the spirit" in Rev 4:2 means "I was caught up by the Spirit."[61] He asserts that "the technical terminology of vision in 4:1 shows that 4:2 cannot be the beginning of a second trance: John is already in the spirit. The context requires that 4:2 refer to John's rapture to heaven."[62] Bauckham appeals to parallels in the phrase, "in the spirit" in Rev 17:3 and 21:10, to Ezek 37:1 and Bel 36. By means of these two passages, Bauckham suggests that "in the spirit" in Rev 17:3; 21:10 represents "transportation by means of the Spirit" which is paralleled by the chariots of wind or of the spirit that transport Enoch in 1 Enoch 70:2.[63]

Bauckham's understanding of "the spirit of prophecy" in Revelation is based on language used in post-biblical Judaism, where "the Spirit is especially the Spirit of prophecy, who speaks through the prophets."[64] According to Bauckham, the term spirit used in Rev 14:13b; 22:17a and in the seven letters of chapters 2 and 3, is "almost exclusively the spirit of prophecy."[65] Thus, according to Bauckham, the spirit in Revelation speaks through the Christian prophetic groups to the churches. However, he adds that prophecy is not only delivered to the Christian prophets, but also to the whole church, which "has a prophetic vocation."[66] Bauckham distinguishes both the action of the spirit speaking and the content of the spirit's speech by analyzing "the witness of Jesus" in Rev 19:10. However, here Bauckham does not seek parallels from other literature outside Revelation, but turns to evidence from "some related expressions" within the book. He observes that the phrase "of Jesus" seems to be always a subjective, not an objective genitive, so that the phrase always means, in some sense, "the witness Jesus bore."[67] Thus the content of "spirit-inspired

61. Bauckham, *Theology of the Book*, 153–54.
62. Ibid.
63. Bauckham, *Climax of Prophecy*, 154–55.
64. Ibid., 160.
65. Ibid.
66. Ibid., 161. Bauckham believes the two witnesses in Rev 11:3 represent the whole church making truthful witness to the world; cf. Deut 19:15.
67. Bauckham, *Climax of Prophecy*, 161.

prophecy," "apocalypse," and "John's prophecy" are related to the witness Jesus himself bore in his earthly life.[68] The witness Jesus offered is the same witness his disciples testify about to the world, whether as small prophetic circles or by means of the whole Christian community.[69] In short, according to Bauckham, the spirit of prophecy "speaks through the prophets to the churches and through the churches to the world."[70] This, of course, means that the message of the book of Revelation is, indirectly and through the witness of the church, addressed to the whole world.

Finally, Bauckham identifies four major roles of the Holy Spirit in Revelation: (1) the Spirit of vision, (2) the Spirit of prophecy, (3) the Seven Spirits, and (4) the Spirit of eschatology.[71] In fact, each of these roles also has several aspects. For example, the Holy Spirit not only inspires John with prophetic vision (thus the expression, "in the spirit"), but also with "prophetic speech and revelation."[72] The Holy Spirit not only moves the prophets to prophesy to the churches, but also grants the churches understanding of what is prophesied.[73] The Holy Spirit thus transmits heavenly revelations and the risen Christ's words to the churches and to the world.[74] The Holy Spirit also inspires the churches and the prophets to pray to God.[75] Further, the Seven Spirits prepare the churches to be witnesses of Jesus Christ even to the point of martyrdom.[76] Additionally, the Holy Spirit leads the saints to obey the Lord's commandments since to bear witness is always correlated with obedience.[77] The Spirit of prophecy inspires the churches in true worship, not the worship of money, power, or any created celestial being, but rather worshipping the Creator through

---

68. Ibid.

69. Ibid. Bauckham uses the concept of the two witnesses in Rev 11:3 to explain that the whole Christian community is called to bear witness to the world.

70. Bauckham, *Climax of Prophecy*, 162.

71. Ibid. Bauckham does not use the terminology of the Spirit of eschatology, but uses the terminology of "the eschatological role of the Holy Spirit" in Revelation.

72. Ibid., 150. Thus, John's witness is established as divinely authoritative since he was in the spirit when he wrote Revelation.

73. Thus, "the spirit" or "the spirit of prophecy." Ibid., 160–62.

74. Ibid.

75. According to Bauckham, Rev 22:17a, "The Spirit and the bride say, 'Come,'" means the bride, that is, the church, prays for Jesus' coming by the leading of the Spirit.

76. Bauckham, *Theology of the Book*, 162.

77. According to Bauckham, the witness is closely related to obedience in Rev 12:7; 14:12. *Climax of Prophecy*, 120.

the Holy Spirit.[78] It is evident from the seven letters to the seven churches that the Holy Spirit searches the reality of the churches, perceiving their members' innermost thoughts and motives. The Holy Spirit thereby brings the churches to a realization of their problems and inspires them to repent of their sins.[79] Thus the Holy Spirit warns of judgment to come. Furthermore, the Holy Spirit provides the churches with spiritual vantage points so that the saints may recognize both the reality of Satan and evil spirits and the promised rewards and punishments associated with conquest in the spiritual warfare.[80]

In addition, Bauckham emphasizes the eschatological role of the Holy Spirit.[81] The Holy Spirit fills the saints both with the remembrance of Jesus Christ's death, resurrection, and ascension, and also the expectation that he will come again. The Holy Spirit thus inspires the churches with an eschatological perspective toward the world.[82] In this way, the Holy Spirit provides "a paradigm of faithful prophetic witness," even for today's readers. The Holy Spirit inspires Christians to prepare for the Parousia: to yearn to be perfected as the true eschatological Church, so as to be a bride clad in white for the messianic feast, made ready for the Bridegroom.

To summarize, Bauckham is able to give considerable unity to his account of the Spirit in Revelation—in contrast with Aune's fragmented analysis. Bauckham is not merely engaging in a historical-critical approach, but also tries to unlock the meaning of the text as it is given. In other words, he does not attempt to find some hidden textual history of Revelation, but rather explores the cross-referencing of the text of

78. Bauckham points to Rev 19:10 warning the church to worship only God (an interest in angelology being a feature of first century Judaism; cf. Col 2:18). The Spirit of prophecy thus leads the church in true worship.

79. There appear to be various problems or wrong attitudes in the seven churches in Asia: complacency, the worship of wealth, idolatry, sexual sinfulness, and the adoption of worldly teachings or philosophy.

80. We find this particularly in Rev 2 and 3. Actually, the Holy Spirit not only empowers the churches to preach the gospel *to the world*, but also faithfully encourages them to endure persecutions and sufferings *in the world*.

81. Bauckham, *Theology of the Book*, 166–73.

82. Ibid. Bauckham interprets Rev 11:8 "spiritually" or "prophetically." He understands that the Holy Spirit provides a prophetic imagination or prophetic viewpoint for the saints. From the prophetical point of view, they can see that the earthly city of Jerusalem is not a holy city, but a version of the sinful city of Sodom and Egypt. From the perspective of the Holy Spirit, the churches may have an inspired prophetic role today.

Revelation to OT texts and other Jewish literature to shed further light on his subject. He is refreshingly concerned with adopting some literary methods such as numerology of apocalyptic literature and literary parallelism. With his more synthetical approach, Bauckham gives a considerable contribution to the study of the Holy Spirit in Revelation. Even though Bauckham tried to overcome the limit of traditional historical-critical approach by adopting a new literary critical approach, his study is still limited in doing it. He did not employ some important literary devices such as the point of view of the narrator, the divine frame of reference, characterization, plot, and structure in his study of the Holy Spirit in Revelation.

R. L. Jeske

Whereas Bruce, Aune, and Bauckham altogether deal with the whole usage of the spirit in Revelation, Jeske is particularly interested in only the phrase "in the Spirit" in Revelation. Jeske takes for granted, without further analysis, that in the Spirit refers to the Holy Spirit. Jeske criticizes the usual scholarly assumption that in the spirit means *ecstatic experience*, by asserting that the phrase is more "a relational symbol than a privately experiential one."[83] He offers five purposes for which John employs the phrase in the Spirit: (1) to represent his own identity as a preacher who gives messages in the Spirit; (2) as a hearing and seeing recipient of the Lord's messages in the Spirit; (3) as a prophet who is called by the risen Lord to take prophetic responsibility for the seven churches in the Spirit; (4) as a participant in the Christian communities in the Spirit who is able to communicate with them in the same Spirit, even if physically separated from them; and (5) to provide literary signposts to the structure of Revelation.[84]

Jeske appeals to similar usages of the expression in the spirit from the Old Testament, the New Testament, and other early Jewish and Christian literature, in order to substantiate his argument. Even though he fails to find an identical usage, he discovers similarities in Mic 3:8 and *Did.* 11:7–12. Both these passages have the same context; namely, to

---

83. Jeske, "Spirit and Community," 464.

84. Ibid., 462–64. In fact, within the five purposes Jeske suggests just two kinds of reasons why John employs the phrase "in the Spirit." One is to show the identity of John himself, the other is to function as a literary signpost for the book.

rebuke false prophets who lay claim to ecstatic vision in the Spirit. *Didache* 11:7–12 indicates that not all prophets who claim the Spirit are true prophets. Micah proclaims that those prophets who experienced ecstasy in the Spirit are not true prophets, although Micah himself received prophetic words and messages for Israel in the Spirit. Thus, Jeske concludes that in the spirit in Revelation refers to the illumination of the Holy Spirit for the prophets to receive prophetic words rather than some putative private ecstatic experience.[85]

Jeske adopts a sociological and anthropological analysis to identify the sociological situation of the seven churches. Appealing to the anthropological concept of "the state of liminality"[86] developed by Turner and reapplied to Christian studies by Gager,[87] Jeske insists that the early church community was a *liminality* community, differing in social structure and norm from the surrounding society. This difference had resulted in persecution and isolation from the prevailing social and religious community. In Revelation, according to Jeske, the seven Asian churches suffered persecution both externally and internally. John responded by writing to encourage and strengthen those Christian communities who faced life-threatening crisis. But he did so by way of a pneumatically inspired communion so that, in the Spirit, he directly participated in their worship services preaching messages received from the risen Christ via the same Holy Spirit. Throughout, John's language is laden with liturgical terminology.

Jeske also appeals to the parallel social background of Paul's ministry to reveal the meaning of in the Spirit in Revelation. Just as Paul encouraged and strengthened the churches through his letters, emphasizing his and their unity in the one Spirit, John adopts the same Pauline model of ministry when he uses the expression "in the Spirit" from the island of Patmos. Jeske asserts that John's usage of in the spirit is intended to represent his unity with these Christian communities. Thus, according to

---

85. Ibid., 453–56.

86. Cultural anthropologists such as A. van Gennup and V. Turner have designated *liminal* as that stage of existence that is on the threshold of the world, in transition from the order of a previous world. Gager has applied the concept of liminality to the early Christian communities and sees the intense emphasis on the unity and stability of Christian congregations in early Christian literature as "an effort to preserve the only meaningful form of social existence for a liminal community constituted primarily by liminal persons." Jeske, "Spirit and Community," 458.

87. Ibid., 463.

his sociological and anthropological analysis, Jeske concludes that John employs the expression in the Spirit to emphasize his joint participation with his addressees in the Holy Spirit in their common crisis.[88]

In short, Jeske attempts to examine cross-references of in the spirit from the Old Testament, the New Testament, and Jewish Literature. He also explores the social situation of the early churches, that is, the Revelation audiences. However, he did not search for the literary effect of the phase "in the spirit" in the plot and structure of Revelation.

J. C. de Smidt and K. de Smidt

We can find quite a different fashion of study method of the spirit in Revelation from the articles of J. C. de Smidt and K. de Smidt. In his article, "The Holy Spirit in the Book of Revelation-Nomenclature," J. C. de Smidt tries to summarize the results of the studies concerned in the Holy Spirit in Revelation in a more collective rather than analytical way.[89] He focuses on surveying the history of the interpretation, especially, of ἐν πνεύματι[90] from Late Jewish and early Christian literature to those in contemporary times.[91] He notes wide scholarly agreement that the author experienced "partial ecstasy" although this ecstasy was accompanied by

---

88. Ibid., 457–60.

89. J. C. de Smidt tends to make use of the data in a more collective way rather than in an analytical one in his writing. This means he largely avoids criticizing others' studies, but instead combines them to build his own perspective. He does, however, criticize the claim that "in the spirit" is "synonymous with Paul's 'outside the body.'" J. C. de Smidt, "Holy Spirit in the Book," 234.

90. J. C. de Smidt briefly comments on the Seven Spirits and the spirit of prophecy. He suggests that the Seven Spirits indicate "the wholeness of life which God continued to mediate through the Spirit within the believing community of Asia Minor" as well as "a symbol for the various manifestations of the Spirit of God which was localized in each of the seven congregations" (ibid., 241). He also suggests that the spirit of prophecy plays an "instrumental" role "in conveying to John the truth which Jesus had revealed" as well as in inspiring the whole book of Revelation (ibid., 242).

91. J. C. de Smidt suggests that *evn pneu,mati* (in the spirit) was a "well-known term in Late Jewish and early Christian literature," which meant that "the specific person had had an experience caused by an activity of the Spirit of God in the sense of the Spirit taking control of him" (ibid., 233). He insists that the contemporary issue in interpreting *evn pneu,mati* is focused on a "state of personal visionary consciousness" (ibid.).

"sober knowledge of his world situation, his congregations, the Scriptures and the artistic characteristics of his book."[92]

J. C. de Smidt then reviews the work of six scholars: R. J. Bauckham, R. L. Jeske, M. E. Boring, J. A. Du Rand, L. L. Thompson, and J. J. Pilch, before offering his own interpretation on ἐν πνεύματι. In fact, he offers six hermeneutical perspectives: (1) psychological and phenomenological, (2) literary, (3) rhetorical, (4) theological, (5) liturgical, and (6) eschatological.

K. de Smidt subsequently developed the approach of J. C. de Smidt, and sought to expound a Christian doctrine of the Holy Spirit on the basis of Revelation in his article, "Hermeneutical Perspectives of the Spirit in the Book of Revelation." K. de Smidt insists that a distinctive "emphasis in the doctrine of the Holy Spirit" is found in Revelation.[93] He is not concerned with identifying the different usages of the term Spirit in Revelation (such as the Seven Spirits, in the spirit, the spirit of prophecy, and so forth), but is concerned with identifying the function of the Spirit in the light of the aforementioned perspective analysis. Thus, he analyzes the work of the Spirit in the light of the following considerations: (1) phenomenology, (2) literary critique, (3) social analysis, (4) congregational dynamic, (5) metaphorical usage of the spirit, (6) psychological and physiological references, and (7) the spirit as interpreter of history through the author.[94]

From these seven perspectives, K. de Smidt explains the functions of the Spirit in Revelation. The Spirit helps John experience the heavenly world in the Spirit in contradistinction to the physical world with a clear capacity to hear and see.[95] The Spirit guides the author in the literary process of casting "his vision in the mould of a specific genre: an apocalypse," incorporating "elements, inter alia, of epistolary art, narrative, prophetic writings, and the principles of rhetoric."[96] The Spirit also strengthens the

---

92. Ibid., 234–35.

93. K. de Smidt, "Hermeneutical Perspectives," 28.

94. Ibid. He uses the terminology of phenomenological experience in that the Spirit moves John phenomenologically from the earthly realm into the heavenly realm when the seer is *in the spirit*. He employs a literary perspective in that the spirit gives the vision to John so that John may be guided to write the apocalyptic vision in the literary form of the letter.

95. Ibid., 28–30.

96. Ibid., 31. K. de Smidt insists that the Spirit allows the author to use not only anthropomorphism and metaphor, but also various rhetorical techniques of ethos, pathos, and logos including "in the spirit" so that the contemporary readers may

Introduction

Christian communities that are experiencing social marginalization, by informing them that they have a central role in building the kingdom of God on earth.

According to K. de Smidt, the Holy Spirit is concerned about the whole life of the Christian congregations: about salvation, sanctification, worship, discipleship, witness, unity, prayer, and constant regeneration.[97] The Spirit is able to gaze into the situations of both the saints and the world, a capacity signified by the language of the Seven Spirits, as the Seven Spirits of God. The Spirit also powerfully assists the Churches' victory over the evil one since the Seven Spirits are the seven horns of power.[98] K. de Smidt does not agree with Pilch's assertion that John's vision is a "psychological symptom" induced by stress.[99] Psychological categories are insufficient to explain the data and if pressed too hard, become reductive. Rather, according to K. de Smidt, the Spirit acts as "an interpreter of history through the author."[100]

In short, the two de Smidts have made significant contributions to our understanding. First of all, they regard the variety of references to the Spirit or spirits in Revelation as indicating the same Holy Spirit. Secondly, they identify the functions of the Spirit in Revelation through the use of several hermeneutical perspectives. In this way, they are able to build a coherent doctrine of the Holy Spirit in Revelation. Thirdly, by applying rhetorical analysis to the narrative of Revelation, they expand the repertoire of literary methods used to unlock its text. By contrast, many scholars of Revelation, including Bauckham and Aune, focus, at most, on three literary characteristics of Revelation, such as the apocalypse, letter, and prophecy. Fourthly, the de Smidts focus on the congregational perspective of the Holy Spirit in Revelation.[101] They are thus able to show, in detail, how Revelation envisages the Holy Spirit not theoretically but by actually working in the lives of believers. Fifthly, they also have shown how the Holy Spirit in Revelation inspires the author so that John may write the revelation of Jesus as well as be moved into another realm when

---

understand. Here he understands in the spirit as a rhetorical principle. He asserts that the author uses "God's audio-visual presentation" in Revelation to produce something like the drama and tragedy of the theatre in Ephesus (32).

97. Ibid., 34–41.
98. Ibid., 41–43.
99. Ibid., 44.
100. Ibid.
101. The congregational perspective of the Holy Spirit is used to indicate how the Holy Spirit relates to the lives of believers.

he was in the Spirit. In addition, the de Smidts have not only gone beyond the usual conventions of historical criticism by adding sociological and rhetorical approaches, but also have employed a *synthetic-hermeneutical analysis* to explore the role of the Holy Spirit in Revelation.[102] They interpret the data appealed to in their study of the Holy Spirit in Revelation from several perspectives.

Summary and Evaluations

The results of scholarly approaches to the subject of the Holy Spirit in Revelation can be examined by means of five tables:

Table 1.1. Methodology Employed for the Study of the Holy Spirit in Revelation

Scholars	Methodology[103]
Bruce	Historical critical
Aune	Historical critical
Bauckham	Historical critical, Canonical, Sociological, Literary-Rhetorical
Jeske	Historical critical, Sociological
J. C. de Smidt, K. de Smidt	Historical critical, Socio-Rhetorical, Synthetic-Hermeneutical

Table 1.2. On the Concept of "the Seven Spirits" in Revelation[104]

The Holy Spirit in its fullness	The seven principal angels of God	Seven astral deities, seven sky powers
Bruce, Bauckham, J. C. de Smidt, K. de Smidt, (Cowley, Beckwith, Sweet, Metzger, Smalley, Talbert, Beale, Wall, Caird, Johnson)	Aune, (Charles, Ford, Thompson, Roloff)	(Malina, Pilch)

---

102. They use historical-critical and socio-rhetorical approaches as their basic methods with ancillary help from socio-rhetorical criticism. Their methodology may be called a *synthetic-hermeneutical approach* in that several perspectives are combined in their study.

103. Actually, scholars, including those in our study, use many kinds of methodology in their books. Here, the prevailing methodology of each is provided.

104. In this table, I have added some other scholars who are not included in this survey, so that the whole concept of "the Seven Spirits," "in the spirit," "the spirit," and "the spirit of prophecy" may be shown.

Table 1.3 On the Meaning of "in the Spirit" in Revelation

As an agent of visionary experience: the ecstatic or trans-like state of John	J. C. de Smidt, K. de Smidt, (Gilbert, Desrosiers)
The identification with prophetic authority => Ezekiel's repeated rapture in the Spirit	Bruce, (Beale)
Social relationship to the seven churches	Jeske
A trance through the agency of the Spirit Transportation by means of the Spirit	Bauckham
In the sky power: altered states of consciousness	(Malina)
Body and spirit dichotomy	Aune

Table 1.4. On the Concept of "the Spirit" or "the Spirit of Prophecy" in Revelation

The Spirit to the seven churches (Rev 2-3)	Responsive Spirit (Rev 14:13, 22:17)	The Spirit of prophecy (Rev 19:10)
Agent to proclaim the prophetic mandate to the Churches (J. C. de Smidt, K. de Smidt). The same as the Spirit of prophecy (Bruce, Bauckham).	The same as the Spirit of prophecy (Bruce, Bauckham).	The Spirit of messianic prophecy (Bruce). The Spirit of witness Jesus bore (Bauckham). The Spirit giving prophecy (J. C. de Smidt).

Table 1.5. On the Functional Role of the Holy Spirit in Revelation

	Bruce	Aune	Bauckham	Jeske	Smidts
Mediating visionary experience	No	No	Yes	No	Yes
Mediating prophecy	Yes	Unclear	Yes	No comment	Yes
Providing power in witnessing	Unclear	No	Yes	No comment	Yes
Inspiring worship and prayer	Unclear	No	Yes	No comment	Yes
Inspiring to keep God's Word	Unclear	No	Yes	No comment	Yes

	Bruce	Aune	Bauckham	Jeske	Smidts
Inspiring eschatological and prophetic worldview	Unclear	No	Yes	No comment	Yes
Spirit of radical Christian life	Unclear	No	Yes	No comment	Yes
Inspiring the author	No	No	Yes	No	Yes
Spiritual relationship between believers	Unclear	No	Unclear	Yes	Yes
Generating life	No	No	No	No	Yes
Recognizing all the world	No	No	Yes	No comment	Yes
Literary signpost	No	No	Yes	No	Yes

As indicated above, these scholars show different interpretations of the Spirit in Revelation even when using similar interpretive techniques: such as the historical-critical approach and socio-rhetorical approaches.[105] As shown in Table 1.1, "historical criticism" is the dominant approach used by scholars studying the Holy Spirit in Revelation. Note that any methodological approach on its own is unable to unlock a literary text.[106] That is why we need "to have as full a set of keys as possible."[107] In this study, I shall attempt a dynamic reading of the Holy Spirit in Revelation with a narrative critical approach as a useful key to unlock the literary text of Revelation.

Towards a Dynamic Reading of the Holy Spirit in Revelation

It is easy to miss the most important feature of Revelation, that the text is a narrative. This mistake is easily made because of too much concentration on interpreting the many obscure apocalyptic images, symbols, and repeated structures. Barr rightly insists on this:

105. For example, the meaning of the genitive in μαρτυρία Ἰησοῦ (the testimony of Jesus) in Rev 19:10 is interpreted by Bruce as objective, but by Bauckham as subjective, using the same historical criticism. Another example is shown in the interpretation of ἑπτὰ πνευμάτων (the Seven Spirits) in Rev 1:4. Aune interprets them as the seven archangels, but Bauckham as the Holy Spirit, with the same historical-critical approach.

106. Powell, *What is Narrative Criticism?*, 101.

107. Ibid.

> Because it is part of the Bible, because it is used in our culture to advocate political agendas both of the left and right, because it utilizes an obscure set of images and ideas, because it is all divided up into neat chapters and discreet verses, because we are so familiar with a few of its symbols (such as the four horsemen or 666), it is easy to miss the most important thing for understanding the Apocalypse: it is a narrative.[108]

As Desrosiers has rightly asserted, from Charles to Beale,[109] Revelation has characteristically been analyzed using the now traditional historical-critical approach.[110] This is true even though some other critical methods such as socio-rhetorical, socio-scientific and reader-response approaches have also been attempted.

Nonetheless, recently, after Bauckham had attempted the literary approach, several Revelation scholars have employed new literary approaches, including narrative criticism. Garrow, in his book, *Revelation*, challenges previous readings of Revelation by attempting to reproduce "the context of the original intended receiver as close as possible."[111] Thus he claims,

> There is little new in a method of approach which gives attention to the original context of the text. However, traditional analyses of the context of Revelation have tended to focus on the text's historical context, while failing to pay sufficient attention to those aspects of context over which John had specific control or "of which he had" particular knowledge: the co-textual context and the context created by the theatre of reception. By studying these neglected aspects of context, in combination with the wider historical context, it should be possible to reproduce with a new degree of accuracy the context in which John's hearers received Revelation. The consequence of this will be an improved understanding of how John's intended hearers interpreted his text.[112]

---

108. Barr, *Tales of the End*, 1.

109. Charles, *Critical and Exegetical Commentary*; Beale, *Book of Revelation*.

110. Desrosiers, *Introduction to Revelation*, 70. He asserts, "For nearly one hundred years, the predominant way of reading and interpreting the book of Revelation has been through the use of the historical-critical or the grammatico-historical method" (ibid.).

111. Garrow, *Revelation*, 3.

112. Ibid., 4.

Garrow attempts to find the story of what must soon take place, contained within the scroll, in the text of Revelation with "careful listening to the co-textual context, and consideration of the influence on the structure of the text exerted by the theatre of reception,"[113] even though the majority of scholars hardly have found the consensus in their studies.[114] Through his analysis, Garrow concludes that Revelation has three storytelling texts, namely, 12:1—14:5 (persecution); 15:6—16:21 (judgement); 19:11b—21:8 (salvation).[115] Other passages, he claims, support and describe "the story contained within the main scroll."[116] To make his point clear, Garrow summarizes the story in diagrams. And in his accompanying analysis, Garrow examines literary elements such as the characters, action, and time of the story. Garrow seems to be successful in finding a part of the story of Revelation. However he fails to discover both the narrator and the point of view of the narrator in Revelation, by means of which we could identify the whole narrative of Revelation.[117]

Desrosiers also, in his *Introduction to Revelation: A Pathway to Interpretation*, uses a narratological method to interpret Revelation. But this is part of "a multi-pronged approach to Revelation" that uses both a diachronic method and a synchronic method.[118] He recommends that "the reader tackles the task of reading Revelation in one or two sittings, paying special attention to characters, plot, and setting."[119] However both Garrow and Desrosiers have not applied narratological analysis to the whole book of Revelation, but only to those sections of the book that they consider amenable to this approach.

In contrast, Barr applies narrative criticism to the whole book of Revelation in his *Tales of the End: A Narrative Commentary on the Book*

---

113. Ibid., 13. Garrow defines "co-text" as "the context created by as much of the text as has already been received." He suggests that "the theatre of reception" is defined as "the exact environment in which a text is going to be received."

114. Garrow concludes this after he reviews scholarly approaches to the story of Revelation. Ibid., 6–13. However, he suggests that "a convincing understanding of the whereabouts and logic of the story" may be revealed by his method.

115. Garrow insists that there are three basic elements of the story of Revelation: persecution, punishment, and salvation. Ibid., 13.

116. Ibid., 61.

117. For this, see sections 3 and 4, "The Narrator of Revelation and the Holy Spirit" and "The Narrator's Point of View in Revelation with Special Reference to the Holy Spirit" in chapter 2.

118. Desrosiers, *Introduction to Revelation*, 100.

119. Ibid., 10.

of Revelation. He attempts to read Revelation consistently as a narrative, "ignoring for the moment its chapters and verses, its political application, its status as scripture, its use in theology."[120] In particular, he identifies three segments of the story in Revelation: the letter scroll (ch. 1–3), the worship scroll (ch. 4–11) and the war scroll (ch. 12–22). In each segment, Barr explores the characters, setting, and plot. He also finds a concentric structure of Revelation with three pairs of frames: letter frame, vision report frame, scroll frame in which the worship scroll is surrounded by the letter and war scrolls.[121] Barr seems to be successful in finding the story and structure of Revelation by using many narrative tools. However, he fails to illuminate the narrative level of the narrator in Revelation despite his ingenious identification of three frames of the Revelation narrative. The various kinds of the narrator are not analyzed in his study.[122]

Resseguie also applies a narrative critical approach in his commentary, *Revelation Unsealed: A Narrative Critical Approach to John's Apocalypse*. Resseguie first observes the whole narrative of Revelation by means of the basic elements of the narrative-critical method: point of view, rhetoric (use of numbers, repetition, figurative language), setting, character, plot, the reader. Then he explores the theological themes of Revelation such as the Church, evil, God, worship, salvation, Christ, and the future.

However, except for Desrosiers, these four scholars barely regard the Spirit as a character in the story of Revelation. Garrow suggests that the Spirit may be identical with "his angel" in Rev 1:1; 22:16.[123] Despite the fact that scholarly debate is quite unresolved about whether "his angel" and "the Spirit" are identical, Garrow fails to argue his case, presumably because he is preoccupied with finding the real story of Revelation.[124] By contrast, Desrosiers recognizes the Spirit as a character who "plays a central role as a communication agent" (especially in the letter scroll), and as the "agent of the visionary experience," as the prophetic Spirit and as the fullness of the Seven Spirits or "seven archangels."[125] Nonetheless,

---

120. Barr, *Tales of the End*, 1.

121. Ibid., 149.

122. For the various kinds of narrator in Revelation, see chapter 2, the section entitled, "Previous Study of the Narrator and the Point of View of the Narrator in Revelation."

123. Garrow, *Revelation*, 30.

124. For this scholarly debate, see Aune, *Revelation 1–5*, 15–19. We will discuss the subject of the identification between "his angel" and "the Spirit" in chapter 2.

125. Desrosiers, *Introduction to Revelation*, 14, 98, 99.

Desrosiers's interest in the Holy Spirit in Revelation is not primarily displayed in his narrative critical analysis.[126] Rather, he treats the Holy Spirit as a theological theme of Revelation to be studied under the heading of the doctrine of the Trinity.[127] Barr says little about the narrative role of the Holy Spirit in Revelation in his otherwise detailed narrative approach. It is rather the absence of reference to the Holy Spirit in the opening declaration that he regards as "strange."[128] Barr tends to identify the voice of the Holy Spirit indirectly as the viewpoint of the rhetor-narrator, but fails to recognize the Holy Spirit as both a character in the Revelation narrative and as a divine frame of reference.[129] Resseguie, like Barr, similarly does not regard the Spirit as a character in the narrative. In fact the Holy Spirit is hardly mentioned in his study of Revelation.

In short, the above-mentioned four scholars have tried to instigate a paradigm shift by introducing the narrative approach into Revelation studies. However, each has failed significantly to identify the Holy Spirit's role in the narrative of Revelation.

Recently, Du Rand has written a promising article entitled, "'Let him hear what the Spirit says . . .': The functional role and theological meaning of the Spirit in the Book of Revelation." His purpose has been to identify the role and theological meaning of the Holy Spirit in Revelation using narrative criticism:

---

126. Desrosiers recommends a "multi-pronged approach" to study Revelation. Ibid., 100–102. With this approach, he explores the Holy Spirit in Revelation.

127. Ibid., 98–99.

128. Barr, *Tales of the End*, 31.

129. Ibid., 36. Actually, Barr does not directly connect the rhetor-narrator's viewpoint with the voice of the Holy Spirit. But while he identifies Jesus with the shifting point of view of the rhetor "in the persona of John-in-the-spirit," and affirms that Jesus speaks as "the voice which is also attributed to the spirit." The connection of the Holy Spirit with the rhetor-narrator's viewpoint is only loosely made. Nevertheless, Barr identifies the term "rhetor-narrator" with "the ultimate narrator" (ibid). In fact, Barr classifies the Spirit as a minor character in the appendix of his *Tales of the End* (181). However, in the main text, the Spirit is apparently not regarded as a character. The Holy Spirit as a divine frame of reference, vindicates as reliable any character who is said to be "in the spirit." Barr does nowhere treat this matter directly but it is implicit in what he says. Ibid., 36. According to Barr, Jesus is considered a character-narrator who is unlimited and completely reliable. The voice of the Spirit is equated with the words of Jesus in ch. 2 and 3 (2:7, 11, 17, 29; 3:6, 13, 22). This means that the Spirit may be regarded as a reliable character. The divine frame of reference will be defined and discussed more fully in chapter 2.

> Therefore, the aim of this contribution is not to count the references but, first of all, to listen to the theological narrative of the book of Revelation trying to describe the organic and functional role of the Spirit. Furthermore, the narratological and theological analyses will try to answer the crucial question of the possible relationship between the Spirit and the Church, as well as between the Spirit and the world. The intention is not to ask such questions from a presupposed Pauline or Johannine (Gospel) projection, but to allow the narrative of Revelation itself to provide the theological answers. This will also bring perspective on the role of the Spirit in the divine eschatological activity to establish the recognition of God's rule on earth.[130]

Du Rand's study makes an unquestionably significant contribution to the understanding of the narrative function of the Holy Spirit. Firstly, Du Rand emphasises the Holy Spirit as an important character in the Revelation narrative. Secondly, in this task, he concentrates on the narrative of Revelation itself, not importing Pauline and Johannine theology to fill out the picture. Thirdly, he pursues his aim by surveying the narrative levels of Revelation according to Eugene Boring's "four levels of narrativity in Revelation."[131] Fourthly, he attempts to explore the role of the Holy Spirit who "functions on all four levels."[132]

Nonetheless, the methodology of his writing could be improved in four ways. Firstly, Du Rand could have used the standard *narrative elements* as a basis: *point of view, setting, characterization, plot, and style*.[133] Instead Du Rand confines his attention to simply the plot. In this process, he fails to discern the role of the Holy Spirit as a divine frame of reference within the narrator's point of view.

Secondly, he fails to make use of the narrative theories of the narrator's point of view and characterization to illuminate the function of the

130. Du Rand, "Let Him Hear," 43–58.

131. Ibid., 49. Du Rand notes that Boring's four levels of narrativity in Revelation are helpful for the readers to understand the functional role of the Spirit in Revelation. Boring suggests that the first narrative level of Revelation is a framework of the letter/apocalypse, representing John's account of his experiences and of the meaning for the Churches. The second narrative level represents the visions of God and Christ, the so-called God's story and Christ's story. The third narrative level deals with the unfolding actions from the visions of the seals, trumpets, and vials. The fourth narrative level contains the comprehensive narrative presupposed by and alluded to by each of the first three narrative levels.

132. Ibid.

133. Tate, *Biblical Interpretation*, 81–97.

Holy Spirit in Revelation.[134] He may be successful in finding the narrator's ideological point of view by investigating a theological framework of Revelation. However, he ignores the perceptual and psychological aspects of the narrator's point of view.

Thirdly, Du Rand fails to consider the interaction between *the implied author or the narrator, the text, and the implied reader*, which would have befitted a narrative analysis.[135] Rather, he explores the Holy Spirit's role in Revelation theologically. Thus he develops a reading derived from messianic war ideas, the eschatological motif, and the reader's context, all within the context of the history of the world. He appears unconcerned with the role of the Holy Spirit as the guide to the narrative reading process, an important point to which this book will later consider.[136]

Overall Evaluation

As implied in Table 1.6 below, the narratological study of the Holy Spirit in Revelation is still at an early stage. Barr and Resseguie attempt a narrative interpretation of Revelation as a whole but deal with the Holy Spirit quite superficially. On the other hand, Du Rand does not apply narrative criticism to the whole of Revelation, but focuses exclusively on the Holy Spirit.[137] Thus, his study is not sufficient from the perspective of narrative approach, even though he made a notable contribution to the study of the Holy Spirit in Revelation. It yet remains for a dynamic narratological reading to be employed across the whole book of Revelation.

---

134. Either Uspensky's five planes point of view model or Rimmon-Kenan's three facets point of view model may be used to verify the narrator's point of view of Revelation. Some character-classification models such as those of Forster, Harvey, Hochman, and some character-presentation models such as those of Booth or Rimmon-Kenan may be applied in this study to find a better understanding of the functional role of the Holy Spirit.

135. Tate, *Biblical Interpretation*, 74–81.

136. For the dynamic reading process in Revelation, see Barr, *Tales of the End*, 159–60. His dynamic reading process is: Real Author => [implied author => narrator => narratee => implied reader] =>Real Reader. For the dynamic reading process, not in Revelation, but in Luke-Acts, see Hur, *Dynamic Reading*, 90.

137. Du Rand is less successful in his study since he has not attempted to analyze the entire book of Revelation with narrative criticism.

Table 1.6 Narrative Approach Employed to the Study of the Holy Spirit in Revelation

Scholars	Methodology	
	The study of Revelation	The study of the Holy Spirit in Revelation
Du Rand		Narrative critical and Historical critical
Desrosiers	Narrative critical	Historical critical (finding the theology of the Holy Spirit in Revelation)
Garrow	Narrative critical	Narrative critical (the relationship between angel and the Holy Spirit)
Barr	Narrative critical	Narrative critical (superficial)
Resseguie	Narrative critical	Narrative critical (superficial)

Methodology

In my study of the Holy Spirit in Revelation, I will engage the literary elements related to the Holy Spirit in Revelation: (1) the narrator's *point of view*, (2) *character-presentation*, (3) *plot-function*, and (4) *structure-function*, in order to attempt to provide a more convincing reading of the Holy Spirit in Revelation.[138] I will also identify the interaction between the implied author (or the narrator), the text, and the implied reader in the reading process. Usually, the significant surveys have been attempted on who the real author is or who the real readers or audiences are. However, they have not been so successful in identifying them. The

---

138. In developing my methodology, two previous studies of the Holy Spirit in Luke-Acts have been helpful: W. H. Shepherd, *Narrative Function*; Hur, *Dynamic Reading*. Shepherd addresses the characterization of the Holy Spirit in Luke-Acts. Hur criticizes Shepherd's study as failing to provide a holistic reading of the Holy Spirit's significance in Luke-Acts. He explores three aspects of the literary traits of the Holy Spirit based on the dynamic reading process: the Lukan narrator's point of view; character presentation; and plot function. In addition, he both provides the literary repertoire of Lukan references to the Holy Spirit and describes the theological significance of the Spirit in Luke-Acts. However, I do not accept all of his methodology. For example, even if I agree that the diachronic analysis, that is, the literary repertoire, is needed to interpret Revelation, nonetheless I have two important reservations. Firstly, it has been already used in the historical-critical approach in the study of the spirit in Revelation. It may be repetitive to use it in this study. Secondly, the synchronic analysis may not only be needed, but also contribute vitally to the study of the Holy Spirit in Revelation.

narrative approach, which proposes the concept of the implied author and readers, opens the door to break through those complicated issues in biblical interpretation. To define the literary elements such as point of view, character presentation, plot, and structure, some literary theories shall be employed in this study.[139] The divine frame of reference concept to affect the ideology of the narrator shall be adopted to explain the role of the Holy Spirit. With this new approach, many aspects of the identity and role of the Holy Spirit in Revelation as well as aspects of the theological significance of the Holy Spirit shall be discovered in connection with the messianic feast and the messianic war, which represents the causality of the plot of Revelation and the fundamental-semantic structure of Revelation.

In chapter 2, the narrator's point of view in Revelation will be discussed in reference to the Holy Spirit in Revelation. In addition, the divine frame of reference will be explored to discover how the Holy Spirit is presented *rhetorically* as a divine frame of reference so as to underline the reliability of the narrator and other characters in Revelation.

Chapter 3 will offer a study of the Holy Spirit as a divine character in the Revelation narrative. The theory of characterization and character-presentation of the Holy Spirit will be applied across the whole narrative of Revelation.

Chapter 4 will explain how the Holy Spirit is presented in the overall plot of Revelation. We will also explore how the Holy Spirit works in the narrative reading process, especially in implied readers or real readers who actualize the text.

Chapter 5 will explore how the Holy Spirit is presented in the structure of Revelation. The characterization of the Holy Spirit in Revelation will be elucidated along five structural perspectives: narrative-syntactic structure, fundamental-syntactic structure, narrative-semantic structure, fundamental-semantic structure, pragmatic structure. In this connection, the functions of the Holy Spirit in the messianic war and feast will become clear.

Chapter 6 will offer some concluding remarks built on the results of the earlier chapters.

---

139. Rimmon-Kenan's theories shall be employed for the narrator's point of view and character presentation. For the plot, Van Dijk's five scheme model shall be employed. For the category of the narrative structure, Patte's category of semio-narrative structure shall be adopted in this study.

2

Narrator, Point of View of the Narrator, and the Holy Spirit in Revelation

Introduction

By employing the narratological approach, we can find out how significantly the Holy Spirit plays a role in the narrative, if the Holy Spirit is proved to be a divine frame of reference of the narrator. How important is the narrator and his viewpoint in the narrative? Does the narrator really adopt the Holy Spirit as a divine frame of reference?

In this chapter, to answer these questions, I shall focus on the narrator of Revelation as well as the narrator's point of view, keeping in mind the Holy Spirit within the divine frame of reference, before discussing the literary presentation of the Holy Spirit in following chapters. First of all, I shall outline the previous studies of the narrator and the narrator's point of view, that is, those of James L. Resseguie and David L. Barr. Then, I shall explore the narrator and the narrator's point of view using the three facets model of Rimmon-Kenan. Finally, I shall elucidate the divine frame of reference of the narrator with reference to the Holy Spirit, based on the literary study of John A. Darr, before offering a summary and conclusion.[1]

---

1. Darr insists, "Much like the narrator's perspective, that the divine frame of

Previous Study of the Narrator and the Point of View of the Narrator in Revelation

David L. Barr

David L. Barr gives more concentrated attention to the narrator than Resseguie.[2] He recognizes the narrative level, the extent of the narrator's participation in the narrative, and the visibility and reliability of the narrator in the story. He explains the movement of the narrative level from the level of the *rhetor* to that of John, and from the level of John to that of Jesus.[3] He also distinguishes the ultimate narrator or the covert narrator from the character narrator or the overt narrator, as provided in the footnote.[4] He finds the shift of viewpoint—or focalization[5]—in Revelation from the standpoint of the ultimate narrator to that of the character narrator such as Jesus, John, and God.[6] In the prologue to his book, Barr explains the temporal and spatial dimensions of Revelation's story in

---

reference provides the audience with a consistent and highly authoritative guide for constructing and/or evaluating characters and their roles in the action." Dar, *On Character Building*, 53.

2. Resseguie shows no particular interest in the narrator of Revelation though he does offer a study of the narrator's point of view.

3. Barr uses the word *rhetor* instead of *narrator*.

4. Barr suggests that the narrative level of the rhetor is different than that of other characters. Further, he adds that the rhetor uses various masks such as the voice of God, John, Jesus, the first person narrator, and even the Spirit. Barr also distinguishes two types of narrators: the covert narrator (ultimate narrator) and overt narrator (character narrator). Readers may find his distinction between the narrator's level and the reader's level confusing. This is probably because he does not distinguish the various literary concepts of narrator such as the extradiegetic narrator, the intradiegetic narrator, and the hypodiegetic narrator in terms of the narrative level, as well as the heterodiegetic narrator and homodiegetic narrator in terms of the extent of participation of the narrator in his book. These various concepts of the narrator can be classified according to three groups: the narrative level and the narrator in Revelation, participation of the narrator in Revelation, and perceptibility of the narrator in Revelation.

5. Rimmon-Kenan usually uses the terminology, "point of view of narrator" as "the focalization of the focalizer," just as Genette prefers. Sheeley, *Narrative Asides in Luke-Acts*, 149; Genette, *Narrative Discourse*, 186–89. In other words, Rimmon-Kenan regards the narrator's point of view as the focalization of the narrator in a similar way to Genette. Rimmon-Kenan describes that "the story is presented in the text through the mediation of some 'prism,' 'perspective.'" Rimmon-Kenan calls this mediation "focalization." Rimmon-Kenan, *Narrative Fiction*, 71. All quotes from Rimmon-Kenan's *Narrative Fiction* are from the 1983 edition.

6. Barr, *Tales of the End*, 35–36.

traditional historical critical terms without reference to the psychological point of view of the narrator.[7] Instead, he reveals the narrator's ideological viewpoint through the study of doxological passages and material related to spiritual warfare.[8] Despite these limitations, Barr provides a significant contribution to our understanding of the narrator's viewpoint.

James L. Resseguie

James L. Resseguie treats the narrator more concretely and systematically than Barr.[9] He uses Uspensky's five planes model to reveal the narrator's viewpoint. Resseguie, by linguistic study, draws attention to the use of "hear and see," divine passives, and the distinctiveness of voices and speeches in Revelation. In relation to the spatial narrator's viewpoint, he studies four binaries: above and below, open and closed, center and perimeter, and inner and outer. As to the psychological viewpoint, Resseguie identifies a single crucial binary: the attitude that gives glory to God and the attitude that curses the name of God. He contrasts the responses of the world populace and John toward the symbolic evil beasts. As to the narrator's temporal viewpoint, he makes three distinctions: the impending eschatological point of view; the mixing of past, present, and future; and numeric symbols—such as forty-two months, three and half years, a thousand and two hundred and sixty days, and a thousand years. As for the narrator's ideological viewpoint,[10] Resseguie suggests six points: Divine determinism of historical events, the universal existential choice between God and the evil one, the need for a dual heavenly-and-earthly perspective to understand events, the imperative to listen to the prophet so as to understand the inner significance of things, the mesmeric deception of evil that fools almost the whole world, the need to consider the present work in the light of the soon-coming eschaton.

---

7. Ibid., 19. He attempts to identify the milieu and date of Revelation.

8. Ibid., 34–35. However, his description of the narrator's ideological viewpoint is sketchy and superficial.

9. Resseguie argues that recent studies of the narrator's viewpoint are focused on "the narrator's stance with regard to space, time and ideology," not on "the mode of narration." Resseguie, *Revelation Unsealed*, 2.

10. Resseguie insists that the ideological point of view is "the most important of various planes because it allows the reader to understand the narrator's belief and value system—what the narrator considers important." Ibid., 3.

Evaluation

Resseguie argues rightly that "being in the spirit" represents both the spatial plane and the psychological plane of the narrator's viewpoint.[11] Although Resseguie gives a credible account of the narrator's perspective, he does not explain how the Spirit relates to it. Barr attempts to explain how the Spirit transforms the narrator's viewpoint, but his attempts in this direction are fragmentary. Such work needs to extend to Revelation as a whole. Serious work is needed on how the narrator's viewpoint relates to the divine frame of reference. Such a work would need to focus on the Holy Spirit in Revelation. We shall begin this work in the next section.

Narrator of Revelation and the Holy Spirit

In this study, Rimmon-Kenan's narrator typology analysis will be used to help classify the relation between the narrator and the Holy Spirit. There are three reasons for preferring Rimmon-Kenan's model in this context. Firstly, it reveals more about the narrator than other models. As Steven M. Sheeley puts it, Rimmon-Kenan's analysis "seems most suited for this examination of the narrator."[12] Secondly, it focuses on the reliability of the narrator by drawing attention to the narrator's divine frame of reference and appealing to the Holy Spirit by establishing the narrator's reliability. Rimmon-Kenan's model is especially useful for explaining why and how the narrator introduces the Spirit onto the narrative stage of Revelation. Thirdly, it is well grounded in literary theory. It is based both on analysis of the three dimensions of the narrative: that is, story, text, and narration, and on analysis of the "narrative communication situation," which consists of four participants: the real author, the narrator, the narratee, and the real reader.[13] In short, Rimmon-Kenan's criteria provide a more coherent picture of the narrator than other studies have.

---

11. This means that John was not only controlled by the Spirit psychologically, but also was moved spatially when he was in the spirit.

12. Sheeley, *Narrative Asides in Luke-Acts*, 151.

13. She emphasizes the dynamic relation between the author and the reader in the narrative communication situation. However, I disagree with her limitation of the narrative communication situation to just four participants: the real author, the narrator, the narratee, and the real reader, which excludes the implied author and implied reader. Rimmon-Kenan, *Narrative Fiction*, 88. The meaning of the text will be found through the whole reading process which includes the implied author and the implied reader. For the interaction between text and reader, see Hur, *Dynamic Reading*, 89; Iser, *Implied Reader; Act of Reading;* and Fish, *Is There a Text?*

She proposes criteria by which to investigate the variety of Revelation's narrators, identification that significantly contributes to "the reader's understanding of and attitude to the story."[14] Thus, she suggests four crucial criteria to understand the narrators in a literary work: the narrative level, the extent of participation in the story, the degree of perceptibility, and the reliability.[15]

> The narrative level to which the narrator belongs, the extent of his participation in the story, the degree of perceptibility of his role, and finally his reliability are crucial factors in the reader's understanding of and attitude to the story. It is therefore according to these criteria that the variety of the narrators will be presented. The criteria are not mutually exclusive and allow for cross-combinations between the different types.[16]

For the purpose of this study, only the reliability of the narrator shall be discussed since it is related to the phrase "in the Spirit."[17]

---

14. Rimmon-Kenan, *Narrative Fiction*, 94.

15. Ibid., 94–103. For the historical development of the study of the narrator in literary theory, see Sheeley, *Narrative Asides in Luke-Acts*, 149–59. He summarizes the various aspects of a narrator's techniques in literary theory, that is, the point of view of the narrator discussed by Uspensky, Chatman, and Genette; the narrator's presence in the narrative; the narrator's personality discussed by Lanser, Sholes, and Kellog; the taxonomic approach discussed by Genette and by Rimmon-Kenan. He, finally, adopts the Rimmon-Kenan model of taxonomy to analyze the narrator of Luke-Acts.

16. Rimmon-Kenan, *Narrative Fiction*, 94.

17. Many kinds of narrators can be found in Revelation, including extradiegetic and intradiegetic narrator, heterodiegetic and homodiegetic narrator, and hypodiegetic and hypo-hypodiegetic narrator. The variety of narrators can be classified according to certain criteria. Rimmon-Kenan asserts, "The narrative level to which the narrator belongs, the extent of his participation in the story, the degree of perceptibility of his role and finally his responsibility are crucial factors in the reader's understanding of and attitude to the story" (ibid.). According to the narrative level, a narrator who is "'above' or superior to the story he narrates" is called an extradiegetic narrator, while a narrator who is "a diegetic character in the first narrative told by the extradiegetic narrator" is an intradiegetic narrator (ibid.). A narrator who is a character in the second narrative told by an intradiegetic narrator is called a hypodiegetic narrator, while a narrator who is a character in the third narrative told by a hypodiegetic narrator is a hypo-hypodiegetic narrator. According to the extent of participation in the story, a narrator who does not participate in the story is called a heterodiegetic narrator, while a narrator who takes part in the story is a homodiegetic narrator. Ibid., 95.

Reliability of the Narrator in Revelation and "in the spirit"

Rimmon-Kenan argues that "a reliable narrator is one whose rendering of the story and commentary on it the reader is supposed to take as an authoritative account of the fictional truth."[18] The degree of a narrator's unreliability depends on "the narrator's limited knowledge, his personal involvement, and his problematic value-scheme."[19] The extradiegetic narrators in Revelation are presented as authoritative.[20] Their knowledge is unlimited, they do not participate in the story, and their value-scheme is not problematic. Almost all of the intradiegetic and hypodiegetic narrators in Revelation also are reliable since they are unlimited in knowledge, have unproblematic value schemes, and yet participate as characters in the story. Nonetheless, as is usually to be expected of participants in a story, the reliability of the intradiegetic and hypodiegetic narrators is less than that of the extradiegetic narrators.

It should be noted, however, that two narrators are less reliable in narratives. One is John, an intradiegetic narrator. The other is Babylon, a hypo-hypodiegetic narrator. John's relative unreliability is due to his role within the story's spatio-temporal horizon, which necessarily limits his knowledge.[21] At the very beginning he is limited to Patmos (Rev 1:9). Furthermore, his knowledge is not superior to that of his brothers in Christ since he has shared their experience (1:9). Thus, Rev 1:9 explains why John is less reliable. But, the real or implied author recovers John's reliability in Rev 1:10 by use of the phrase, "in the spirit." In other words, this phrase is a rhetorical device used to reinforce John's narrational reliability.

How does this rhetorical device—"in the spirit"—work? Firstly, besides overcoming John's limited knowledge as such, the phrase specifically overcomes John's spatial constraints. John is carried "in the spirit" to the heavenly place in Rev 4:2 so that he might be able to see God, the Lamb, and other heavenly beings, and learn the significance of the

---

18. Ibid., 100.

19. Ibid.

20. In my study, the extradiegetic narrator concept among many concepts of narrator shall be focused on since it represents an authoritative and omniscient one like a divine character in the spiritual writings.

21. The value-scheme of John was not problematic since he shared the common value-scheme to suffer because of the word of God and the testimony of Jesus (Rev 1:9) with the extradiegetic narrator.

forthcoming events. In Rev 17:3, John is similarly transported "in the spirit" into a wilderness to see the judgment of the great whore. In Rev 21:10, John is again carried to a great, high mountain to see the bride, the Lamb's wife, that is, the holy city Jerusalem descending from heaven. Secondly, it is evident that John, when he was "in the spirit," was considered to have the value-scheme or norm of the implied author or the narrator.[22] In other words, John's veracity shares the norm of the implied author or the narrator whenever he is in the spirit. In the spirit, John can not only hear the exalted Jesus' message to the seven churches, but also see the visions and hear the heavenly voices, which represent the value-scheme of the overall narrator.

On the other hand, the rhetorical device, "in the spirit," importantly transforms the intradiegetic narrator, John, into a sort of "semi-extradiegetic" narrator.[23] However, John, even "in the spirit," cannot directly become the extradiegetic narrator because as a terrestrial human being he lacks the narrator's *intrinsic* omniscience. For example, in response to the question of the mighty angel in Rev 5:2, John weeps because he cannot find anyone who deserves to open the seven seals. However, it seems reasonable to suggest that John wept because "in the spirit" he realized how important opening the seven seals was. Thus John may be identified as a "semi-extradiegetic" narrator. Another example of John's limited knowledge is found in the repeated episode in which John attempts to worship the angel (Rev 19:10; 22:8b). However, John's obeisance to the angel might not seriously compromise his narration reliability, for at least two reasons. Firstly, it is only a lapse of judgment in the face of numinous glory rather than a moral or spiritual error expressing a distorted value-scheme. Secondly, it can be interpreted as a literary technique of the implied author, intended to emphasize the importance of worshipping only God.[24] To summarize: the rhetorical phrase, "in the spirit," functions to reinforce the reliability of John's testimony and visions.

22. Rimmon-Kenan confesses that the norm or value of the implied author is usually hard to find. The point of view of the narrator in Revelation shall be discussed in the next part of this chapter.

23. For the sake of convenience, "semi-extradiegetic narrator" shall be used in this study, even though no literary scholar names it as such. The level of his knowledge is laid at some point on the continuum between that of an extradiegetic narrator and of an intradiegetic narrator.

24. Rimmon-Kenan insists that the readers do not feel as if the narrator is unreliable when the error of the narrator can be considered as ironical or momentary. Ibid., 102–3.

Meanwhile, Babylon—which becomes the dwelling place of every evil demon and foul spirit in 18:7b—is contrasted with John, who is "in the spirit," as an unreliable narrator contrasted with a reliable narrator. Firstly, Babylon operates at a different narrative level, being a hypo-hypodiegetic narrator—a narrative level associated with lower reliability—rather than as an intradiegetic narrator, like John. Secondly, Babylon becomes a dwelling place of demons (18:2b), which negatively affects all three factors of reliability, that is, knowledge, involvement, value-scheme. Her knowledge is extremely limited in that she is unaware of her imminent destruction and grief (18:7). Furthermore, she celebrates her permanent security as a queen (18:7). Her arrogance, boastfulness, and sins do not conform to the norm of the implied author of Revelation (18:5–7). Thus, the rhetorical effect of the description of Babylon in 18:7 contrasts to that of the phrase of "in the spirit."

Summary

The implied reader of Revelation experiences four narrators in terms of each narrative level: the extradiegetic, the intradiegetic, the hypodiegetic, and the hypo-hypodiegetic narrator. Other kinds of the participant-narrator can be found in Revelation: the heterodiegetic and the homodiegetic narrator. John's use of the rhetorical phrase, "in the spirit," reinforces his reliability. The unreliability of Babylon is reinforced by using the phrases, "dwelling place of demons" and "every foul spirit," and by her deluded comment about her prosperity and security immediately before her impending crisis.

In short, a narrator might just be comprehended as a storyteller by whom a story is narrated in the narrative. However, the narrator's role can be classified into many different kinds of the narrator according to four criteria given by Rimmon-Kenan. Based on these definitions, this study shall be narrowed to focus on the extradiegetic and heterodiegetic narrator as a representative narrator in the following sections since these are the most reliable and distinguishable from the narrative characters.

Narrator's Point of View in Revelation with Special Reference to the Holy Spirit

Introduction

What is a point of view or focalization? Chatman insists that it is the "perspective" of a narrator or a character within the narrative.[25] In this study, Rimmon-Kenan's model will be adopted to clarify the narrator's viewpoint. In her book, *Narrative Fiction: Contemporary Poetics*, she distinguishes the focalization from the narration as well as external focalization from internal focalization.[26] In this study, as declared above, since my purpose is to find the relationship between the narrator and the Spirit in Revelation, the extra-heterodiegetic narrator as narrator-focalizer or external narrator will be given more attention than the intradiegetic and hypodiegetic narrator as character-focalizer or internal narrator.[27] However the shifts between an external focalization and internal focalization shall be observed in each facet of the narrator's viewpoint. Rimmon-Kenan analyzes the focalization or point of view of the narrator with three facets: the perceptual, psychological and ideological facets.[28] Her analysis is a revised version of Uspensky's model.[29]

---

25. Chatman, *Story and Discourse*, 151–52.

26. She prefers to use the terminology of focalization rather than point of view. She adopts the terminology of "narrator-focalizer" from Bal to represent the agent of external focalization as well as "character-focalizer" to represent the agent of internal focalization. Rimmon-Kenan, *Narrative Fiction*, 74; Bal, *Narratologie*, 37.

27. The extra-heterodiegetic and the extra-homodiegetic narrator can be created if we consider both criteria of narrative level and the participation of the narrator in the story. The extra-homodiegetic narrator in Revelation will be excluded since it appears just in Rev 1:5b–6a and is not so meaningful in the study of the point of view of the narrator in Revelation.

28. These three facets in the narrator's point of view are not mutually exclusive, but overlapping. Hur, *Dynamic Reading*, 92.

29. She insists that Uspensky does not always distinguish between narration and focalization, nor between the narrator and the author. Rimmon-Kenan, *Narrative Fiction*, 139. That seems to be why she tries to suggest her own three facets model of focalization. In this study the three facets of the narrator's point of view will be discussed.

Perceptual Facet of the Narrator's Point of View in Revelation

The perceptual point of view is "determined by two main coordinates: space and time."[30] With regard to "space," there are two different narrative positions: the external position and the internal position. According to Rimmon-Kenan, the external "takes the form of a bird's-eye view," while the internal takes the view of "a limited observer."[31] The former yields either a "panoramic view" or a "simultaneous focalization of things 'happening' in different places."[32] The latter is limited to the observer's location. She insists that the narrator's spatial point of view may change from external to internal or from internal to external.[33] Now we will examine more closely the narrator's spatial positions in Revelation.

First of all, Revelation starts with a panoramic view of the process of transmission from God to Jesus Christ to the servants of Jesus (Rev 1:1–2). The beatitude (1:3) and the coming of Jesus (1:7) are declared from the external position. This beatitude appears again at the very end of the narrative (22:14–15) with more specific information, namely, of the right to eat from the tree of life and to enter the heavenly city (contrasted with the curse of exclusion from the New Jerusalem).

Meanwhile, the external narrative position provides a simultaneous view to the readers. The process of transmission—from God to Jesus to His angel to John to the seven churches—unites several different places. The locations of reading, listening, and keeping the revelation of Jesus, are different. The positions, from which all the tribes of the earth see of the second coming of Jesus, will be different. The interior of the city of the New Jerusalem differs from the exterior. However, the external narrator of Revelation can observe all these places simultaneously.

Secondly, the narrator's viewpoint is also spatially associated with some character-narrators (intradiegetic narrator), John, Jesus, angels, and heavenly beings. As previously discussed, John's viewpoint is limited. John is located on Patmos and is specifically writing to the seven churches in Asia Minor. He can view only his earthly place. However, John overcomes this limitation in the Spirit and is transported into heaven. The narrator projects his viewpoint to John with the phrase, "in the spirit." On the other hand, the narrator projects his simultaneous and panoramic

30. Ibid., 77.
31. Ibid.
32. Ibid.
33. Ibid., 78.

spatial viewpoint onto another character-narrator, Jesus, who knows the seven churches both simultaneously and panoramically.[34] Finally, and remarkably, the narrator also projects his viewpoint onto angels and heavenly beings who give heavenly information to John.

Thirdly, it should be noted that the narrator's viewpoint shifts from the external to the internal or from the internal to the external. The external viewpoint in Rev 1:1–3 moves to an internal one in Rev 1:4. The internal focalization shifts again to the external one in Rev 1:7. The external viewpoint moves again to the internal one in Rev 1:9. From the isolation of Patmos, John ascends into heaven in the spirit in Rev 4:1–2. The unique expression, "in the spirit," is adopted by the author of Revelation to represent the change of viewpoint of John, from the internal and earthly one to the external and heavenly one. In Rev 17:3, the phrase, "in the spirit," is used again to indicate the shift of John's spatial viewpoint from heaven to the wilderness. In Rev 21:10, the spatial viewpoint is changed again from the wilderness to a great, high mountain to provide a panoramic view of the New Jerusalem. With the same spatial viewpoint, Revelation ends with the hopeful wish of Jesus' coming and the blessing for all saints in Rev 22:20–21.

In short, the external narrator has an omnipresent and panoramic viewpoint. Even the internal character-narrator, John, has the panoramic point of view *in the spirit*, as do angels and heavenly beings in the narrative. It is notable that the shifts of spatial viewpoint in Revelation are related to the rhetorical phrase, "in the spirit."

On the other hand, in terms of "time," Rimmon-Kenan insists:

> External focalization is panchronic in the case of an unpersonified focalizer, and retrospective in the case of a character focalizing his own past. On the other hand, internal focalization is synchronous with the information regulated by the focalizer.[35]

The external narrator covers all the temporal dimensions of the narrative, that is, the past, present, and future. However, the internal narrator is limited to the present time dimension.[36] The extra-heterodiegetic narrator of Revelation has a panchronic point of view. The passages concern-

34. Jesus can be recognized as the omniscient and omnipresent Son of God from the perspective of Christian readers. However, here Jesus is regarded as a character in the literary perspective.

35. Rimmon-Kenan, *Narrative Fiction*, 78.

36. Uspensky, *Poetics of Composition*, 67, 113.

ing the transmission of revelation (Rev 1:1–2), of blessing (1:3; 22:14), and of the coming Jesus (1:7) are narrated by the unpersonified narrator who has a panchronic focalization. John, who is "in the spirit," uses external focalization that allows a retrospective viewpoint on his own past experience throughout the narrative of Revelation.

To sum it up, "in the spirit" plays a significant literary role in expanding John's spatio-temporal viewpoint. When, therefore, the phrase, "in the spirit" is used, it indicates that John is briefly granted some share in the divine attribute that overcomes the limitations of time and space. In the spirit, John participates in the omnipresent and retrospective point of view as a creature made divine by grace.

Psychological Facet of the Narrator's Point of View in Revelation

Rimmon-Kenan suggests that the narrator's psychological viewpoint has two components:

> Whereas the perceptual facet has to do with the focalizer's sensory range, the psychological facet concerns his mind and emotion. The determining components are two: the cognitive and the emotive orientation of the focalizer towards the focalized.[37]

In terms of the narrator's cognitive orientation, he knows everything. His omniscience is presented both through direct narrative description as well as through the mouths of reliable characters. The direct presentation unveils the whole of Revelation of Jesus Christ, the benediction on those who receive the revelation, and the coming of Jesus for the readers. He knows: (1) the identity of God, who is and who was and who is to come; (2) the Seven Spirits who are before God's throne; and (3) Jesus, the faithful witness, the firstborn of the dead and the ruler of the kings of the earth. However, in general, the narrator prefers to communicate important information through reliable characters. Thus, the narrator presents the identity of God as the Alpha and the Omega not through narrative description but through direct divine self-description (Rev 1:8). Again, through the words of Jesus himself, the narrator reveals Jesus' identity as the first and the last, and the living one who has the keys of Death and Hades (1:17–18), and also the spiritual situation of the seven churches in Asia ("I know" in Rev 2–3).

---

37. Rimmon-Kenan, *Narrative Fiction*, 78.

Narrator, Point of View of the Narrator, and the Holy Spirit in Revelation

The narrator provides knowledge of the heavenly topography through John, who is in the spirit, so that John acts for the reader, as a spatio-temporal lens through which the majesty of heaven can be viewed; hence, John's repeated phrase, "I saw and I heard." However, how can it be understood when John, who is in the Spirit, experiences the recognitional limitation in the narrative of Revelation? We can figure out that the author often creates a "shock effect" by limiting John's perception to one of an internal narrator.[38] This is evident in Rev 1:17–20. When John saw the risen Christ, he fell at His feet as if dead since he was so afraid. John was so spatio-temporally limited at that moment that he needed help identifying the glorified Jesus and understanding the mystery of the seven stars and seven golden lampstands. By this device, readers participate in the shock and thereby pay closer attention to the message. A similar shock effect is used when John weeps at not being able to find anyone sufficiently worthy to open the scroll (5:1–5). John's mistaken angel worship in Rev 19:10, 22:8b creates a similar shock effect.[39]

In terms of the narrator's emotive orientation, he yields both objective and subjective focalization.[40] He is neutral in describing the revelation of Jesus Christ, the benediction, and the coming of Jesus. However, he registers his subjective emotions through the characters. Thus, through the character-narrator, Jesus, he indicates his attitude towards the seven churches. He approves of their patient endurance, faithfulness in suffering, love and service, and keeping the word of Jesus in the churches. He disapproves of the abandonment of the first love, holding the teaching of Balaam and the Nicolaitans, tolerating Jezebel, not waking up, and being lukewarm. Through John, he informs readers of the awesome fear appropriate before the risen and glorified Jesus, the worthiness of the Lamb to open the scroll, the heart desire of the second coming of Jesus (which is also expressed by the Spirit and the bride; Rev 22:7). The narrator also provides important information about other heavenly characters through the angels' actions and voices, thereby using a multi-perspective approach.

---

38. Rimmon-Kenan explains the shock effect of Faulkner's "A Rose for Emily" in her *Narrative Fiction*, 78–79. This relates to the psychological aspect of the narrator's viewpoint.

39. This shock effect comes from the contrast with the usual reliability of John as narrator.

40. The emotive psychological point of view (as a literary strategy) is related to the ideological point of view of the narrator in Revelation.

In short, it is reasonable to assert that the narrator is omniscient, and conveys knowledge by both objective and subjective means. He informs the readers of the characters' intentions, thoughts, and feelings. He shows his preference towards the risen Jesus and the Lamb of God as well as toward the faithful acts of the seven churches in Asia, while rebuking their unfaithful acts. He expresses a strong desire for the coming again of Jesus through speeches by the Spirit and the bride, as well as other heavenly beings. In other words, the narration, which is produced by the narrator through the Holy Spirit, presents that the narrator as *omniscient* as well as *reliable* and *authoritative*.

Ideological Facet of the Narrator's Point of View in Revelation

The narrator's ideological viewpoint is essential to understand since the narrator not only "controls the overarching point of view of the story," but also "presents the differing points of view of the characters in the course of telling the story" through his value and belief system.[41] Rimmon-Kenan describes the ideological viewpoint:

> This facet, often referred to as "the norms of the text," consists of "a general system of viewing the world conceptually," in accordance with which the events and characters of the story are evaluated. In the simplest case, the "norms" are presented through a single dominant perspective, that of the narrator-focalizer. If additional ideologies emerge in such texts, they become subordinate to the dominant focalizer, thus transforming the other evaluating subjects into objects of evaluation.[42]

The narrator's ideological viewpoint shapes the narrative according to his standards of judgement. Thus, the narrator is neither neutral nor impartial.[43] He leads the readers via his prejudices or biases.[44] Rhoads, Dewey, and Michie correctly observe:

> When a narrator is omniscient and invisible, the reader tends to be unaware of the narrator's biases, values, and conception of

---

41. Rhoads et al., *Mark as Story*, 43.

42. Rimmon-Kenan, *Narrative Fiction*, 81. Quotes in the first sentence are from Uspensky, *Poetics of Composition*, 8, quoted in Rimmon-Kenan, *Narrative Fiction*, 81.

43. Culpepper, *Anatomy of the Fourth Gospel*, 32.

44. The terms "bias" and "prejudice" here must necessarily have non-pejorative meanings since they are unavoidable in any narrative.

the world and therefore tends to trust the narrator as a neutral, "objective" teller of the events. But the narrator is not neutral. Rather, the narrator functions like the director of a film, who is responsible for the presentation of the whole story.[45]

To reconstruct the narrator's ideological viewpoint, it is necessary to analyze "the asides, manner of describing characters and events, choice of the words, order of episodes, literary techniques," quotations from the writings, the words and actions of the characters that "the narrator has established as reliable or unreliable."[46] It is also necessary to think about the "conflict world" embedded in the narrative to identify the narrator's ideological or theological worldview.[47] Based on such analysis, the narrator's ideological viewpoint of Revelation emerges as follows.

COSMOLOGICAL PERSPECTIVE

Firstly, the narrator has clear evaluations of both parties in the cosmological conflict he describes: God is good and both Satan and human beings are bad.[48] Thinking in "God's terms," is considered the reliable viewpoint, while thinking in "Satan's terms" or "human terms" is regarded as unreliable and incorrect.

Secondly, the following attitudes to God are commended: keeping the words of the prophecy (Rev 1:3; 12:17; 14:12; 22:9), testifying to or prophesying the word of God (1:2; 10:11; 11:3; 12:17; 22:10), holding the first love (2:4, 19), patient endurance in the persecution (1:9; 2:2; 13:10; 14:12), being in the spirit (1:10; 4:2; 17:3; 21:10), love (2:4; 19), faith (2:10, 13, 19; 13:10; 14:12; 17:14), service (1:6; 2:19; 5:10), worship toward God (4:8, 10, 11; 5:9–10, 12–13; 7:15; 11:1, 15–18; 14:7; 15:3–4; 19:1–10; 22:3, 9), prayer to God (5:8; 8:3–4), martyrdom (6:9, 11; 12:11; 13:15; 18:24; 20:4), awakening (2:10; 3:1, 3, 16–17; 16:15), repentance (2:5, 16, 21, 22; 3:3, 19; 9:20–21; 16:9, 11), wearing white robes and linen (righteous deeds; 3:4; 6:11; 7:9, 12–13; 14:4; 16:15; 19:8, 14; 22:14), wisdom (5:12;

---

45. Rhoads et al., *Mark as Story*, 43.
46. Ibid., 44–45.
47. Hur, *Dynamic Reading*, 98.
48. Human beings who are not overtly serving God are ultimately allied with Satan. However the narrator is economic with references to Satan and instead characteristically appeals to human responsibilities. In this study there is, therefore, an explicit conjoining of "satanic" with distorted human attitudes and actions.

7:12; 13:18; 17:9), and conquering (2:7, 11, 17, 26, 28; 3:5, 12, 21; 12:11; 21:7).

Thirdly, so far as Satan and deluded human activities are concerned, the reader is warned to avoid: false teachings (Rev 2:2, 14–15, 20; 22:18–19); fornication (2:14, 20, 22; 9:21; 14:8; 17:2, 4; 18:3, 9; 19:2; 21:27; 22:15); self-deception (3:17–18); worshipping demons, idols, angels, and the beast (9:20; 13:12, 15; 19:10; 21:8; 22:8, 15); murdering the saints (6:10; 9:21; 16:6; 17:6; 18:24; 19:2; 21:8; 22:15); sorcery (9:21; 21:8; 22:15); deception (13:14; 19:20; 21:8; 21:27; 22:15); cursing the name of God (16:9, 11, 21); refusal to repent (2:5, 16, 21–22; 9:20–21; 16:9, 11); and self-glorification (18:7).

Fourthly, the narrator's ideological viewpoint is supported through two contrasting character types. Those who follow God are presented as positive and conquering characters who transcend time and the space. Those who follow Satan and distorted human ways are described as destructive and, eventually, defeated characters. The former group, who are allied to God, include: those who keep and testify to the word of God (Rev 1:3; 22:7); the churches in Smyrna (2:8–11) and Philadelphia (3:7–13); the twenty-four elders (4:10–11; 5:8–10); those slaughtered for the word of God (6:9; 18:4; 20:4); the 144,000 sealed people (7:4); a great multitude from every nation, tribe, people, and language (7:9); the prophets who announce the mystery of God (10:7); the two witnesses (11:3–13); a woman who gives birth to a son and her children who keep the commandments of God and hold the testimony of Jesus (12:1–17); the 144,000 people standing on Mount Zion (14:1–5); those who had been victorious over the beast and its image (15:2); and the bride of the Lamb (19:7; 21:9; 22:17). The narrator noticeably favors these people as God's sincere servants, whereas he disfavors those associated with Satan. Those who obey Satan and distorted human ways are the kings of the earth, the magnates, the generals, the rich, and the powerful (Rev 6:15); every slave and free person who are is sealed on their forehead (9:4); the beast that comes up from the bottomless pit and kills the two witnesses (11:7); the angels following Satan (12:3–17); the beast from the sea (13:1–8); the beast from the land and the false prophet (13:11–17; 19:20); those who worship the beast and its image and receive a mark on their forehead (14:9); those who refuse to repent and who curse God (16:9, 11, 21); the great whore and the kings of the earth (17:1–18); those who are not written in the book of life (20:15); and the cowardly, the faithless, the polluted, the murderers, the fornicators, the sorcerers, the idolaters, and all liars (21:8).

Besides two contrasting groups, we find some characters who float uncertainly between these opposite poles in the Revelation narrative. In fact, the ideological conflict only allows temporarily for any such middle ground. For example, the five churches in Asia (Rev 2-3) might have responded positively to God.[49] But now they float toward the evil side. The narrator in Revelation challenges them to repent and to follow God, giving them the choice between eschatological promise and doom. More generally—through the use of narrative asides—he calls all the saints for wisdom, faith, and endurance of Revelation (13:10; 13:18; 14:12; 17:9).[50] Adding the majestic description of the heavenly throne (Rev 4-5) and awesome judgment of those who follow satanic and distorted human ways (Rev 6-16) reinforced this challenge. A climax is reached with the announcement of destruction for Babylon, the dragon and the two beasts (Rev 17-20), and then the descent of the New Jerusalem (Rev 21-22), the bride of the Lamb, who is faithful to God. In literary terms, the narrator uses various rhetorical devices to persuade his readers to conform to what he regards as God's ways. Those who live on the earth are thus challenged to worship, fear, and give glory to God when the eternal gospel is proclaimed (14:6-7). This challenge is issued to both unconverted and converted readers.[51] This appeal goes out even for very late repentance (9:20-21; 11:13).

---

49. The five churches in Asia mean the churches in Ephesus, Pergamum, Thyatira, Sardis, and Laodicea. Actually, the two model churches in Smyrna and Philadelphia create a rhetorical contrast.

50. According to Sheeley, narrative asides are defined as *material necessary to understand the story*: explanation, identification, context, commentary on story and on character, custom; *general information*; *inside views (characters)*; *self-conscious narration*: narrator's relationship to story, narrator's relationship to reader; reader's relationship to story. Sheeley, *Narrative Asides in Luke-Acts*, 42. For the narrative asides in Revelation, see Dal Lee, *Narrative Asides*, 91-157.

51. This book was originally designed to be read in church by believers. Therefore, strictly speaking, it was directed at "the converted," though indirectly through their faithful witness, also to the unconverted.

A Dynamic Reading of the Holy Spirit in Revelation

Apocalyptic perspective

The narrator in Revelation adopts an apocalyptic worldview as his own ideological starting point. David Barr summarizes as follows[52]:

1. The world is under the control of evil for the duration of this age. Thus, the primary forces of history are not human action but supernatural forces. This is a strongly dualistic way of thinking.
2. There are two ages and the age to come will be the complete opposite of this age: good will prevail; evil will be judged. All apocalypses posit this dualism, but some do not project it as an historical epoch of the future; rather they see it as retribution beyond death. Again, we note the strong dualism.
3. God will bring about this change through some decisive act of intervention.
4. We should be prepared for the change for it is near at hand.

The narrator in Revelation shows some traits of dualism. With respect to cosmic battle, he counters the satanic trinity with the Divine Trinity, which Satan mimics.[53] With respect to the spatial dimension, the narrator has a threefold contrast: heaven, earth, and hades. With respect to the temporal dimension, he contrasts this age to the coming age.

However, on the one hand, it should be noted that he offers a modified dualism. For example, he indicates that God cannot be compared with the dragon. In other words, the conflict between two powers is asymmetric. In the heavenly war narrative Michael and his angels defeat the dragon and his angels. More fundamentally still, he characterizes God as sovereign over both the supernatural and the entire spatial dimension whether heaven, earth, or hades. God also controls all historical events within the entire temporal dimension. The narrator presents his ideological viewpoint by using the divine passive as well as by presenting

---

52. Barr, *Tales of the End*, 156. Barr rightly insists that Revelation assumes this worldview.

53. Revelation claims that the dragon inspires the two beasts and they worship him. The first beast from the sea shows its power so that all the people worship and follow it. The second beast from the land supports the first beast by deceiving all people to worship the image of the first beast. Bauckham names these three satanic entities as the satanic trinity in his *Theology of the Book*, 89.

the heavenly throne as having power for universal judgment.[54] In this way, he presents his own absolute theocentric ideology.

On the other hand, the narrator offers another modified dualism between the satanic trinity and the Divine Trinity. To scrutinize this contrast, the dragon and the first beast of satanic trinity may be contrasted with the Divine Trinity. However, the narrator does not contrast the second beast with Divine Trinity by commenting that the second beast is the false prophet, not the supernatural one in Rev 16:13; 19:20; 20:10. Rather, we find that he intends to contrast the false prophet with the faithful prophetic witness, that is, the church. However, the narrator does not refuse to contrast the satanic trinity with the Divine Trinity by describing that the dragon and two beasts are said to have their own demonic and foul spirits in Rev 16:13–14.

In relation to the spatial dimension, he broadens the use of the word heaven from referring only to the mysterious spiritual place where the saints dwell. Thus, in Rev 12:11–12, heaven is contrasted with the earth and the sea. *It is notable that those who dwell in heaven cannot be separated from those who dwell in the earth since the latter can be included in the former.* The narrator again blurs the distinction between heaven and earth in Revelation 21–22 by including the episode of the New Jerusalem descending on earth. In this way, the narrator transcends the dualistic concept of apocalyptic space. Barr rightly argues that "John's spiritual geography imagines a clear link between realms, but we should avoid oversimplifying, for it is not a one-dimensional link."[55] The narrator proposes that the "great city" in Rev 11:18 represents not only Roma (the patron deity of Rome), but also Sodom, Egypt, and Jerusalem. This mixing of imagery allows the narrator to highlight the primal decisions that the urban Christians of East Asia faced—to decide between God and Satan in their daily lives.

In relation to the temporal dimension, he overcomes the contrast between the present age and the age to come. He presents his prophetic-ideological viewpoint by intensively gathering past and future motifs into the present time of decision. This collision of temporalities is evident in the name of God "who is who was and who is to come."[56] He characterizes Jesus as one who is coming in the present time. He challenges the readers to adopt a prophetic perspective on their present lives, by

---

54. For the divine passive, see Resseguie, *Revelation Unsealed*, 37–38.
55. Barr, *Tales of the End*, 65.
56. For this, see Bauckham, *Theology of the Book*, 28–30.

remembering the past and anticipating the age to come. Thus, for the narrator, the present world represents the battlefield where the saints are called to "fight" alongside Christ in the messianic war as his prophetic army.[57]

THEOCENTRIC, CHRISTOCENTRIC, AND PNEUMATOCENTRIC PERSPECTIVE

The extradiegetic narrator in Revelation counts Jesus as a fundamentally reliable character. This narrator allies himself to Jesus. Since God gave the revelation to Jesus (Rev 1:1) and Jesus served as *the faithful witness*, Jesus became the standard scale by which all other characters are to be weighed. Alliance with Jesus is regarded as the key to the future. (14:1; 21:22–27). In effect, the narrator identifies his own ideology with that of God and Jesus. He challenges his readers to abandon their existing ideology in favor of his own theocentric or christocentric worldview.

It should be noted that the narrator also has a pneumatocentric ideology. He identifies the Seven Spirits with God and Jesus, and describes the Seven Spirits as one of three sources of grace and peace with God and Jesus in Rev 1:4–5. The Seven Spirits are identified with God not only by the possessive phrase "of God" in Rev 4:5 and Rev 5:6, but also by their location in front of God's throne in Rev 1:4 and 4:5. On the other hand, they are also allied to Jesus who is said to have the Seven Spirits in Rev 5:6. The extradiegetic narrator metaphorically refers to the function of the Seven Spirits by speaking of the seven horns and seven eyes of the Lamb. In other words, the Seven Spirits are closely identified with Jesus. He also elucidates the close relationship of the Seven Spirits to both God and Jesus by using a divine passive, "sent out into all the earth" (Rev 5:6). They are sent out into all the earth by God and Jesus. In the letters to the seven churches, the Spirit is described as working with Jesus in the same phrase, "what the Spirit is saying to the churches." The voice of the Spirit and the voice of Jesus are associated.

However, the narrator also attempts to distinguish the Spirit from the Seven Spirits by delineating a different ministry for each. The Spirit appears dominantly in the ministry for the Churches, whereas the Seven

---

57. It is important to emphasize that this conflict is not a physical war, but a spiritual combat against evil principles within the lives of the saints. In fact, the author rejects physical violence as a means; cf. Rev 13:10.

Spirits focus on the ministry for all the earth. For example, when the heavenly voice announces, "blessed are the dead who from now on die in the Lord," the Spirit says, "Yes, they will rest from their labours, for their deeds follow them" (Rev 14:13). The Spirit is concerned about the lives of the saints even after their death. In Rev 22:17, the Spirit shares the same hope with the bride of Jesus, the ideal Church. The Spirit says, "come" *together with* the bride. The narrator challenges his readers to participate in the eschatological hope through the Spirit. Similarly, he identifies the Spirit as the Spirit of prophecy in Rev 19:10 and emphasizes that the Spirit not only witnesses to Jesus, but also to the prophetic words that Jesus witnesses. Furthermore, he emphasizes that the Spirit comes from God who then gives it to Jesus. Founding the worshipping community is a decisive fruit of the ministry of Jesus and of the Spirit in the narrative of Revelation.

Furthermore, the narrator uses the phrase "in the Spirit" to highlight John as a reliable character who shares his own viewpoint and also God's viewpoint.[58] In other words, the Spirit takes control of John and guides him to a reliable viewpoint. All reliable visions and voices John sees and hears happen under the auspices of the Spirit. The narrator is able to challenge his readers since John allegedly narrates the whole story of Revelation when he is in the spirit. Hence, the narrator not only tells the reader of the functions and identity of the Holy Spirit, but also of John, who is inspired by the Holy Spirit to narrate the whole story of Revelation.[59]

It is also necessary to note the binary contrast between the Seven Spirits and the three evil spirits. The Seven Spirits are closely related to God and the Lamb, Jesus, whereas the three foul spirits are closely related to the dragon and false prophet (Rev 16:13).[60] The Seven Spirits of God are sent out into all the earth (5:6), whereas the three foul spirits are sent

---

58. As for "in the Spirit," we will discuss it again in "The Divine Frame of Reference and the Spirit in Revelation" in this chapter, especially in the section, "Four big visions."

59. Actually, the narrator in Revelation does not adopt the terminology of the Holy Spirit at all in his narrative. However, it seems to be clear that the Spirit is represented as the "Holy" Spirit since the Seven Spirits are in front of God's throne. It also seems to be clear that the Spirit speaks to the churches just as Jesus does. Thus we can propose that the narrator presents the Spirit or the Seven Spirits as the "Holy" Spirit through the whole narrative in Revelation.

60. For the false prophet is meant as the second beast. See Bauckham, *Theology of the Book*, 38, 78, 91, 102, 106, 112, 114–15, 123–24, 155.

out to the kings of the whole world. Three foul spirits "go abroad to the kings of the whole world, to assemble them for battle on the great day of God the Almighty" (16:14). Both sets of spirits are working in the world. However, their purposes of mission are diametrically opposed. The three foul spirits are sent to assemble all the world's kings to war against God, whereas the Seven Spirits work for God as the seven horns, the seven eyes, and the seven flaming torches (4:5; 5:6). Another contrast between the three foul spirits or demonic spirits and the Divine Spirit, that is, the Seven Spirits and the Spirit is as follows. The three foul spirits are sent to speak to the worldly kings whereas the Seven Spirits are sent to address the seven churches. But in fact, the contrast is wider than this. Three demonic spirits influence the world's kings, whereas the divine spirit addresses—in symbolic form—the worldwide church.[61] Furthermore, the numerical contrast between the "three" evil "spirits" and "every" foul "spirit" (18:2) needs to be considered. The narrator is making a deliberate, not an accidental, distinction in order to make sure that the "Spirit" and seven "Spirits" represent the same identity as three evil "spirits" and every foul "spirit." By using the word "foul" or "demonic" to describe these evil spirit(s), he implicitly and pejoratively contrasts them with the seven "divine" and "holy" spirits. Additionally, phrases like "who are before his throne" (1:4), "the seven flaming torches burning in front of the throne" (4:5), "seven horns and seven eyes" (5:6), serve further to contrast the divine holy spirit(s) with the evil spirit(s) that are described as "like frogs," "coming from the mouth of the dragon, from the mouth of the beast, and from the mouth of the false prophet" (16:13). By such literary devices, readers are persuaded to see the Seven Spirits (and the spirit) as holy, worthy, divine, and transcendent, and their demonic counterparts as repellent and doomed. The attention these matters are given in the narrative confirms the narrator's pneumatocentric theology.

In short, one can justly claim that the narrator has not only a "theocentric" and "christocentric" viewpoint, but also a "pneumatocentric" perspective.[62] Additionally, by setting up a contrast between the two spiritual opponents (albeit, these are asymmetric in significance and

---

61. Although the seven letters are sent to seven historic Asia Minor churches, these churches also stand representatively for the churches of the whole world.

62. The pneumatocentric viewpoint shall be clarified more in later parts of this book, especially as we examine the divine frame of reference provided by the Spirit in this chapter and chapter 3.

power), the narrator's *prophetic* and *spiritually "combative"* viewpoint is displayed.[63]

Divine Frame of Reference and the Spirit in Revelation

The narrator's viewpoint is "complemented and authenticated by a carefully and tightly constructed divine frame of reference."[64] Darr insists that the narrator's viewpoint is "the most significant, all-encompassing frame of reference."[65] The divine frame of reference and the narrator's viewpoint are "two utterly reliable, authoritative, and mutually-reinforcing frames of reference that condition everything (including other point of view) in the story."[66] Darr asserts the critical role of the divine frame of reference in the following:

> Much like the narrator's perspective, the divine frame of reference provides the audience with a consistent and highly authoritative guide for constructing and/or evaluating characters and their roles in the action.[67]

The narrator uses the "external reference" to visions, angels, heavenly voices, heavenly beings, and even the Spirit to provide a "divine frame of reference."[68] In what follows, I shall note how the divine frame of reference plays a role throughout the narrative of Revelation and in particular the function of the Spirit in the divine frame of reference.[69] In addition,

---

63. This will be discussed in chapter 5. See also H. Y. Lee, "Concept of the Messianic War," 33–62. In this thesis, I assert that Revelation is strongly orientated by a messianic war concept that calls the readers and the churches to be participants in the spiritual combat. Bauckham also insists that Revelation may be recognized as a war scroll. See Bauckham, *Climax of Prophecy*, 210–37.

64. Darr, *On Character Building*, 51.

65. Ibid., 50.

66. Ibid.

67. Ibid., 53.

68. Darr indicates some kinds of divine frame of reference, such as the Spirit, visions, heavenly voices, angels, reliable characters, and quoted Scriptures, from his study of the Gospel of Luke. Ibid., 51–53. However, in Revelation, heavenly beings such as the four living creatures, the twenty-four elders, and the slaughtered souls also are employed. Adopted Scriptures are not employed in Revelation as a divine frame of reference, even though many allusions are used in Revelation.

69. In this study, we focus on the Spirit and on the relationship between the Spirit and the other divine frame of references such as angels, visions, heavenly voices, heavenly beings. However, the study of the other means of establishing the divine frame

we will note that *character reliability* is linked with the character's place in the divine frame of reference. In other words, if the narrator treats a character in a positive way in relation to the divine, this indicates that he/she is trustworthy and shares the narrator's ideology.

The Spirit

The Revelation narrator employs the spirit as divine frame of reference. As Table 2.1 shows, he tries to elucidate that the spirit has a strong relationship to the church, whereas the spirit used in the phrase of "in the spirit" affects the whole narrative of Revelation. The spirit speaks to the seven Asian local churches with the revelatory messages of the exalted Jesus in Rev 2:7, 11, 17, 29; 3:6, 13, 22. The spirit explains the life after the death of the saints in Christ. The spirit proclaims that they will take rest and get rewards from God according to their labors in this world. The spirit also invites the second coming of Jesus as well as the people of God in 22:17.[70] Thus, it is notable that the spirit has the same ideological point of view as the Revelation narrator.

Table 2.1 Divine Frame of Reference of Narrator in Revelation: The Spirit

Speaker	Related characters	Related verse(s)	Content of messages
Narrator	Seven churches	2:7, 11, 17, 29; 3:6, 13, 22	Let anyone who has an ear listen to what the Spirit is saying to the churches.
Narrator		14:13	"Yes," says the Spirit, "they will rest from their labors, for their deeds follow them."
Narrator		22:17	The Spirit and the bride say, "Come."

of references—angels, visions, heavenly voices, heavenly beings—can be additional topics to be researched respectively. We will discuss the characterization of the Holy Spirit in chapter 3. Our focus will be on how the Spirit is related to the main characters such as Jesus, God, John, and the heavenly beings including angels, churches, the two witnesses, the woman who gave birth to a son, the dragon and the two beasts, evil spirits, and the woman sitting on a scarlet beast.

70. For an interpretation of this verse, see Aune, *Revelation 17–22*, 1227–28.

Narrator, Point of View of the Narrator, and the Holy Spirit in Revelation Visions: Four Visions and Other Small Visions[71]

FOUR BIG VISIONS

According to Darr, visions are usually used as divine frame of reference. Two different groups of visions are found in Revelation: four visions headed by the same literary signpost, "in the Spirit"; and small visions within the big four visions. In Revelation, four big visions can be literary signposts to outline the whole single vision of Revelation, as Table 2.2 shows us.[72] In order to draw the readers' attention to the divine frame of reference that expresses his ideological viewpoint, the narrator employs several literary devices before the four visions (prologue) and after the four visions (epilogue).

---

71. Here four visions represent the four vision sets that can be identified by the four time usages of "in the Spirit" in the Revelation narrative. The first set is found in Rev 1:10—3:22, the second in 4:2—16:21, the third in 17:3—21:9, and fourth in 21:10—22:6. Small visions represent individual visions in Revelation.

72. A big vision includes many small visions. Here I shall examine the four big visions first. Then small visions will be considered in the next section, including exploration of heavenly voice(s), angel(s), and heavenly being(s). I shall discuss the structure of Revelation in chapter 5. Bauckham insists that "the whole of the book between prologue and epilogue is recounted as a single visionary experience." He admits that the single visionary is divided with the technical phrase, "in the spirit." Bauckham, *Climax of Prophecy*, 3. I name this single visionary as four big visions, since they not only are headed by four repeated phrases of, "in the spirit," but also need to be separated from small visions.

Table 2.2 Divine Frame of Reference of the Narrator in Revelation: Four Big Visions[73]

Seer	Related characters	Related verse(s)
John	One like a Son of man, Spirit, the angel of the seven churches	1:10—3:22
John	One on the throne, the Lamb, the Spirit, the heavenly beings, the angels, the two witnesses, the woman, the Dragon, the beasts, the 144,000 people	4:2—16:21
John	Woman sitting on a scarlet beast, God, the Lamb, demon, evil spirit, the Rider on the white horse, Satan, the Spirit of prophecy,	17:3—21:9
John	The Bride, the New Jerusalem, God, the Lamb	21:10—22:6

Firstly, the narrator describes the transmission of the revelation of Jesus Christ in 1:1–2: "The revelation of Jesus Christ, which God gave him to show his servants what must soon take place; he made it known by sending his angel to his servant John, who testified to the word of God and to the testimony of Jesus Christ, even to all that he saw." He explains that five third-person characters—God, Jesus Christ, an angel, John, and His servants—are involved in the transmission process. This is also indicated in a more direct literary way by Jesus speaking in the first person in Rev 22:16a: "It is I, Jesus, who sent my angel to you with this testimony for the churches." By these means, readers understand that the four vision cycles are the revelation of Jesus as well as that of God.

Secondly, the narrator immediately emphasizes the significance of listening and obedience to this prophetic revelation. Thus, 1:3 says, "Blessed is the one who reads aloud the words of the prophecy, and blessed are those who hear and who keep what is written in it; for the time is near." The importance of the revelation is again intensified with the first person declaratory blessing of the returning Jesus, "I am coming

---

73. Many commentators argue that the prologue and seven letters to the churches are the main address of Revelation, and the next vision cycles fill out the context and meaning of the message of these seven letters. According to literary analysis with a view to four visions and four repeats of the phrase "in the Spirit," the prologue after 1:10 and seven letters are regarded as merely one of the four episodes. However, with considering the cumulative effect, the first vision of the messages from the glorious Jesus is related to the coming next three visions that explain them more fully.

soon" in Rev 22:7, "See, I am coming soon! Blessed is the one who keeps the words of the prophecy of this book," which is the parallel saying of 1:3. In addition to these two beatitudes, the narrator adds another promise, "See, I am coming soon. My reward is with me, to repay according to everyone's work," in 22:12, which is parallel to Rev 22:7 with the same phrase, "See, I am coming soon." By means of this literary tool of parallelism, readers are strongly recommended to attend to the messages included in the four visions.

Thirdly, the narrator adopts two other literary forms.[74] The first is the proclamation of Jesus' coming by means both of third-person (Rev 1:7) and first-person witness (Rev 22:7, 12). The second is the self-descriptions of God and Jesus (Rev 1:8; 22:13, 16). Rev 1:7 uses the third-person announcement to express the coming of Jesus, whereas Rev 22:7, 12a twice uses the stronger first-person form, "I am coming."[75] With this first-person form, the narrator generates a literary effect to intensify the reader's attending to the revelation in the four visions. Here the narrator employs Jesus like a narrator.[76] The prophecy of Jesus' coming, both before the four visions (Rev 1:7) and after the four visions (22:7a, 12a), function to intensify the reality both of Jesus' coming and of the whole sweep of Jesus' revelations in the four visions. Moreover, this pivotal literary form functions to awaken the readers to take seriously the revelations in the four visions which result from (and in) the revelation of Jesus who gives this message to a prophet, John and the seven churches. Therefore, the coming of Jesus becomes a significant literary signpost that shapes the four visions into the narrator's divine frame of reference for the readers.

On the other hand, besides the coming of Jesus, the self-definitions of God and Jesus are another strong literary signpost to shape the four visions into the narrator's divine frame of reference for the readers. In

74. Besides the two literary forms, it seems that the narrator combines the four visions with a letter form in Rev 1:4–6, 22:21. If it is true, the four visions may be the content of the letter. With this combination of the four visions with the form of the letter, the four visions would be understood as reliable in that they are written to the real local seven churches in Asia, even though they are visions, which may not be considered to be real.

75. "Look! He is coming with the clouds; every eye will see him, even those who pierced him; and on his account all the tribes of the earth will wail. So it is to be. Amen" (Rev 1:7).

76. In Rev 1:7, the narrator reports Jesus' coming, whereas in Rev 22:7a, 12a, the narrator does not introduce Jesus as a character. Jesus takes His position as a narrator and proclaims His coming directly.

Rev 1:8, God—acting as self-proclamatory narrator—reveals himself as "the Alpha and the Omega," "who is and who was and who is to come," and "the Almighty."[77] In the second vision, in Rev 4:8; 11:17; 15:3; 16:5, 7, the same "God Almighty" and "who is and who was and who is to come" appears as one who deserves to be worshipped by all heavenly beings and angels.[78] In the fourth vision, in Rev 21:6, God declares, "I am the Alpha and the Omega." In the first vision in Rev 1:17; 2:8, Jesus declares, "I am the first and the last." In the second vision in Rev 5:5, Jesus introduces himself as "the Root of David." In Rev 22:13, 16, Jesus (again, *as the narrator*) introduces himself as "the Alpha and the Omega, the first and the last, the beginning and the end," "the root and the offspring of David," and "the bright morning star." In short, the narrator emphatically uses the same expression of both God and Jesus. He intends to identify the giver of the four visions, Jesus, with the giver of the revelation in Rev 1:1, God. By such divine declarations and their third-person affirmation, the narrator makes his four-vision narrative both authoritative and reliable due to its origin. Therefore, his readers are alerted to the importance of the revelation given through four visions since its origin is from the Alpha and the Omega, that is, he who is and who was and who is to come, the Seven Spirits, and Jesus Christ who is coming in Rev 1:5–8.

Fourthly, the narrator uses an internal character, John, so as to gain a first-person perspective. John is the one who sends the letters to the seven churches in Asia in Rev 1:4. In Rev 1:9–10, the internal narrator, John, presents himself as the recipient of four visions on the island of Patmos. Using first person and the form of a letter, the narrator shapes the four visions into more reliable divine frame of reference to the readers.

Fifthly, the narrator warns the readers neither to add nor remove words from the four-vision prophecy (Rev 22:18–19). The literary role of this warning is to underwrite the divine authority of the prophecy's words. This authority is further reinforced by the contrasting beatitudes on obedience in 22:7, 12, and 14. This literary technique prompts readers to be alert to read and obey four visions.

Sixthly, John was commanded by Jesus not to "seal up the words of the prophecy of this book, for the time is near" (Rev 22:10b).[79] The

---

77. In Rev 1:8, God takes His position like a narrator and introduces himself directly as a first person.

78. In Rev 11:17; 16:5, "who is and who was" is used. For this, see Bauckham, *Theology of the Book*, 29–30. Only God Almighty is used in Rev 15:3; 16:7.

79. For the allusion of sealing up, see Aune, *Revelation 17–22*, 1216–17.

phrase, "for the time is near," parallels 1:3: "Blessed is the one who reads aloud the words of the prophecy, and blessed are those who hear and who keep what is written in it; for the time is near."[80] Despite the negative form of this commandment, "Do not seal up the words of the prophecy of this book," its import seems primarily positive—namely a command to broadcast the contents of the prophecy to the whole world. This impression becomes cumulative with the successive open seal narratives.[81] In the first of the four visions, Jesus asked John to write the message in a letter written to the seven churches. In the second of the four visions, the uniquely qualified Lamb of God opened the seven seals in the heavenly court (Revelation 4–8). After being asked to eat the (little) scroll,[82] John is told, "You must prophesy again about many peoples and nations and languages and kings" (Rev 10:11). By contrast, he must seal up what the seven thunders had said, whereas he must proclaim the prophecy of the scroll. Thus, it is clear that the narrator emphasizes the significance of proclaiming the prophecy that concerns Jesus to the whole world. The narrator persuades the readers with being concerned in the four visions that reflect the contents of the prophecy.

Finally, it should be noted that the narrator employs the literary device of "in the Spirit," in each of the four visions, to give them a "divine frame of reference." The narrator emphasizes that the internal narrator, John, who received the four visions (as shown in Table 2.2), is "in the Spirit" in Rev 1:10; 4:2; 17:3; 21:10. This emphasis on John being "in the Spirit" has three literary effects. The first is to give authority to the narrative since the Divine Spirit is the means by which the four visions are conferred. The second is to lend reliability to John who is under the control of the Spirit throughout the four visions. The third effect is to identify the Spirit as the origin—or at least the *mediated origin*—of the four visions from God (the Father) and Jesus since John receives all four visions "in the Spirit."[83] Thus, the expression "in the Spirit" lends divine authority to the visions and places them firmly in a divine frame of reference.

80. Most commentators of the book of Revelation agree with this. For more, see ibid., 1205–6.

81. For the literary cumulative effect, see Darr, *On Character Building*, 42–47. Many commentators argue that it is alluded from Daniel 12:9, "He said, 'Go your way, Daniel, for the words are to remain secret and sealed until the time of the end.'"

82. For this, see Bauckham, *Climax of Prophecy*, 243–66. In his book, Bauckham argues rightly that the two are the same scroll, even if here has been a sharp discussion on whether the scroll in Revelation 5 is the same as the little scroll in Rev 10.

83. It is notable that the revelation of Jesus Christ in 1:1 was given him by God (the

A Dynamic Reading of the Holy Spirit in Revelation

To summarize, the narrator, by using a first-person character, John, who is declared to be "in the Spirit" when he receives the four visions, has linked the visionary narrative of John integrally to the threefold God.[84] The narrator thereby provides his text with credentials of reliability and authority, confirming that if the readers obey the visions, they will receive blessed eternal life, but if they disobey the visions, they will be subject to eternal ruin.

Small Visions

Just as "in the Spirit" is used as a literary signpost to the four *big* visions in Revelation, "I saw" (εἴδω) is used as a literary signpost to the *small* visions. In each case this phraseological formulation indicates to the reader that the visions have a divine frame of reference.[85] The narrator usually has John first seeing the visions, and then hearing the explanatory voices. However, in some exceptional cases, John first hears and then sees. One such exception occurs in the first vision in Rev 1:10–12. John first hears a loud voice like a trumpet, and only when he turns around does he see whose voice it is. A similar exception also occurs in the description of the seven bowls. John first hears a loud voice from the temple saying to the seven angels, "Go, pour out the seven bowls of God's wrath on the earth" (16:1). Only then does he see the seven angels pouring out the seven bowls. Another such exception occurs when the great whore is judged in 17:1–2. John first hears the voice of one of the seven angels with the bowls. Then he sees a woman sitting on a scarlet beast in the wilderness. In each of these cases, the voices play the role of introducing the coming visions. In most cases, however, the voices retrospectively interpret the previous

---

Father) and that he is the faithful witness of this revelation which is then communicated to John by the Spirit or, to use the terminology of Revelation, when John is "in the Spirit." This creedal pattern accords with the orthodox Christian understanding of the Father as the increate source and of the Son as eternally generated by him and the Spirit eternally proceeding from him. It was later explicitly stated at the Councils of Nicea (AD 325), Constantinople, Ephesus, and Chalcedon. Such a triune understanding of the divine is already anticipated in the Pauline and other New Testament writings (e.g., Eph 4:4–6; 1 Cor 8:5–6; Matt 28:19) and reflects early Christian worship

84. The first-person character can make the narrative more reliable in general than the third-person character because his own experiences are usually presented.

85. Rev 11:15–19 is an exception. Some visions appear with a hidden "I saw." For this, see Aune, *Revelation 6–16*, 635–40. Rev 12:1–18 and 22:1 adopt other expressions, "a great potent appeared," and "angel showed me," rather than "I saw."

visions.[86] However, this particular kind of explanatory voice needs to be distinguished from the heavenly voices[87] that are more directly related to the divine frame of reference. In fact, the narrator summarizes the whole revelation given throughout the book in two words joined by the copula, "heard and saw," in 22:8. This phrase "heard and saw" constitutes a literary signpost to the narrator's ideological viewpoint. In other words, by this phrase, the narrator highlights the divine frames of reference of *both* the small and large visions of Revelation.

Table A.1 in the appendix shows us that the narrator depicts John as seeing visions and hearing voices accompanying the visions. Further, the narrator depicts an authoritative heavenly *topos* (place) from which issue messages of the risen Lord Jesus to his churches. Whilst John is "in the Spirit," he is brought into the palpably majestic presence of both the glorified Jesus and God Almighty. There he understands from the unsealed scroll that the world will be subject to an escalating series of judgements designed to bring it to repentance. Those saints who are sealed with a heavenly sign on their forehead will receive ultimate protection. Meanwhile, they are called to digest and proclaim the message of the unsealed scroll to the whole world. Their mission will be a costly one involving possible martyrdom at the hands of opposing spiritual, political, or economic powers.[88] In order to be sincere witnesses to the world, prayer (Rev 5:8; 8:3, 4), endurance (2:2, 19; 3:10; 13:10; 14:12), faith (2:10, 13, 19; 13:10; 14:12; 17:4), wisdom (13:18; 17:9), love (2:4, 19), and pure deeds (14:13; 19:8, 14) are called for.[89] Ultimately, after a time of witnessing and suffering, the Messianic Warrior, the Risen Jesus, will deliver the saints and judge those who have opposed them. Finally, a new heaven and a new earth will be granted to the faithful witnesses through the work of Jesus.

---

86. For this, see Resseguie, *Revelation Unsealed*, 33–37. He argues that what John hears interprets what John sees.

87. We will discuss the heavenly voices in a specific section later in this chapter.

88. The spiritually-related visions are those of a beast in Revelation 11, the dragon and the second beast in Revelation 13, and the whore in Rev 17–19. The politically-related visions are those of Babylon, kings, and the first beast from the sea. The economically-related visions are those of the first beast, Babylon, and the merchants.

89. These factors represent how the saints in the churches should take part in the messianic war in this world. For this, see H. Y. Lee, "Concept of the Messianic War," 36–62. These core values of the saints are proposed by the narrator as narrative asides in Revelation. For the narrative asides in Revelation, see Dal Lee, *Narrative Asides*, 119–61.

In short, the narrator of Revelation employs both the four visions and the small visions as the divine frame of reference that represents his ideological viewpoint. In doing this, he employs a repeated literary phrase, "in the Spirit" which is related to all visions. In all four vision cycles, the narrator describes the first-person character, John, as "in the Spirit," in such a way as to identify John with his own ideological commitment. Each individual vision, all of which are cast in a divine frame of reference, bears the narrator's ideological viewpoint.[90]

Heavenly Voice(s)

Besides the visions and the voices related to the visions, the narrator uses heavenly voices to indicate the divine frame of reference that gives his narrative reliability and authority. Table A.2 in the appendix shows that the narrator uses heavenly voices twelve times. The places from which the voices come are reported as heaven (seven times), the divine throne (three times), and the temple (two times), though with the variation of the voice of a great multitude in 19:6-8.[91] Heavenly voices speak to John ten times, whereas they speak on one occasion each to the two witnesses and to the seven angels.

The narrator reveals God's sovereign plan to his readers through heavenly voices. What is noteworthy is that the heavenly voice focuses on the witness of the Church to the world. It deals with John's writing of the scroll, his sealing up of what the seven thunders said, and then his digesting the scroll in order to witness to all the peoples of the earth (Rev 10:4). After the two witnesses have completed their mission, the heavenly voice summons them to ascend (11:12).

The heavenly voice also focuses on what happens on earth and in heaven after the two witnesses have ascended. "The kingdom of the world has become the kingdom of our Lord and of his Messiah, and he will reign forever and ever" (Rev 11:15b). The devil, who accuses the saints before God day and night, is thrown down (12:10-12). The seven bowls of divine wrath will be poured out on earth (16:1) and the great corrupting whore shall be judged because of her part in persecuting God's

---

90. Of course, individual visions are one of the factors used to describe the ideological point of view of the Revelation narrator. For this, see Rhoads et al., *Mark as Story*, 44–45.

91. Actually, a loud voice came from both the temple and the throne in Rev 16:17.

servants (19:1–2). God's home shall be among mortals—his dwelling with them; they will be his people, and God *their* God. God will wipe every tear from their eyes. Death will be extinguished; mourning, crying, and pain likewise (21:3–4). The people of God shall rejoice and glorify God, because the messianic marriage will be accomplished. The bride, that is, the Church, will be granted fine linen to wear, bright and pure (19:6–8).

The heavenly voice also reveals the church's task in this world. It proclaims the arrival of God's salvation, power, and kingdom, and of the Messiah's reign (11:15; 12:10–12). The people of God should separate from the world so as to avoid complicity in worldly sins, and the consequent punishing plagues that the world will experience (18:4). The saints are called to conquer Satan, by Christ's sacrifice and by their own fearless testimony in the face of mortal threat (12:11). They are to worship God and Jesus with faith in the future messianic victory (19:5–8).

As a result, the characters who are addressed by the heavenly voice(s)—that is, John, the two witnesses, and the seven angels—are regarded as "reliable characters" since they are evidently God's servants and witnesses. It should also be noted that John is the *receiver* of the heavenly voice who also becomes the *transmitter* of what he has heard to the seven churches.

Thus, like the visions, the heavenly voices, which reveal the divine frame of reference, also reflect the narrator's ideological viewpoint. In other words, the narrator uses the heavenly voices to underwrite his ideology with divine authority. Added to the fact that the voices are themselves an address from heaven, John hears them when he himself is "in the Spirit." Thus, in a double sense, his testimony is presented as reliable.

Angel(s)

Both the overall narrator and the internal narrator, John, report the appearance, speeches and actions of the angels in Revelation. The angels, whose presence also indicates the divine frame of reference, function in various ways.[92] For example, they act as questioners who highlight the

92. Not all angels are employed as a divine frame of reference in Revelation. Only twenty uses of fifty-six uses of "angel" in Revelation work as a divine frame of reference, whereas only one use of twenty-three uses of "angels" in Revelation works as a divine frame of reference. About the role of the angel in Revelation, see Munger, *Rhetoric and Function*, 282–93. He analyzes the functions of angels in Revelation theologically, such as revealer, interpreter, guardian, priest, military leader, manager, helper, herald, announcer, God's personal ambassador, mediator of judgment, controller over angels

fact that Christ alone is qualified to open the seven seals of the scroll in 5:2. They are the agents who protect God's servants by sealing them on their foreheads so that they avoid the divine judgement of 7:3. They are also charged with everlasting worship of God in heaven (in which they model behavior for the saints) in 7:11–12. They are God's spiritual agents who reveal his will to the readers, concerning the final fulfilment of the divine plan in 10:1–7; they show what must soon take place in 22:6.[93] They act as God's ambassadors, explaining events such as when John is told to eat the scroll in 10:9. They can be prophetic heralds proclaiming the eternal gospel to all peoples in 14:6, explaining its essential content as fearing God and worshipping him in 14:7. They can mediate divine judgment on rebellious powers such as Babylon in 14:8, or warn of the dangers of idolatry in 14:9–11, or announce Satan's destruction for his deception in 20:1–3, or herald the soon-coming judgment of the world in 14:15–19, or proclaim the just judgment of God on evildoers in 16:5–6. They can describe the fitting destruction of the whore Babylon for its oppressive power, wealth, violence, and deception in 17:1–2, 7; 18:1–3, 21–24; 19:17–18. They can pronounce the heavenly blessing concerning the blood of martyrs in 16:6; 18:24, and the blessing of those invited to the messianic supper in 19:9. They can introduce the messianic bride in 21:9, and reveal the river of the water of life in 22:1.

The narrator utilizes the angel, within the divine frame of reference, not only to reinforce his own ideological viewpoint, but also to lend the narrative reliability and authority. Both the narrator and John, the first-person character, usually talk about "the angel(s)" retrospectively, not prospectively, since Revelation describes John's past visions. Angelic manifestations correlate with John's state of being "in the Spirit." Both powerfully underline the divine reliability of the narrative and its commands.

---

to bring judgment, and scroll transmitter. However, he does not separate angels who were adopted as divine frames of reference by the Revelation narrator from those who were not adopted as divine frames of reference in Revelation.

93. The Revelation narrator clearly describes angels as God's spiritual agents who show what must soon take place to God's servants in Rev 22:6.

Narrator, Point of View of the Narrator, and the Holy Spirit in Revelation

Heavenly Being(s)

The twenty-four elders, along with the four living creatures and souls beheaded share (and thereby underwrite) the narrator's ideological viewpoint. The narrator particularly uses these figures to tell readers of the worthiness of worship and praise to God, in 4:10–11; 11:16–18; 19:4 (twenty-four elders); 4:8; 19:4. In the case of the four living creatures, the focus is on the holiness of God, whereas the focus of the twenty-four elders is the eternity, creation, glory, honor, power, almightiness, sovereignty, rewards, and judgments of God. In addition, the narrator emphasizes the spiritual worthiness of worship and praise toward Jesus Christ, in 5:8–10.[94] The twenty-four elders and four living creatures also illuminate the identity of the Lamb of God and his deeds in 5:5, 8–10. Thus, they introduce the Lamb of God as the Lion of the tribe of Judah, the Root of David, as well as one who is worthy to take the scroll and to open its seals. The narrator explains Christ's worthiness for this task because of his sacrificial death for the salvation of God's people, who become a nation of priests in 5:9–10. The narrator uses two other heavenly entities to achieve his goal: the slaughtered martyrs and the altar. Indeed, he implies that it is the heavenly martyrs who call for God's righteous judgment on earth—thereby bringing its injustice to an end. The justice of God is thus revealed as true and just not only because God is holy and true but also because the righteous martyrs call for God's justice from heaven. Then the altar proved it in 16:17, "Yes, O Lord God, the Almighty, your judgments are true and just!"

The narrator, thus, suggests that his narrative is reliable and authoritative through his use of the twenty-four elders, the four living creatures, and the righteous martyrs, as well as the altar. The first-person character, John, who is "in the Spirit," mostly reported these characters and their messages. There is, therefore, a close relationship between the heavenly beings and the Holy Spirit in the narrative of Revelation. All alike are coordinated to lend authority to the narrator's message.

---

94. For this, see Bauckham, *Theology of the Book*, 118–49; Aune, *Revelation 1–5*, 319–67.

A Dynamic Reading of the Holy Spirit in Revelation

Summary

I have explored the narrator's use of the divine frame of reference to lend credence to his ideological viewpoint. What has become clear is that the divine frame of reference given to the text by its reported visions, heavenly voices, angels, heavenly beings, and the Spirit, conspire to reinforce the narrator's ideological viewpoint. Such characters as John, who are allied positively with the divine frame of reference "in the Spirit," can be considered "reliable and authoritative." Consequently, readers can hardly differentiate the messages of such characters as John from the message of the narrator. In one sense, the narrator can be regarded as an ideal character who is able to employ the divine frame of reference without restraint. In short, the divine frame of reference functions to suggest that Revelation's narrative, and its main character, John (who is inspired by the Holy Spirit), are reliable and authoritative.

Conclusion

The key phrase "in the spirit" plays a significant literary role in reinforcing three facets of the narrator's viewpoint. When John is in the spirit, he shares the omnipresent, retrospective (in the perceptual dimension), omniscient, objective or subjective (in the psychological dimension), and reliable, as well as authoritative (in the ideological dimension) narrator's viewpoint. More specifically, I have pointed out that the narrator's ideology is "theocentric," "christocentric," and "pneumatocentric." He evaluates or judges all characters and incidents in these terms. That is why, if any characters' visions, speeches, or actions in the narratives are approved or sanctioned by the narrator, the readers are meant to understand that they are reliable and authoritative. It is notable that the Spirit plays a role as the divine frame of reference. Thus, the reader is encouraged to consider that not only the Spirit but also any character inspired and guided by the Spirit is God's reliable agent whose testimony is to be trusted and obeyed.

So far, we have proved that the narrator plays a significant role in the whole narrative through his point of view and adopts the Holy Spirit as a divine frame of reference. In other words, it can be asserted that the Holy Spirit himself affects the narrator directly as a divine frame of reference. Furthermore, the Holy Spirit influences the narrator indirectly through other divine frame of references: visions, heavenly voice(s), angel(s), heavenly being(s). Thus, it can be claimed that the Holy Spirit has a strong and wide impact over the whole narrative of Revelation. Now we need to observe how the Holy Spirit is presented as a character in the following chapter.

3

Character Presentation of the Holy Spirit in Revelation

Introduction

I S THE DIVINE SPIRIT a character in Revelation? If so, how is the Divine Spirit presented as a character in Revelation? To find the answer to these questions, in the first section of this chapter, I shall survey briefly the previous study of characterization of the Divine Spirit in Revelation with two narratological commentaries of Revelation: those of Barr and Resseguie.[1] In the next section, on the basis of the narrative theories of "character" and "characterization,"[2] which were proposed by Rimmon-

---

1. For the convenience of understanding for the general readers, I use the term of "the Holy Spirit" in the titles of each chapter, even though there is no such direct definition of the Divine Spirit in Revelation. However, I employ the term of "the Divine Spirit" to refer to the various ways in which the Spirit(s) or Spirits of God, that is, Seven Spirits, Spirit, Spirit of prophecy, and in the Spirit are represented in Revelation.

2. For the narrative theory of character and characterization, see Rimmon-Kenan, *Narrative Fiction*, 29–42, 59–70. For the applied narrative theory of character in biblical narrative, see Hur, *Dynamic Reading*, 113–22. He attempts to reshape the description of Rimmon-Kenan about character with "a dynamic reading" process. After he adopted Abrams's classical definition of character, he proposed two issues related to the narrative theory of character: word or person; being or doing. For word or person, he summarizes two different opinions on "a character's mode of identification or existence in a narrative." One, which is derived from "mimetic criticism," claims that

Kenan and Ju Hur, I shall analyze the Spirit(s) in Revelation as "Being" in terms of the character-presentation.[3] First of all, the various expressions of the Divine Spirit in Revelation shall be observed briefly. Then, the direct definition of the Spirit(s) in Revelation, which shows direct presentation of the Spirit(s), will be explored according to four factors: adjectives, abstract nouns, other kinds of nouns, and parts of speech. In the following section, indirect presentation of the Divine Spirit in Revelation shall be explored according to four factors: speech, action, external appearance, and environment. And, then, the analogy of the Divine Spirit will be explored according to four factors: repetition, similarity, contrast and comparison. Finally, I shall observe whether the Spirit(s) in Revelation can be regarded as a literary character.

"characters are equivalent to people in life." The other, which is derived from "semiotic criticism," claims that "characters are equivalent to 'segments of a closed text.'" Hur accepts two opinions, that is, two models, about character both as "word or person" and as "being or doing." But he also adopts a dynamic reading process to identify the readers' role in two models. Hur argues that "characters portrayed by words in literature are generated by the readers' consciousness or experience so as to become living people." Furthermore, he attempts to apply his theory to the biblical narratives. He insists that characters in biblical narratives are "conceived as textualized persons or personified texts" and "re-constructed as 'real people' by readers" in the reading process. Finally he concludes that characters in the biblical narratives possess "person-likeness" such as thinking, speaking, acting, and having names, whereas the divine characters possess both "person-likeness" and "person-unlikeness." For being or doing, he summarizes two different opinions on "characters' relationship to the plot." One views characters as "plot functionaries." The other regards characters as "autonomous or independent beings apart from the plot." He admits that the first one is a traditional concept and the other one is a modern concept. With his acceptance of the two different views over the character in relation to the plot, Hur emphasizes the role of the readers by this argument that "characterization is, after all, dependent upon readers as the final cause." Furthermore, Hur applies this concept to the biblical narrative, especially Luke-Acts. He concludes that characters are considered in the biblical narratives both as "plot functionaries" and as "autonomous or independent beings," that is, actors.

For the narrative theory of characterization, see Hur, *Dynamic Reading*, 123–28. Hur sums up that "the literary approach to characterization has, to some extent, shifted recently from a text-centered definition to a reader-centered one, influenced by reader response criticism." He explains that the text-centered approach usually employs character-classification, whereas the reader-centered one employs character-presentation. After he criticizes character-classification approaches, he examines, with a character-presentation approach, the character, the Holy Spirit, in Luke-Acts, as an autonomous being.

3. Chapter 4 shall deal with the Spirit(s) in the light of the overall plot of Revelation as "doing" or "functioning."

Previous Study of Characterization of the Divine Spirit in Revelation

D. L. Barr

Barr admits that the Spirit is a character, whereas it is hard to determine whether Resseguie recognizes the Spirit as a character. Barr classifies the Spirit as a minor character.[4] However, he does not attempt to characterize the Spirit(s), although he tries to characterize other characters such as Jesus, God, heavenly creatures, and demonic entities. Nevertheless, he characterizes the Divine Spirit, especially the Seven Spirits, even if partially, while he describes the characterization of Jesus.[5]

Barr characterizes the Seven Spirits in connection with three usages in Rev 1:4, 4:5, and 5:6. He insists that the Seven Spirits, who are before God's throne (1:4), are employed in chapter 4 where "throne imagery will dominate the vision."[6] Barr argues rightly:

> That there are *the Seven Spirits* would be puzzling, if we were not familiar with the conventions of visionary, symbolic writing in John's time, which used numbers to signify qualities not quantities. The quality of the number seven is a divine quality, signifying fulfilment, perfection, and completion. John signifies the quality of the spirit as seven/perfect not a quantity of spirit by this symbol.[7]

He also explains that the Seven Spirits have the literary and dramatic effects reminding the readers of ancient cosmology and astrology.

> Setting the scene with the Seven Spirits has a certain dramatic effect recalling both an ancient cosmology and a biblical scene. The Seven Spirits are also found in a picture of the world deriving from Babylonian astrology, which taught that the cosmos consists of seven spheres or seven heavens, presided over by the Seven Spirits of God and visible in the five planets, the moon, and the sun.[8]

---

4. Barr, *Tales of the End*, 181. He shows a list of characters in Revelation in the appendix.

5. He describes the characterization of the Seven Spirits while he explains the characterization of Jesus in 1:4; 5:6.

6. Barr, *Tales of the End*, 31.

7. Ibid.

8. Ibid., 32.

In addition, he explains that John characterizes the Seven Spirits of God as the seven eyes that Jesus has. He emphasizes that the Seven Spirits represent the Holy Spirit.

> He tells us that the seven eyes are "the Seven Spirits of God sent out into all the earth" (5:6). Now we have already met these Seven Spirits (1:4) and understood that they are a figure of the Holy Spirit. Thus to say that Jesus has seven eyes is to say that Jesus fully possesses the spirit of God—seven being the quality of fullness and perfection.[9]

J. L. Resseguie

Resseguie classifies all characters of Revelation into two kinds: apocalyptic and demonic imagery.[10] He characterizes characters such as God, Jesus, and demonic animals through the speech, actions, narrator's description, and the descriptions of other characters. Even if he employs mainly the method of indirect presentation, he also adopts direct definition for characterization. Unfortunately, he does not recognize the Divine Spirit as a character. Nor does he attempt to do the characterization of the Divine Spirit.

Summary

In the study of Revelation, characterization of characters starts to be employed and applied for the main characters such as Jesus, even if the full literary concept of characterization is not adopted.[11] However, for the Divine Spirit in Revelation, characterization has hardly been found in the narrative study of Revelation. In my study, I shall briefly survey the expressions used in relation to the Divine Spirit in Revelation before discussing the characterization of the Divine Spirit.

---

9. Ibid., 69.

10. Resseguie, *Revelation Unsealed*, 103. He adopts two categories from Northrop Frye, *The Great Code*. Frye states that apocalyptic imagery is "idealized imagery," whereas the counterpart is "demonic imagery."

11. Barr uses only indirect presentation to discover the characterization. Other ways of characterization such as direct definition, repetition, similarity, comparison, and contrast are not employed.

Expressions for the Divine Spirit in Revelation

Is there any expression for the Holy Spirit in Revelation even though there is no usage of the term, "the Holy Spirit"? If so, how many usages appear in the narrative of Revelation? What kinds of expressions for the Holy Spirit appear? In this section, I shall explore various expressions for the Holy Spirit. In the following sections, I shall discuss these questions: How are various expressions for the Holy Spirit related to each other? Are they able to be identified with the Holy Spirit?

Bauckham argues that the description of the Divine Spirit appears eighteen times in Revelation.[12] I propose that one more case should be added from 11:11: "But after the three and a half days, the breath [Spirit: KJV] of life from God entered them, and they stood on their feet, and those who saw them were terrified (Καὶ μετὰ τὰς τρεῖς ἡμέρας καὶ ἥμισυ πνεῦμα ζωῆς ἐκ τοῦ θεοῦ εἰσῆλθεν ἐν αὐτοῖς, καὶ ἔστησαν ἐπὶ τοὺς πόδας αὐτῶν, καὶ φόβος μέγας ἐπέπεσεν ἐπὶ τοὺς θεωροῦντας αὐτούς)." The narrator adds two phrases, "of life," and "from God" specifically to represent it as the Divine Spirit. The Spirit derives from God, and the function of the Spirit is to give life to the two witnesses. The breath needs to be translated into the Spirit as KJV does. The narrator or John in the Spirit narrates God's breathing into the two witnesses with the Spirit of life causing them to stand on their feet (11:11). This work of the Spirit makes those who see them terrified to be prepared for repentance (11:13).

The narrator or reliable characters such as John in the Spirit, the risen Jesus, and the angel narrated all of the descriptions of the Divine Spirit, as Table 3.1 shows. With this, readers may have an impression that the Divine Spirit is reliable. The Seven Spirits in Rev 1:4 are narrated by John as a narrator-like character. The exalted Jesus narrates the Seven Spirits in 3:1. John who is in the Spirit narrates the Seven Spirits in 4:5; 5:6. The narrator attempts to describe that the Seven Spirits are authoritative and divine since they have a close relationship to both God in the throne and the risen Lamb, Jesus.

John narrated all four usages of "in the Spirit." The narrator attempts to represent that John himself feels and experiences the control of the Spirit over him with the description of John. He was not lost in his mind, but clear in his mind enough to describe and remember what

---

12. Bauckham, *Climax of Prophecy*, 150; *Theology of the Book*, 109.

had happened in his spiritual journeys. He heard and saw the exalted and glorified Jesus in the Spirit in 1:10. He journeyed to the heavenly court and saw the heavenly throne (4:2), was carried into the wilderness (17:3), and was carried to the New Jerusalem (21:10).

Furthermore, the narrator attempts to introduce the Spirit through the exalted Jesus as the divine character who speaks to the local churches with the repeated phrase, "Let anyone who has an ear listen to what the Spirit is saying to the churches" (2:7a, 11a, 17a, 29; 3:6, 13, 22). He describes the role of the Spirit as a spokesman of Jesus as well as an advisor to the churches. In other words, the Spirit not only says to the churches what Jesus is saying as a spokesman of Jesus, but also guides the churches or individual followers of Christ at any time and place as an advisor. The narrator also emphasizes that the Spirit continues to speak to all the churches. The narrator encourages readers to be attentive to what the Spirit is saying or the guidance of the Spirit in their lives.

The narrator employs an angel as an introducer of the Spirit of prophecy or advisor to John. He characterizes an angel as a reliable character in Rev 19:10. In other words, an angel is characterized as a fellow servant with John, who holds the testimony of Jesus. Moreover, the narrator characterizes the angel as an advisor of John not to worship him, but to worship God. The angel is described as a character who knows whom everyone should worship (God), to whom everyone should give witness (to Jesus), and with whom everyone should share a testimony of Jesus (with the Spirit of prophecy). With this reliability of an angel in characterization, the narrator makes the angel proclaim about the Spirit of prophecy in 19:10b, "the testimony of Jesus is the Spirit of prophecy." Through the logic of this proclamation, the Spirit of prophecy is characterized as having a relationship not only to Jesus, but also to the Lord's servants, like John who hold the Spirit of prophecy.[13] The narrator attempts to adopt the expression of a causal connector, *gar* (for), in order to emphasize not only the role of the Spirit of prophecy in the testimony of Jesus, but also the cooperation of the Spirit of prophecy with servants of the Lord Jesus. The Spirit of prophecy is said to work with them when the Lord's servants witness to Jesus. Whenever they give testimony to Jesus, the power of the Spirit of prophecy is with them. In other words, without the Spirit of prophecy, there is no testimony of Jesus. Even more, without

13. This relationship can be logically traced in 19:9–10. One who holds the testimony of Jesus is the one who holds the Spirit of prophecy since the testimony of Jesus is the Spirit of prophecy.

the Spirit of prophecy, there are no witnesses, nor servants of Lord. In short, the narrator shows that the main role of the Spirit of prophecy is to witness to Jesus and what Jesus says, according to Rev 19:10.

On the other hand, with this expression, "the testimony of Jesus is the Spirit of prophecy" (19:10b), the narrator especially emphasizes the relationship between the Spirit of prophecy and the angel. The angel also gives a testimony about Jesus with the Lord's servants in 19:10. The angel works with the Spirit of prophecy since the servant of the Lord, like John, works with the Spirit of prophecy. We can deduce that Jesus supports the collaboration between the angel and the Spirit since Jesus holds the angel in 2:1 as well as the Seven Spirits in 5:6. Thus, the angel, the servants of the Lord, and the Spirit of prophecy have the same purpose, which is to witness to Jesus.

Aune confirms his interpretation of "the spirits of prophets" by finding its similar usage from 1 Cor 14:32: "And the spirits of prophets are subject to the prophets." For the interpretation of the spirit and the spirits, he uses the same approach. However, he never attempts to ask why the narrator employs "the spirits" of prophets in the context of this phrase. He never tries to understand it with a view to the literary aspect. In fact, inserting "the spirits" seems to be redundant or even confusing as a way to describe the God of the prophets. In other words, just God of the prophets is a complete enough way to describe the God of prophecy. So why does the narrator intend to insert "the spirits" in this context? What kind of literary effect is expected in using the phrase, "the spirits"? Even though Aune's interpretation of "the spirits" is not considered a false one, it remains insufficient. I propose that inserting "the spirits" is intended to reflect "the Spirits of prophecy." In other words, at least, the closed door against reflecting "the Spirits of prophecy" through the spirits of prophets can be opened when we look at it with a view to the literary perspective. The narrator implicitly intends to reflect "the Spirits of prophecy" who work in the prophets or the spirits of prophets by employing a kind of word play in the literary perspective. The same context of writing and transmitting prophecy of God of the two parallel verses Rev 19:9–10 and 22:6–7 supports this reflection. Once this kind of understanding of "the spirits" in this verse is opened, the shadow in which the role of the Spirit of prophecy was veiled in the revelation process of Rev 1:1 may be eliminated.[14] In short, without the Spirit of prophecy, there is no revelation transmission.

With the indirect conversation between the heavenly voice and the Spirit about the fortune of the dead in the Lord after death in 14:13, the narrator attempts to illuminate the role of the Spirit. Firstly, the Spirit hears and talks with the heavenly voice. Secondly, the Spirit confirms what the heavenly voice says. When the heavenly voice talks to John, "write this: Blessed are the dead who from now on die in the Lord," the Spirit responds and confirms what is said by heavenly voice with "yes." Thirdly, the Spirit knows the reason why the dead in the Lord are blessed. Even the Spirit understands and proclaims what will happen after the death of the dead in the Lord. Fourthly, the Spirit is deeply concerned with the destiny of the saints after death. The personal eschatology of them is that they will take rest and be rewarded according to their deeds. Thus, the narrator persuades the reader to believe that the Spirit knows the world after death.

The narrator indicates that the Spirit is working with the bride, that is, the church in 22:17. He shows that the Spirit not only articulates the eschatological hope for personal death in 14:13, but also has the same hope for the ultimate eschatology, that is, the second coming of Jesus as the church in 22:17.

So far, I have discussed some significant issues of which are related to some expressions for the Holy Spirit. However, the whole expressions of the Holy Spirit shall be summarized in Table 3.1. Some questions noted earlier in this section can be answered with this table and explanations in this section as well as the following sections.

---

14. In turn, the understanding of the role of the Spirit of prophecy in the revelation process in Rev 1:1 helps readers accept the appearance of Seven Spirits in the Trinitarian description in Rev 1:4.

A Dynamic Reading of the Holy Spirit in Revelation

Table 3.1 Expressions for the Divine Spirit in Revelation[15]

Speaker	The Spirit	Verse	Context
John / The narrator	The Seven Spirits	1:4	Grace and peace from *the Seven Spirits* who are before God's throne => related to God
The exalted Jesus	The Seven Spirits	3:1	These are the words of him who has the *Seven Spirits* of God and the seven stars. => related to the exalted Jesus
John in the Spirit	The Seven Spirits	4:5	In front of the throne burn the seven flaming torches, which are the *Seven Spirits* of God. => existing in front of the throne in appearance of the seven flaming torches
John in the Spirit	The Seven Spirits	5:6	A Lamb standing as if it had been slaughtered, having seven horns and seven eyes, which are the *Seven Spirits of God* sent out into all the earth. => related to the Lamb and portrayed with seven horns and seven eyes
John	In the Spirit	1:10	I was in *the Spirit* on the Lord's day, and heard behind me a great voice, as of a trumpet, => at Patmos, saw and heard the exalted Jesus
John	In the Spirit	4:2	At once I was in *the Spirit*, and there in heaven stood a throne, with one seated on the throne! => journey to the heavenly throne
John	In the Spirit	17:3	So he carried me away in *the Spirit* into a wilderness, and I saw a woman sitting on a scarlet beast that was full of blasphemous names, and it had seven heads and ten horns. => journey to wilderness
John	In the Spirit	21:10	And in *the Spirit* he carried me away to a great, high mountain and showed me the holy city Jerusalem coming down out of heaven from God. => journey to the New Jerusalem

15. See a related verse to the Spirit of prophecy: "These words are trustworthy and true, for the Lord, the God of *the spirits of the prophets*, has sent his angel to show his servants what must soon take place" (Rev 22:6; italics in the original).

Speaker	The Spirit	Verse	Context
The exalted Jesus	The Spirit	2:7	Let anyone who has an ear listen to what *the Spirit* is saying to the churches. To everyone who conquers, I will give permission to eat from the tree of life that is in the paradise of God.=> speaking to local churches
The exalted Jesus	The Spirit	2:11	Let anyone who has an ear listen to what *the Spirit* is saying to the churches. Whoever conquers will not be harmed by the second death.=> speaking to local churches
The exalted Jesus	The Spirit	2:17	Let anyone who has an ear listen to what *the Spirit* is saying to the churches. To everyone who conquers I will give some of the hidden manna, and I will give a white stone, and on the white stone is written a new name that no one knows except the one who receives it.=> speaking to local churches
The exalted Jesus	The Spirit	2:29	Let anyone who has an ear listen to what *the Spirit* is saying to the churches.=> speaking to local churches
The exalted Jesus	The Spirit	3:6	Let anyone who has an ear listen to what *the Spirit* is saying to the churches.=> speaking to local churches
The exalted Jesus	The Spirit	3:13	Let anyone who has an ear listen to what *the Spirit* is saying to the churches.=> speaking to local churches
The exalted Jesus	The Spirit	3:22	"Let anyone who has an ear listen to what *the Spirit* is saying to the churches."=> speaking to local churches
The narrator /John in the Spirit	The Spirit	14:13	And I heard a voice from heaven saying, "Write this: Blessed are the dead who from now on die in the Lord." "Yes," says *the Spirit*, "they will rest from their labors, for their deeds follow them."=> giving explanation why the dead in Christ will be blessed

Speaker	The Spirit	Verse	Context
The narrator	The Spirit	22:17	*The Spirit* and the bride say, "Come." And let everyone who hears say, "Come." And let everyone who is thirsty come. Let anyone who wishes take the water of life as a gift. => ministering together with the Bride, the Church
The angel=> John in the Spirit	The Spirit of prophecy	19:10	Then I fell down at his feet to worship him, but he said to me, "You must not do that! I am a fellow servant with you and your comrades who hold the testimony of Jesus. Worship God! For the testimony of Jesus is *the spirit of prophecy*." Worship, prophecy, and testimony
The narrator /John in the Spirit	The Spirit of life from God[16]	11:11	But after the three and a half days, *the breath of life* from God entered them, and they stood on their feet, and those who saw them were terrified. => the two witnesses were breathed into by the Spirit of life of God

Direct Definitions of the Divine Spirit in Revelation

Rimmon-Kenan argues that there are two types of character-presentation in the narrative.

> There are two basic types of textual indicators of character: direct definition and indirect presentation. The first type names the trait by an adjective (e.g., "he was good-hearted"), an abstract noun ("his goodness knew no bounds"), or possibly some other kind of noun ("she was a real bitch") or part of speech ("he loves only himself"). The second type, on the other hand, does not mention the trait but displays and exemplifies it in various ways, leaving to the reader the task of inferring the quality they imply.[17]

16. The NRSV translates it as the breath of life from God, whereas the KJV has it as the Spirit of life from God. The Greek means the spirit of life (*pneu/ma zwh/j evk tou/ qeou/*). Aune does not explain the exact meaning of the spirit of life in his commentaries.

17. Rimmon-Kenan, *Narrative Fiction*, 59–60. The first sentence is from Ewen, "Theory of Character" and *Character in Narrative*, 47–48, quoted in Rimmon-Kenan, *Narrative Fiction*, 59–60.

Definitions are more frequently employed in the ancient literature including biblical scripture, whereas an indirect definition is more frequently used in modern literature since "suggestiveness and indeterminacy are preferred to closeness and definitiveness."[18] A definition produces "a rational authoritative and static impression" since it represents "explicit and supra-temporal" "generalization and conceptualization."[19] The authority of the definition also depends on who narrates it. Usually definitions narrated by the narrator are the most authoritative. The reader is implicitly forced to accept the definitions narrated by the authoritative narrator.

The Revelation narrator also uses many kinds of direct definitions to characterize the Divine Spirit. All direct definitions are narrated by the narrators and reliable characters, such as Jesus, and John, who is in the Spirit. With this, the narrator designs the readers to accept the direct definition of the Divine Spirit. As shown in Table 3.1, only adjectives and other kinds of nouns are used for direct definitions of the Divine Spirit, whereas abstract nouns and parts of speech are not found in Revelation.

In what follows, I shall explore five expressions for the Divine Spirit in Revelation as direct definitions: (1) the *Seven* Spirits, (2) the Seven Spirits *of God*, (3) the Spirit *of prophecy*, (4) the Spirit *of life from God*, and (5) the *testimony of Jesus*.

"Seven" Spirits

The word πνεῦμα (Spirit) occurs twelve times in Revelation.[20] The word *pneu,mati* (in Spirit) occurs four times in Revelation. The phrase τὰ ἑπτὰ πνεύματα (the Seven Spirits) occurs three times, in 3:1; 4:5; 5:6, and the phrase τῶν ἑπτὰ πνευμάτων (the Seven Spirits) occurs one time, in 1:4, whereas there is no occurrence of the "Holy" Spirit in the narrative of Revelation. For the analysis of the "Seven" Spirits, three aspects will be considered: (1) Who narrates or describes the *Seven* Spirits?, (2) In what narrative contexts do the *Seven Spirits* appear?, and (3) What are the implications of the term *seven*? The first two questions have been

18. Rimmon-Kenan, *Narrative Fiction*, 61.
19. Ibid., 60.
20. Among twelve times, one used in 13:15 indicates the breath to the beast. The other used in 11:11 indicates the breath to the two witnesses. However, the latter can be characterized as the Divine Spirit. It shall be discussed later in this chapter, especially in the section,"Spirit of Life."

answered briefly in Table 3.1. John or the narrator, the exalted Jesus, and John in the Spirit narrated the Seven Spirits.

In the context of *the Seven Spirits* shown in Table 3.1, we notice that the narrator of John as *the Seven Spirits* who *bless the seven churches with grace and peace before God's throne* understands the Divine Spirit in 1:4. After the process and agents of revelation, transmission in 1:1–2 and the first beatitude in 1:3 are presented, John or the narrator then blesses the seven churches in 1:4 with the traditional letter-form blessing of New Testament literature. In that blessing, *the Seven Spirits* appear with God, who is and who was and who is to come, and with Jesus as blessing-giver. In this context, readers face the apocalyptic descriptions of God, the Divine Spirit, and Jesus. God is described as the one who is and who was and who is to come in 1:4, 8. Jesus appears as the Son of man in apocalyptic literature in 1:13–16. In that context, the Spirit is described as "the Seven Spirits" in 1:4. Naturally readers understand *the Seven Spirits* as an apocalyptic narrative indicator since the number seven usually represents divine attributes in the apocalyptic literature. The word, ἑπτὰ (seven), occurs fifty-five times in Revelation as an apocalyptic document among eighty-eight times in the New Testament. Thus, we can figure out that the narrator designs to persuade the readers, who may understand apocalyptic codes in their Greco-Roman situations, that the Seven Spirits represent the Divine Holy Spirit[21] since "the quality of the number seven is a divine quality, signifying fulfilment, perfection, and completion."[22] John or the narrator "signifies the quality of the spirit as seven/perfect, not a quantity of spirit by this symbol."[23]

The second *Seven Spirits* appear in the context of seven letters of Jesus to one of the seven churches, the church in Sardis in Rev 3:1. Especially it is used in the passage introducing who Jesus is. The Seven Spirits are described as being owned or held by Jesus with the seven stars, which are explained as angels of the seven churches in 1:20. The narrator leads readers to form some impressions from the second usage of "the Seven Spirits" in 3:1. Firstly, the relationship of the Seven Spirits to Jesus is emphasized in 3:1. The Seven Spirits are described as belonging to Jesus since Jesus holds or has the Seven Spirits. Rev 3:1 contrasts to 1:4 in that

---

21. This can be supported with another definition of the Seven Spirits "of God" in 4:5. God is characterized as one who is praised to be "holy, holy, holy" in ch. 4. For this, see the following section.

22. Barr, *Tales of the End*, 31.

23. Ibid.

Character Presentation of the Holy Spirit in Revelation

the relationship of the Seven Spirits to God is emphasized in 1:4 with the expression of "who are before the throne of God." Secondly, the narrator intends to distinguish the Seven Spirits from the seven stars, that is, angels of the seven churches, in 3:1. Jesus is described to have both the Seven Spirits and the seven stars. The narrator makes this distinction of the two more clearly by adding different descriptive words: "of God" in 3:1 (for the Seven Spirits) and "of the seven churches" in 1:20 (for the seven stars). In fact, "of God" looks redundant to describe the Seven Spirits in 3:1 since they have already been described in 1:4 with the expression, "who are before the throne of God." One of the purposes for using the phrase, "of God" in 3:1 is to clearly distinguish between the Seven Spirits and the seven stars.[24] In contrast, Aune argues that the Seven Spirits are the seven archangels in his commentary.[25] He criticizes commentators who understand the Seven Spirits as the Holy Spirit in their lack of searching Qumran literature for the usages of the spirits as the angels. He insists that the Seven Spirits can be identified to represent seven archangels from his research of the publication of the Dead Sea Scrolls.[26] However, Aune, in turn, may be criticized for his failure to search the final text as a whole. He neglects to recognize the narrator's literary effort to make a distinction between the Seven Spirits and the seven stars, that is, the angels by using "of God" and "of the seven churches."[27] As God cannot be identified with the seven churches, the Seven Spirits cannot be identified with the seven archangels in 3:1. In short, the Seven Spirits can be understood as God's Holy Spirit working with Jesus.

The third *Seven Spirits* appear in Rev 4:5. In the context of the description of the throne, John or the narrator understands the seven flaming torches burning in front of the heavenly throne as *the Seven Spirits* of God. The narrator emphasizes the location of the Seven Spirits where they abide and come out of the heavenly throne in 4:5, whereas the equal

---

24. The phrase, "of God," shall be dealt with in detail in the next section.

25. Aune, *Revelation 1–5*, 219.

26. Ibid., 33–36. Aune merely attempts to find evidence from similar usages of "spirits" and "seven" respectively in other Jewish literature, especially Qumran literature. He does not concern himself with how the words are used in relation to the final text.

27. That is why Aune interprets "and" (καὶ) as "namely." Aune, *Revelation 1–5*, 219. Bauckham argues that the Divine Spirit is used separately from angels in Revelation. Bauckham, *Theology of the Book*, 110. Bauckham insists that spirit "very rarely has this meaning in early Christian literature and never in Revelation," even though "the term 'spirit' could certainly be used of angels (as frequently in the Dead Sea Scrolls)" (ibid.).

level of the Seven Spirits with God and Jesus (1:4) and the relationship to the glorified and speaking Jesus (3:1) are emphasized in the former two cases of 1:4 and 3:1. The narrator also attempts to remind readers that the Divine Spirit is related to the fire of the heavenly throne. In short, the Seven Spirits in 4:5 reflects the holy fire of the Spirit in the heavenly throne.

The fourth usage of *the Seven Spirits* is shown in Rev 5:6. In the immediate context of the scroll and the Lamb of God, John or the narrator understands seven horns and seven eyes that are owned by the Lamb to be the *Seven Spirits* of God.[28] The narrator emphasizes the relationship of the Seven Spirits to the scroll and the Lamb who takes the scroll from God and opens the seven seals. The narrator focuses on the role of the Seven Spirits as powerful watcher with the phrases, "seven horns and seven eyes."[29] We need to consider whether the Seven Spirits may be a transmitter of the scroll to all the earth when they are "sent out into all earth" (5:6). This position seems to be supported in that they are sent to accomplish the Word of the Lamb on earth by the Lamb who holds the Scroll, even though it is not clearly noted. If so, we can propose that the Seven Spirits in 5:6 reflect the Holy Spirit who is sent out into all the earth to witness to the word that Jesus commands.

In short, the implications of "seven" of the Seven Spirits can be summarized with four points. First of all, the word seven implies the "fullness and perfection" of the Divine Spirit in 1:4. Secondly, seven implies the "holiness" of the Spirit. Thirdly, seven implies the "purity" of the heavenly Spirit. Fourthly, seven implies the "wholeness" of the Spirit who sees everything in all the earth.[30]

---

28. Bauckham argues that not only the seven eyes, but also the seven horns represent Seven Spirits. *Theology of the Book*, 110–15.

29. See ibid.

30. The four implications of "seven," which are employed in the Seven Spirits, can also be employed in the other usages of "seven" as related to the characters in Revelation. For example, the seven churches (lampstands), seven stars (the angels of the seven churches), seven seals, seven trumpets, and seven thunders reflect the "fullness and perfection." The seven thousand people who were killed in the earthquake (11:13); a great red Dragon, with seven heads and ten horns, and seven diadems on his heads (12:3); the seven heads and ten horns of the beast (17:3, 7); the seven heads (seven mountains 17:9); and seven kings (17:11) all reflect the "wholeness" of the Spirit.

The Seven Spirits "of God"

Another direct definition of the Divine Spirit in Revelation is that of the Seven Spirits "of God." It is notable that the narrator applies the direct definition of the expression, "of God," only to the Seven Spirits, not to other expressions of the Divine Spirit such as the Spirit, the Spirit of prophecy, or the Spirit of life. What purposes make the narrator employ "of God" just to the Seven Spirits? What are the implications of "of God" for the Seven Spirits? First of all, these words imply the unity of the Seven Spirits with God in Rev 3:1, 4:5, and 5:6. "Of God" is not used of the Seven Spirits in 1:4 because the narrator intends to illuminate the separated identity from God. Secondly, "of God" also implies the separation of the Seven Spirits from other heavenly beings such as the seven stars, which denotes angels; four living creatures; and twenty-four elders.[31] Thirdly, it also implies that the term, "Seven Spirits," is not a person-like character, but a person-unlike character. In other words, the narrator intends to clarify the person-unlikeness of the Seven Spirits in the characterization of the Seven Spirits. The Seven Spirits are described as a God-like heavenly character. Since the Seven Spirits are a God-like Spirit, they function as God. The Seven Spirits bless the seven churches in all the earth with God and Jesus. They work with Jesus to guide the local churches in the world. They also are sent to watch over all the earth with their God-like power. Fourthly, using "of God" implies that the Seven Spirits share the same personality or attributes with God. The Seven Spirits can be characterized as the "Holy" Spirit and the "Almighty" Spirit since God is characterized as "holy, holy and holy" and as "almighty" in the praise of the four living creatures in 4:8 as I mentioned in discussion of 4:1. Fifthly, it implies that the Seven Spirits participate in the work of God, such as his creation. They can be characterized as the Spirit of creation since God is characterized as the One who "created all things" in 4:11. In short, the narrator attempts to describe the Seven Spirits as the Holy God-like Spirit with the direct expression of "of God."

---

31. There are 56 usages of "angel" and 23 usages of "angels" in Revelation. However, among them there is not any expression of the direct definition of "of God." In 8:2, seven angels are depicted as standing before God. However, this does not represent a direct definition, but an indirect expression of their mission to receive the seven trumpets. Exceptionally, two of 56 usages of "angel" in 1:1 and 22:6 employ "His" (αὐτοῦ), which is equivalent to "of God" (τοῦ θεοῦ) in meaning, even though the form is different. They represent the separation from other usages of angel in that God gave a separate mission of transmitting his revelation to an angel.

Spirit "of prophecy"

Another direct definition of the Divine Spirit is "of prophecy" in Rev 19:10. The expression, "τῆς προφητείας" (of prophecy), is used seven times in the Revelation narrative (1:3; 11:6; 19:10; 22:7, 10, 18, and 19). In five times among them, it is used to show the direct definition of the "word" (τοὺς λόγους) or "book" (τοῦ βιβλίου), whereas the "day" in 11:6 and the "spirit" in 19:10. The attribute of word or book is prophecy. What the two witnesses are witnessing is the prophecy. Those who read, hear, and keep this prophecy must be blessed. If this is the correct interpretation, what is the implication of the Spirit "of prophecy" in 19:10? It is notable that the context of the Spirit "of prophecy" is related to the word of God in 19:9 ("And the angel said to me, 'Write this: Blessed are those who are invited to the marriage supper of the Lamb.' And he said to me, 'These are true words of God'").

The Spirit "of prophecy" inspires the saints to have a prophetic imagination. They shall be persuaded to be alert during the present time and the God who is coming to the present time. They shall do their best in everything here and now with the prophetic imagination. They shall be motivated to follow the life of prophets by the Spirit of prophecy.

On the other hand, the Spirit "of prophecy" is related to the written book of Revelation. In the process of writing and confirming Revelation, the Spirit of prophecy has inspired one who writes. That is why the narrator emphasizes the determination of the book of Revelation in that nobody is allowed to change the book of Revelation (22:18–19). With the expression of determination, the narrator implies that the Spirit of prophecy of God inspired Revelation, not human efforts.

In short, the Spirit "of prophecy" is involved in inspiring the word of prophecy of God, especially the book of Revelation. On the other hand, the Spirit of prophecy is implicated not only in making nonbelievers become converts of Jesus Christ, but also in equipping believers to become witnesses or spiritual warriors in their lives. In other words, the Spirit of prophecy is involved in the whole process of witnessing on earth.

Spirit "of life"

Another direct definition of the Divine Spirit is "of life." The expression, "ζωῆς" (of life), is employed seventeen times in the Revelation narrative.

Character Presentation of the Holy Spirit in Revelation

It is used four times each to describe the tree of life (2:7; 22:2, 14, 19) and water of life (7:17; 21:6; 22:1, 17). It is used a total of six times to describe the book of life (3:5), of the Lamb (13:8; 21:27; 20:12, 15), from the foundation of the world (17:8). It is used one time each to describe the crown of life (2:10) and every living thing in the sea (16:3). The narrator tries to clarify the role of the Spirit as the Spirit of resurrection in the immediate context of 11:11.

The Spirit of life to resurrect the two witnesses is described as the same Spirit of life to resurrect Jesus from the grave by the following the ascension passage of the two witnesses in 11:12. Readers may understand that the Spirit of life has a role to resurrect the churches or people of God after their death. On the other hand, readers may figure out that the Spirit of life has another role, to revive the churches or people of God spiritually, not only from the persecution of the nations or kings, but also from spiritual depression. In addition to reviving the two witnesses or witnessing people of God, the Spirit of life gives spiritual revival in the witnessing ministry itself.

It is notable that the Spirit of life is not from man or Satan, but *from God* (11:11). God, the Creator and the Almighty, breathes the Spirit of life into the two witnesses so that they may be alive. As God resurrected Jesus with the Spirit of life, he resurrects the two witnesses or the two prophets (11:10) with the Spirit of life. The Spirit of life can restore the two witnesses from any damage caused by the beast coming up from the bottomless pit to kill them since the Spirit of life comes from God. In a sense, the narrator intends to describe that the Spirit of life from God has the power to break the power of the beast and of Satan who inspires the beast. The readers in Greco-Roman may have an impression that the Spirit of life from God is the same Spirit of God who was breathed by God to Adam (human being) and by the proclamation of Ezekiel who was led by God to dry bones (Ezek 37:1–10).

Testimony of Jesus

As Table 3.2 shows, all direct definitions of the Spirit in Revelation are adjectives, including "seven," "of God," "of life from God," and "of prophecy." The only usage of an abstract noun phrase to define the Spirit directly in Revelation is "the testimony of Jesus" in 19:10b.[32] The expression, "the

32. The noun phrase, "the testimony of Jesus" also has an adjective phrase, "of

testimony of Jesus" is found four times in Revelation: once each in 12:17 and 14:12, and twice in 19:10.

We should note that in 19:9–10, the narrator implies that the Spirit of prophecy cannot be separated from "worship to God." It is within the context of "false worship" to the angel that the angel then tells John "the testimony of Jesus is the Spirit of prophecy" and that this is why servants of Jesus should worship only God. In other words, the servants of God who hold the Spirit of prophecy, that is, the testimony of Jesus, are called to avoid false worship and to follow the true worship. The true worship of God's servants is to worship God only. The Spirit of prophecy gives the servants of God the divine wisdom to discern whom to worship as well as how to worship. The Spirit of prophecy leads all of the worship services on the earth. He inspires the preachers, prayers, those who give praises, and all congregations in worship services. From the true worship services, all people of God can understand how to keep the commandments of God as well as how to give testimony to Jesus with the word of God by the help of the Spirit of prophecy.

Moreover, the narrator implies that foul spirits, which come out of the dragon and beasts in 16:13–14, lead the inhabitants of the earth to worship the beast in 13:8, 12. However, the Spirit of prophecy guides the servants of God to worship God. The narrator emphasizes that the judgments or wrath of God will be poured out on those who follow false worship, that is, to worship not God, but the beast or the dragon in 14:9–11. The narrator insists that true worship leads human beings to the true blessing of God as well as to escape from the disaster or judgment of God. It means that the Spirit of prophecy guides the servants of God to true blessing from true worship.

Evaluation of Readers and Summary

Then, what is the role of readers to accept the direct definitions of the Divine Spirit? Readers are supposed to consider the characters' relative reliability in constructing their characterization of characters in each narrative context. However, the narrator attempts to give the high reliability of characters such as John (1:4; 4:5; 5:6), Jesus (3:1), and the angel (19:10b) so that readers should accept the direct definitions of the Divine Spirit.[33]

Jesus," which represents the subject or the object to give the testimony.

33. Rev 1:4 can be narrated by either the narrator or by John.

To do this, the narrator employs some specific literary instruments such as phrasing and contexts. For example, as I have mentioned in chapter 2, the human character, John, the narrator adopts a specific phrase, "in the Spirit." For Jesus and the angel, the narrator adopts each context to shape Jesus and the angel as highly reliable characters. Jesus is described as Yahweh (God)-like Son of man in 1:13–16. The narrator not only describes the appearance of Jesus, but also gives the specific description of both the worshipping attitude of John toward glorified Jesus (1:17a) and the narration of Jesus about his identity and messages to seven local Churches (1:17b–20). For the angel, the narrator exploits a subtle context of John's mistake in worshipping the angel. With this context, the narrator intends to persuade readers to consider the angel who narrates about the Spirit of prophecy as a more reliable character than John who is in the Spirit. On the other hand, 11:11 is narrated by the narrator himself. Rev 1:4 may be considered to be narrated by the narrator. In short, readers can accept all direct definitions of the Divine Spirit with high reliability, even though evaluating the quality of reliability of characters depends on the readers themselves.

In summary, the narrator adopts four adjectives and one noun phrase to give direct definitions of the Divine Spirit. "Seven," "of God," "of life from God," "of prophecy" are the four adjectives. "The testimony of Jesus" is one noun phrase. With these direct definitions, readers can take the clearest traits of the Divine Spirit in Revelation and apply them among any of the presentations of the Spirit in Revelation. Therefore, the Spirit in Revelation is the divine, holy, complete (or perfect), life-giving, and prophetic Spirit of God and Jesus. Until now, we have discussed the direct definitions of the Divine Spirit in Revelation. From now on, we shall discuss the indirect definitions of the Divine Spirit in Revelation.

Table 3.2 Direct Definitions of the Spirit(s) in Revelation

Book of Revelation	Adjective(s)	Abstract noun	Other kind of noun	Part of speech
1:4	Seven Spirits			
3:1; 4:5; 5:6	Seven Spirits[34] of God			
11:11	Spirit of life from God			
19:10	Spirit of prophecy		The testimony of Jesus	

[COMMENT: Please note that although there is nothing listed under "Abstract noun" and "Part of speech," the author would still like to include the columns to illustrate that these possibilities exist, but in this case all of the words/phrases being examined fall into only two of four available categories.]

Indirect Presentations of the Divine Spirit in Revelation

Besides the direct presentation of the Divine Spirit, the narrator employs indirect presentations in Revelation. Before we discover them, we need to figure out what differences there are between direct definition and indirect definition. We can find the answer from Rimmon-Kenan's description:

> A presentation is indirect when rather than mentioning a trait, it displays and exemplifies it in various ways.[35]

In addition to the Rimmon-Kenan's definition of indirect presentation, Ju Hur insists that indirect presentation is "less explicit than definition, and therefore, possibly less concrete."[36] He argues that it is "useful

---

34. The reference of the spirits besides the four time usages of Seven Spirits (1:4; 3:1; 4:5; 5:6) can be found in 16:13–14; 22:6. However, the spirits in 16:13–14 does not represent the Divine Spirits in that it represents the foul spirits. For the second in 22:6, it represents partially the human spirit (Aune, *Revelation 17–22*, 1182) and also reflects the Seven Spirits.

35. Rimmon-Kenan, *Narrative Fiction*, 61.

36. Hur, *Dynamic Reading*, 127.

and even indispensable in building a character."[37] Of note is that indirect presentation leaves the task of inferring the quality of characters as well as more chances of inferring them to the readers than does direct definition. Thus, indirect presentation displays and exemplifies the traits of characters, whereas direct definition mentions the traits of characters. Indirect presentation is less explicit and concrete in building a character than direct definition, even though it is useful and indispensable.

In Revelation, as Table 3.3 shows, four indirect presentation factors such as (1) speech, (2) action, (3) external appearance, and (4) environment are employed to build a character, the Divine Spirit. We shall discover each in the following paragraphs.

Speech of the Divine Spirit

The Divine Spirit in Revelation is depicted nine times, including as a speaking actor by the narrator (two times, 14:13; 22:17) and character, Jesus (seven times, 2:7, 11, 17, 29; 3:6, 13, 22).[38] In 14:13 and 22:17, the narrator portrays the Spirit as a direct speaker, whereas Jesus depicts the Spirit indirectly as a speaker to the seven churches in 2:7, 11, 17, 29; 3:6, 13, and 22. In the two narrative contexts of both 14:13 and 22:17, the narrator attributes the ongoing witness of blessing to the Spirit. In other words, the Spirit is characterized by the narrator as a reliable and authoritative witness to the eternal blessing of saints. The narrator characterizes the Spirit as an announcer of the good news after the death of the saints who keep the commandments of God in faith in 14:13. Furthermore, the Spirit is not only characterized as an announcer, but also as a motivator or an encourager who strengthens the faith and endurance of the saints until death, as we see in the immediate context of 14:12–13:

> Here is a call for the endurance of the saints, those who keep the commandments of God and hold fast to the faith of Jesus. And I heard a voice from heaven saying, "Write this: Blessed are the dead who from now on die in the Lord." "Yes," says the Spirit, "they will rest from their labors, for their deeds follow them." (Ὧδε ἡ ὑπομονὴ τῶν ἁγίων ἐστίν, οἱ τηροῦντες τὰς ἐντολὰς τοῦ θεοῦ καὶ τὴν πίστιν Ἰησοῦ. Καὶ ἤκουσα φωνῆς ἐκ τοῦ οὐρανοῦ λεγούσης· γράψον· μακάριοι οἱ νεκροὶ οἱ ἐν κυρίῳ ἀποθνῄσκοντες ἀπ' ἄρτι. ναί, λέγει τὸ πνεῦμα, ἵνα ἀναπαήσονται ἐκ τῶν κόπων αὐτῶν, τὰ γὰρ ἔργα αὐτῶν ἀκολουθεῖ μετ' αὐτῶν.)

37. Ibid.
38. There is no speaking Spirit among "Seven Spirits" and "in the Spirit."

From the immediate context of Rev 14:12–13, we can discover some characterizations of the Spirit. The Spirit is depicted as a wonderful counselor who counsels the saints with eschatological hope and heavenly rewards. The Spirit is also portrayed as a spiritual mentor who guides the spiritual direction of the saints. The Spirit is described as an ethical guide who helps the saints to balance present ethical deeds on earth as well as eschatological hope. Moreover, the Spirit is revealed as a comforter who consoles those who face the death of the saints caused by persecutions.

On the other hand, the narrator depicts the Spirit as an evangelist or a missionary in Rev 22:17:

> The Spirit and the bride say, "Come." And let everyone who hears say, "Come." And let everyone who is thirsty come. Let anyone who wishes take the water of life as a gift. (Καὶ τὸ πνεῦμα καὶ ἡ νύμφη λέγουσιν· ἔρχου. καὶ ὁ ἀκούων εἰπάτω· ἔρχου. καὶ ὁ διψῶν ἐρχέσθω, ὁ θέλων λαβέτω ὕδωρ ζωῆς δωρεάν.)

The immediate context of 22:17 indicates that the Spirit is inviting those who are thirsty. The narrator implies that those who are thirsty are nonbelievers by the addition of four intended words and phrases: the bride, that is, the believers or the church; anyone who wishes; the water of life; and as a gift. Readers may be able to infer that they are nonbelievers in that those who are doing the inviting are the Spirit and the bride. This invitation is open to anyone who does not refuse, but wishes. Those who do not have the water of life are nonbelievers. The content of the gospel is grace, that is, a free gift of Jesus. Thus, the narrator, as an evangelist who invites nonbelievers on earth to receive the gospel, describes the Spirit.

The Spirit is also portrayed as a mission mobilizer in 22:17. The narrator describes that the Spirit knows how to conduct mission work. The Spirit does the mission or evangelism not only by himself, but also together with the bride of Jesus, that is, the church. The Spirit, who encourages faithful saints who keep God's commandments in 14:12–13, is portrayed in 22:17 as one who motivates them to do mission work with Him by inviting the nonbelievers. The narrator elucidates the role of the Spirit as a mission mobilizer more clearly by employing the second phrase, "And let everyone who hears say, 'Come.'" Readers may be able to infer that everyone who hears are the faithful saints since they have already read it in the whole narrative of Revelation. The narrator has already placed many indicators to the meaning of one who hears. One who hears is blessed in 1:3. One who hears is anyone who listens to

Character Presentation of the Holy Spirit in Revelation

what the Spirit is saying to the churches in seven repeated phrases of 2:7, 11, 17, 29; 3:6, 13, 22. Along with these seven repeated phrases, the narrator inserts specifically that one who hears the voice of the Spirit is one who hears the voice of Jesus in 3:20. The narrator determinately clarifies the meaning of one who hears by identifying one who hears with John who is in the Spirit in 22:8. Moreover, the narrator illuminates one "who hears as one who hears the words of the prophecy of this book" in 22:18. Thus, the Spirit mobilizes the faithful saints, that is, one who hears, to say "come," so that they may invite nonbelievers. In another sense, the Spirit mobilizes all the churches to be mission-oriented churches. The Spirit takes part in the world mission with the churches. The Spirit also calls the churches to participate in the world mission.

Besides the characterization of the Spirit as a type of direct speaker, the narrator adopts another type of characterization of the Spirit as a type of semi-direct speaker through the description of Jesus. In other words, the Spirit is not portrayed directly by the narrator as a speaker to the seven churches, but described indirectly as a speaker by Jesus in His letters given to the seven churches. Even though the Spirit is depicted indirectly, the narrator is considerate in several ways lest this approach by a semi-direct speaker be regarded as less important. The narrator thus employs the apocalyptic literary device of seven repetitions to increase the significance of the fact that the Spirit is speaking to the church. So to speak, the narrator attempts to emphasize that the Spirit is speaking at all times, to all the local churches, and all the church members by adopting the apocalyptic number "seven." In addition to the seven repeated phrases, "what the Spirit is saying to the churches" (τί τὸ πνεῦμα λέγει ταῖς ἐκκλησίαις), the narrator also employs another rhetoric device, "Let anyone who has an ear listen to" (Ὁ ἔχων οὖς ἀκουσάτω). This statement implies that the Spirit is speaking at all times to all the churches, but only anyone who has an ear shall listen to what the Spirit says. The Spirit speaks not only what Jesus says in Revelation, but also what is necessary for the life of saints. Readers are persuaded to do their best to listen to what the Spirit says to them. They need to practice listening to the voice of the Spirit. To do this, it is essential for them to pay attention, read, hear, and keep the word of Jesus and God, since the Spirit is the Spirit of God and Jesus, as well as the Spirit of prophecy. Thus, the Spirit is described as an ongoing speaker to the saints or churches.

In addition, the Spirit is portrayed as a co-worker with Jesus in the immediate context of seven repeated sentences. Readers are expected to understand that the Spirit has the same concern with Jesus since the Spirit is working together with Jesus. Therefore what the Spirit says to the churches is the same as what Jesus says to them.

It should be noted that the narrator characterizes the speaking of the Divine Spirit as both a "person-like" character and a "God-like" character. In other words, the Spirit is characterized as a "person-like" character in that the Spirit speaks as a person does. The Spirit speaks to the churches, saints, and all people groups on earth like a being. In contrast, the Spirit is also characterized as a "God-like" character in that the Spirit transcends space and time. The Spirit transcends time and knows what shall happen after the death of human beings (14:13). The Spirit is characterized as a "God-like" spirit, that is, the Spirit of eternity like the eternal God who is omniscient. The Spirit also transcends space and is not limited in a place at a time, and so is also like an omnipresent God. The Spirit speaks to all the churches all at the same time or to each church one by one respectively in seven repeated phrases of 2:7, 11, 17, 29; 3:6, 13, 22. The Spirit invites all people groups from all places, simultaneously as well as individually, in 22:17. Thus, the narrator and Jesus in Revelation characterize the Spirit as an enigmatic divine character who embodies person-likeness as well as God-likeness.

From my examination of the speech contexts of the Spirit in Revelation, I can infer the following six important characteristics:

1. The Spirit is depicted as a speaking actor by the reliable narrator and character.
2. The Spirit also speaks of eternal blessing of the saints as a witness of blessing, an announcer of eternal blessing after death of the saints, and as an encourager of saints to keep faith and endurance in times of persecution.
3. The Spirit is also portrayed as a wonderful counselor, a comforter, spiritual director or mentor, and an ethical guide of the saints on earth.
4. The Spirit is revealed as an evangelist or a missionary, a world mission mobilizer.
5. The Spirit is described as the Spirit whose speaking voice should be heeded by all saints at all times.

6. The Spirit is depicted as has an enigmatic divine character who holds both person-likeness and God-likeness.

Action of the Divine Spirit

There are two ways of showing the action of the Divine Spirit in Revelation at large: (1) the Divine Spirit as acting, and (2) the Divine Spirit as acted upon. However, from my examination, it is useful to divide the two into four types, for it appears unclear whether some action types are absolutely active or absolutely passive. Hence, I insert two more types: (3) the Divine Spirit as an active co-agent, and (4) the Divine Spirit as a passive co-agent. In this way, the narrator attempts to portray the action of the Divine Spirit more clearly to the readers.

It should be noted that two groups of the Divine Spirit, acting and acted upon, are characterized as "God-like," or "person-unlike" characters in general, whereas the Divine Spirit from the two other groups, an active co-agent and a passive co-agent, are not clearly classified. Along with four types of action of the Divine Spirit, this shall be discussed.

THE DIVINE SPIRIT AS ACTING

We can notice that the unique reference of the Divine Spirit's active action appears in 11:11, where God breathes life into two witnesses. Unlike other presentations of the Divine Spirit, the Spirit of life is active enough to enter the dead bodies directly. The narrator depicts that the entering event of the Spirit of life into the two witnesses is very decisive and urgent in the immediate narrative of 11:11. After the testimony of the two witnesses has been finished with the prophetic power of the Old Testament prophets such as Moses and Elijah, the beast coming up from the bottomless pit makes war against them and kills them. The inhabitants of the earth, that is, "members of the peoples and tribes and languages and nations" (11:9) look at their dead bodies and celebrate by exchanging presents. Their death is the very dangerous event which can nullify all the prophetic ministry of the two witnesses. At this point, the Spirit of life reverses all the situations on earth. The Spirit of life from God suddenly enters their bodies. The witnesses are resurrected by the power of the Spirit of life and then ascend into heaven. Due to the work of the Spirit of life, many people on earth give glory to God of heaven. Readers understand that the ministry of the two witnesses is completed and accomplished by the Spirit of life. In sum, the narrator characterizes the Spirit of life as the Spirit of resurrection and ascension who completes all salvation history. Through the description of the active work of the Spirit of life in 11:11, the Spirit of life is characterized as the Spirit not only to resurrect Jesus from the grave, but also to resurrect all faithful saints.

Additionally, the narrator focuses on the activeness and timeliness of the ministry of the Spirit of life. The Spirit of life is uniquely active among all other presentations of the Divine Spirit. The Spirit of life moves at the right time or the most effective time to make the two witnesses alive. In short, the narrator characterizes the Spirit of life as the Spirit of activeness and timeliness who moves anywhere at anytime to make all faithful saints alive. In another sense, we can imagine this from the perspective of prophetic imagination since the immediate context of 11:11 turns out to be prophetical in addition to the prophetic characteristic of Revelation. Accordingly, the Spirit of life fills the saints with the Spirit at anytime and anywhere to restore them prophetically and spiritually.[39] Thus, the Spirit of life is characterized as the Spirit of restoration or fullness.

Furthermore, the narrator depicts the Spirit of life as a "God-like" character in 11:11. The resurrecting work of the Spirit of life is not like that of human beings. It is a God-like divine character who makes the two witnesses come alive from death. The Spirit of life knows everything about who needs His help and where to go to help, like the omniscient God. He knows what happens on earth such as the war between the two witnesses and the beast coming from bottomless pit. He even knows what happens in both the bottomless pit and heaven. The Spirit of life transcends time and space. In control of His own timing, He enters into the two witnesses after three and a half days have passed. The implication that the Spirit of life transfers the two witnesses from Jerusalem to heaven to enable them to ascend occurs when a heavenly voice says, "come up here." Hence, the Spirit of life is characterized as a God-like Spirit. The narrator proves it by adopting the phrase, "from God" to describe that the Spirit of life comes from God.

It is notable that the Spirit of life is the Spirit who pays His attention to the churches and especially the mission or witnessing ministry of the

---

39. In the immediate context, the great city of Jerusalem is described to be prophetically called Sodom and Egypt in Rev 11:8, even though there is no connection between two descriptions.

churches. That is why the Spirit of life moves quickly when the two witnesses as witnessing church community have a problem by the attack of beast. Thus, we find that the narrator characterizes the Spirit of life as the *church-centric* or *ekklesia-centric* Spirit.

THE DIVINE SPIRIT AS ACTED UPON

The unique reference to the Divine Spirit as a character who is acted upon by another character, God, or Jesus, is found in Revelation.

> Then I saw between the throne and the four living creatures and among the elders a Lamb standing as if it had been slaughtered, having seven horns and seven eyes, which *are the Seven Spirits of God sent out into all the earth*. (Rev 5:6; italics mine)

After the narrator depicts the location of the Seven Spirits as "in front of His throne" (1:4) and "in front of the throne" (4:5), here in 5:6, he narrates that the Seven Spirits "are sent to all the earth." The Seven Spirits are characterized as *cosmological beings or God-like, not human-like, Spirits* since they move from the heavenly throne to all the earth. It is not quite clear who sends the Seven Spirits to all the earth in 5:6; however, we can infer from the immediate context of 5:6 that Jesus, that is, the Lamb of God, and God together send them. The Seven Spirits belong to the Lamb who ransomed the saints from "every tribe and language and people and nation" (5:9) for God by His blood. Readers may infer that it is quite reasonable for the Lamb to send the Seven Spirits to all the earth since the concern of the Lamb is to save people from every tribe and language and people and nation. The narrator intends to depict that the Seven Spirits are sent by God by adopting the phrase of "of God" to present the Seven Spirits. Hence, readers may understand that God and the Lamb send the Seven Spirits to all the earth.

On the other hand, it should be noted that the Seven Spirits must receive missions from God and the Lamb when they are sent to all the earth. From the immediate context, readers may infer that the missions that are given by God and the Lamb must be related to the salvation of the people on earth. Moreover, their missions should not be limited to just a certain people group, but be expanded to all the people from every tribe and language and people and nation on earth. Furthermore, their missions are related not only to save people, but also to build the church of Christ Jesus since Jesus is concerned with the seven churches in Asia. In addition, their missions cannot be separated from the judgment of God and the Lamb, which is written in Revelation (ch. 6, 8–9, 15–20). Those who accept the ransom of the blood of Jesus shall be saved forever. Otherwise, they shall be judged and punished forever.

In sum, the Seven Spirits of God are characterized as the God-like Spirit(s) who is working for all the people on earth as the agent(s) to be sent by God and the Lamb.

The Divine Spirit as a Co-Agent

It is notable that the narrator prefers both an active co-agent (1:4, 10; 4:2; 17:3; 21:10; 19:10) and a passive co-agent (3:1; 4:5; 5:6) to acting and acted upon characters to describe the action of the Divine Spirit in Revelation.[40] The frequency of the usage proves it. The narrator employs the Divine Spirit as an active co-agent six times and as a passive co-agent three times, whereas both the acting and the acted upon Divine Spirit are employed only one time each in Revelation. What does this preference mean in relation to the Divine Spirit? From my examination, I infer that the narrator intends to present that the Divine Spirit prefers working together with other characters such as God, Jesus, John and churches (the bride) rather than working alone. For example, the narrator employs the expression of the Divine Spirit as an active co-agent from "in the Spirit" four times (1:10; 4:2; 17:3; 21:10) in Revelation to present that the Divine Spirit works in the human character, John. The Spirit is characterized as being active in John, whereas John is active enough to hear and see all visions in the Spirit. The Spirit is depicted to be active to control or move John in that John, who is in the Spirit, may be able to see the glorified Jesus (1:10) and to visit the heavenly place (4:2), desert (17:3), and a great, high mountain to see the New Jerusalem (21:10). However, the narrator does not show how much the Spirit controls John. The Divine Spirit as a passive co-agent is found in 3:1 and 5:6, which show that the Seven Spirits belong to Jesus. The Seven Spirits work together with Jesus, not by themselves. Here also the narrator does not clarify how much the Seven Spirits are controlled by Jesus. The narrator also employs the passive form

---

40. In the NRSV, Greek, καιόμεναι, is translated as an active tense, "burn." However, καιόμεναι (being burned) is a participle present passive. That is why Rev 4:5 is sorted as semi-acted upon, even if the meaning is active.

Character Presentation of the Holy Spirit in Revelation

to depict the seven torches of the Divine Spirit in front of the throne of God in 4:5 to show how the Seven Spirits are working with God, indicating slightly the initiative of God in their co-operation.

The first case of the Divine Spirit as an active co-agent is found in 1:4. In the blessing of a formal letter, the Seven Spirits are depicted as the benefactor or the source of grace and peace to the seven churches in Asia. Here they are not portrayed as a unique benefactor or source of grace and peace, but as one of three benefactors or sources. The narrator characterizes the Seven Spirits who are before the throne as the Divine Spirit who is actively giving grace and peace to all churches in the world. However, the narrator does not present how the Seven Spirits give this grace and peace to the seven churches. In addition, the Spirit of prophecy in 19:10 can be classified in this group. The Spirit of prophecy is characterized as being active for the witness to Jesus. The narrator does not show clearly how much the Spirit of prophecy is active for the testimony of Jesus as the Spirit of "in the Spirit" in 1:10; 4:2; 17:3; 21:10 is not clearly described as to how much the Spirit affects John.

It should be noted that the Divine Spirit of both an active and a passive co-agent is not clearly classified as a "personal being" or as an "impersonal being" or as a "God-like being" except in 1:4. In fact, The Seven Spirits in 1:4 can be classified clearly as God-like Spirit(s) since they bless the seven churches with grace and peace together with God and Jesus. However, there is inadequate evidence to define others either as a "personal being" or as an "impersonal being" or as a "God-like being." First of all, the Divine Spirit as a passive co-agent (3:1; 4:5; 5:6) is characterized as belonging to Jesus (3:1; 5:6) and things being burnt in heaven (4:5 passive). Hence, three descriptions of the Divine Spirit as passive co-agents can be classified as "impersonal beings," neither "God-like" nor "person-like" beings. Secondly, the Spirit from the expression of "in the Spirit" of the Divine Spirit as an active co-agent (1:10; 4:2; 17:3; 21:10) can also be classified as both "God-like being" and "impersonal force," rather than a personal being. The Spirit of "in the Spirit" may be characterized as "God-like" character in that He allows John to experience many spiritual experiences such as meeting the glorified Jesus (1:10), and visiting the heavenly place (4:2), desert (17:3), and great, high mountain to see the New Jerusalem (21:10).[41] In another sense, the Spirit of "in the Spirit"

---

41. Those who emphasize this view usually insist that the use of capitalization, such as "Spirit," shows the God-likeness of the Spirit.

may be also characterized as an "impersonal spiritual force" in that the spirit allows John to experience many spiritual things.[42] In my opinion, two different attributes of the Spirit in the Spirit are united, rather than separated. In conclusion, the Spirit in the Spirit can be characterized as a *God-like impersonal force*.[43] Thirdly, the Spirit of prophecy in 19:10 is hard to be defined as a "personal being" or as "God-like being" or as an "impersonal force." In other words, the narrator of Revelation does not seem to tell us whether or not the Spirit of prophecy is a person or God. He is not so concerned with what kind of personality the Spirit of prophecy has in this indirect presentation sentence. Rather he represents the Spirit of prophecy *metaphorically, as a character in the narrative* to be identified with the testimony of Jesus. In another sense, readers understand that the Spirit of prophecy is a metaphorical character to be replaced with the testimony of Jesus. For example, the expression of those who hold the testimony of Jesus may be replaced with those who hold the Spirit of prophecy. We cannot discover the direct action of the Spirit of prophecy from the last sentence in 19:10: "the testimony of Jesus is the spirit of prophecy." However, from the whole verse—"Then I fell down at his feet to worship him, but he said to me, 'You must not do that! I am a fellow servant with you and your comrades who hold the testimony of Jesus. Worship God! For the testimony of Jesus is the spirit of prophecy'" (19:10)—we discover the action of the Spirit of prophecy in that the Spirit of prophecy is active in those who hold the testimony of Jesus. The narrator attempts to draw the activity of the Spirit of prophecy from a metaphorical sentence and a metaphorical character, even though indirectly. In this way, readers can be convinced that the Spirit of prophecy is involved in the testimony of Jesus.

In short, all usages of the Spirits in the expression of "in the Spirit" are described to be an active co-agent. The Spirit of life is depicted to be active. All three uses of the Seven Spirits in 3:1; 4:5; 5:6a are narrated to be a passive co-agent. The one time usage of the Seven Spirits in 5:6b is said to be passive. Another usage of the Seven Spirits in 1:4 is understood to be an active co-agent. Thus the Divine Spirit is characterized as Enigmatic God-like Spirit(s), Church-centered Spirit(s), God-centered Spirit(s), and Jesus-centered Spirit(s).

---

42. Those who emphasize this view usually insist on using the lowercase letter, such as "spirit," to show the nature of the impersonal force of the spirit.

43. The capital letter of "Spirit" is preferred in this united view.

Character Presentation of the Holy Spirit in Revelation

External Appearance of the Divine Spirit

Besides speech and action, external appearance is also employed in Revelation as an indirect presentation of the Divine Spirit. There are only two instances in the Revelation narrative that readers might consider as descriptions of the external or the physical appearance of the Divine Spirit. Both cases in Revelation are apocalyptic and both are narrated by John who is in the Spirit:

> Coming from the throne are flashes of lightning, and rumblings and peals of thunder, and in front of the throne *burn seven flaming torches,* which are the Seven Spirits of God. (Rev 4:5; italics mine)[44]

> Then I saw between the throne and the four living creatures and among the elders a Lamb standing as if it had been slaughtered, having *seven horns and seven eyes,* which are the Seven Spirits of God sent out into all the earth. (Rev 5:6; italics mine)

Seven burning fire torches
(ἑπτὰ λαμπάδες πυρὸς καιόμεναι)

In the first instance, the Divine Spirit, expressed as "the Seven Spirits of God," is said to be in front of the throne with the appearance of the seven flaming torches burning (ἑπτὰ λαμπάδες πυρὸς καιόμεναι) in 4:5. In the context of the heavenly throne, the narrator depicts the seven Spirit(s) with the divine number "seven" (ἑπτὰ), "keep burning" (καιόμεναι), "torches or lamps" (λαμπάδες), and "fire" (πυρὸς). Among the four words, the essential word is fire. The other three describe it more concretely. In other words, the Divine Spirit in front of the throne is fire. This fire is never quenched, but is burning forever, and is in the torch or is torch-like (4:5). In the immediate context of chapter 4, there is no other fire to depict a character directly in the heaven but the Divine Spirit.[45] Moreover, the fire is employed to describe the Divine Spirit directly only in 4:5 in the whole of Revelation.[46] Besides the Divine Spirit, there are four

---

44. KJV is more literal provided that we understand that it is the lamps that are burning and not the fire that is burning.

45. Flash of lightning in 4:5 is not fire.

46. The word "fire" (πυρὸς), is exploited fourteen times in Revelation among twenty-eight times in the New Testament. Besides being used five times for character

usages of "fire" to describe characters in Revelation: three times for Jesus' eye (1:14; 2:18; 19:12), and one time for a mighty angel's leg (10:1). However, all four cases are metaphorical descriptions, not direct descriptions: *like* a flame of fire (1:14; 2:18; 19:12), *like* pillars of fire (10:1).

On the other hand, the narrator makes a room for readers to fill the literary gap in order to understand the relationship between fire from the altar and that in front of the throne.[47] In other words, without any direct description from the narrator, readers have to deal with the question whether the fire, which was thrown on the earth in 8:5, can be identified with the fire in front of the throne, that is, the Divine Spirit in 4:5. Readers may collect the information that the two have the same position, that is, *before the throne*, from the observations of Rev 8:3, 5; 4:5.

> Another angel with a golden censer came and stood at the altar; he was given a great quantity of incense to offer with the prayers of all the saints on *the golden altar that is before the throne*. (8:3; italics mine)

> Then the angel took the censer and filled it with *fire from the altar* and threw it on the earth; and there were *peals of thunder, rumblings, flashes of lightning, and an earthquake*. (8:5; italics mine)

They may also discover that temple is in the throne.[48]

> The seventh angel poured his bowl into the air, and a loud voice came *out of the temple, from the throne*, saying, "It is done!" (16:17; italics mine)

With these two clues, readers may infer that the fire before the throne, that is, the Divine Spirit, can be identified with the fire sent from

---

descriptions (1:14; 2:18; 4:5; 10:1; 19:12), fire is used five times for judgment descriptions (9:18; 19:20; 20:10, 14, 15), two times for natural description of fire (3:18; 14:18), and one time for fire from the altar (8:5). Besides πυρὸς (fire), Rev includes two different cases of πυρὸς πῦρ (five times: 8:7; 9:17; 11:5; 13:13; 20:9) and puri. (seven times: 8:8; 14:10; 15:2; 16:8; 17:16; 18:8; 21:8). Among twelve times, ten times are used for judgment descriptions of fire. The fire in 13:13 is used by the beast to deceive people. The fire in 15:2 is used for fire in heaven. The last one shall be discussed in the paragraph that follows.

47. For literary gap, see Darr, *On Character Building*, 18–23.

48. Furthermore, Aune interprets that the temple is the same place as the throne. Aune, *Revelation 6–16*, 899. Aune translates 16:17b, "and a loud voice came from the temple, that is, from the throne, saying, 'It is finished.'" He emphasizes the identification of the temple with the throne by using, "that is."

Character Presentation of the Holy Spirit in Revelation

the altar to the earth. The narrator intends for the readers to understand some points through the process of filling the literary gap from the narrative: (1) The fire of the Divine Spirit is involved in the judgment of God toward the earth, (2) the fire of the Divine Spirit is sent by God to respond to the prayers of all the saints, and (3) the fire of the Divine Spirit works with the power of God sitting on the throne. The result of sending fire to the earth supports point three since the powerful phenomena of the heavenly throne in 4:5 repeats again in 8:5b, "peals of thunder, rumblings, flashes of lightning, and an earthquake on earth."[49]

Another "fire" mixed with sea of glass in heaven in 15:2 ("sea of glass mixed *with fire*") is designed by the narrator to stimulate the imagination of readers to fill the literary gap to figure out the identity of fire. The narrator gives two phrase-linking clues, that is, "in front of the throne" in 4:5; 4:6 and "sea of glass" in 4:6; 15:2 to help readers to imagine the identity of fire. With these clues, it is not hard for the implied readers to find out that fire in 15:2 can be identified with the fire of the Divine Spirit in front of the throne in 4:5. Both "burning fire" and "sea of glass" are located in front of the throne. In 15:2, both are mingled to be "sea of glass mixed with fire," beside which conquerors in the messianic war are standing with harps of God in their hands.[50] In this way of imagination, the implied readers can draw five significant conclusions: (1) the fire of the Divine Spirit has a vast impact in heavenly court, including more than the torch or lamp in that it flows like the river or sea of fire from the throne; (2) the fire of the Divine Spirit is involved in the messianic war in that conquerors must have been supported by the Divine Spirit who is sent to earth, since they cannot conquer the beast and its image and the number of its name without the help; (3) the fire of the Divine Spirit is involved in the praise and worship of the saints in that they are standing beside the fire of the Divine Spirit; (4) the fire of the Divine Spirit is

---

49. The first three phenomena are the same as those in the throne of God. The last one, the earthquake, can be understood as a sign of theophany. Thus, we infer that the power of heaven comes down on the earth with the form of fire through the Seven Spirits of God who were sent to the earth.

50. Aune argues, "In 15:2 a 'sea of glass mingled with fire' combines the motifs of a celestial sea above which the throne of God is set and the river (or rivers) of fire that flows from his throne." *Revelation 6–16*, 870–71. He does not attempt to discover the identity of fire in his commentary. However, Beale associates the fire in 15:2 with the "fire" in 4:5. He concludes that "therefore, 'fire' in 4:5, which is part of a description of the 'Seven Spirits,' associates those spirits with judgment." Beale, *Book of Revelation*, 792.

involved in the world mission in that they praise the conversion of all nations (Rev 15:4b: "All nations will come and worship before you"); and (5) the fire of the Divine Spirit is involved in the judgment of God (Rev 15:4c: "for your judgments have been revealed").

Seven Horns and Seven Eyes

In the second instance, the Divine Spirit is spoken of as the "seven horns and seven eyes" in 5:6. There have been two interpretations concerning the Seven Spirits of God in 5:6 as just "seven eyes" or as both "seven horns and seven eyes."[51] As Bauckham argues, seven horns and seven eyes stand for "the power of the victory" of the Lamb. "The Seven Spirits are sent out into all the earth to make his victory effective throughout the world."[52] How do the Seven Spirits do it? To find the answer, I read this verse in the way of dynamic reading without historical background from the perspective of the narrator and the implied readers. The narrator draws readers' attention to what and how the Seven Spirits are doing in the world by the expression of "sent out into all the earth" (5:6b). The first story in which readers may discover the work of the Divine Spirit

---

51. Aune supports the first view. *Revelation 1–5*, 353–54. Bauckham supports the second view. *Climax of Prophecy*, 164–65. Both Aune and Bauckham find the allusion of this verse from Zechariah 4. However, Bauckham attempts to discuss more about the seven horns. Finally he argues that "probably Revelation 5:6 identifies the Seven Spirits with both the seven horns and the seven eyes of the Lamb." *Climax of Prophecy*, 164. To draw this conclusion, he adopts the following question and answer method:

> Question: "The seven horns and the seven eyes belong to the description of the Lamb when he first appears in Revelation: as the slaughtered Lamb who has conquered (5:5–6). They represent the power of his victory. The Seven Spirits are sent out into all the earth to make his victory effective throughout the world. How do they do so?"
>
> Answer: "The answer is best found in the implicit relationship that exists between the Seven Spirits and the two witnesses of Rev 11:3–13." Ibid., 165

Then he attempts to focus on the allusion to Zechariah 4 to find some relationship between the two. I agree that finding allusion may illuminate the clearer meaning of Revelation. However, in this study, I shall attempt to conduct the dynamic reading without finding historical background as mentioned in the part of methodology of chapter 1.

52. Ibid.

Character Presentation of the Holy Spirit in Revelation

after the Seven Spirits are sent out into all the earth in 5:6 is that of the two witnesses in 11:3–13.[53]

It is notable that the narrator depicts how the two witnesses prophesy on earth by the expression of "τὴν ἐξουσίαν" (ruling power, supernatural power or authority) to control even nature such as sky, rain, water, and earth in 11:6. Before we discuss this expression, more general issues need to be investigated in view of the relationship between the story of the two witnesses and the Divine Spirit. The narrator provides two clues to help readers understand how the Divine Spirit works with the two witnesses: the identity of the two witnesses as "the two olive trees and the two lampstands that stand before the Lord of the earth" (11:4) and the expression of "fire" (11:5). The first clue in 11:4 is related to the Divine Spirit implicitly, whereas the second one in 11:5 is related more explicitly. Readers understand that both the olive tree and lampstand should be "anointed with the oil of the Spirit" to play their roles.[54] In other words, the Divine Spirit is indispensable for the churches to prophesy as witnesses. The Divine Spirit was already sent by the Lord Jesus to all the earth where the two olive trees and the two lampstands stand before the Lord who has seven horns and seven eyes. If the churches can prophesy with authority and supernatural power on earth, they must be filled with the Divine Spirit, that is, the Seven Spirits. The second clue for the Divine Spirit is found in the word, "fire" in 11:5. The word, "fire," must remind readers of the fire, which represents the Divine Spirit, that is, the Seven Spirits of God, in front of the throne in 4:5. In short, the Divine Spirit of "fire" works when the prophets and saints prophesy the word of God to witness to Jesus in their mouths.

Now we need to focus on the issue of the expression of "τὴν ἐξουσίαν" (ruling power, supernatural power or authority) in view of

---

53. After the Seven Spirits are sent into all the earth in 5:6, the story continues with the opening of the seven seals of the scroll by the Lamb, the judgment against the world, the protection of the saints, and the attention to the saints' prayers in chapters 6–9. In chapter 10, the opened scroll is given to John to eat and to prophecy to many peoples and nations and languages and kings. Then the story of the two witnesses, representing witnessing churches, is narrated. Here, readers may discover how the Divine Spirit works with the churches in the world.

54. See Bauckham, *Theology of the Book*, 113. Bauckham argues that "the two anointed olive trees" is "the two anointed ones [literally: 'sons of oil']." He also insists that John emphasizes the role of the seven Spirits by employing "the two olive trees and the two lampstands" (Rev 11:4). We understand that the readers might understand apocalyptic literature like the book of Zechariah.

the probable interpretation of the seven horns as the identity of the Seven Spirits. If the apocalyptic expression of the killing power over the enemies of the two witnesses is the "fire" which represents the Seven Spirits of God, what is the apocalyptic expression of "τὴν ἐξουσίαν" in the Revelation narrative? There are three possibilities to address this question: "fire" in 4:5, "seven eyes" in 5:6, and "seven horns" in 5:6. By way of filling the gap, readers can discover that there is no other expression but "seven horns." Fire is related to kill enemies. The seven eyes are described to watch over all creatures like the omniscient God. However, it is not satisfactory for both the fire and the seven eyes to represent a ruling power or authority. Thus readers accept both the seven horns and the seven eyes as the identity of the Seven Spirits.

On the other hand, once seven horns is adopted as the identity of the Seven Spirits, a synergic meaning can be drawn in relation to the Divine Spirit. The Divine Spirit is depicted as the Seven Spirits who work not just to watch over the saints and nonbelievers, but also to rule over them with authority that is shared with Jesus.

Thus, the Divine Spirit is characterized through indirect presentation indicator, external appearance, as the omnipotent and omniscient authority to rule over all creatures both in heaven and on earth.

Environment of the Divine Spirit

Besides speech, action, and external appearance, the narrator employs the environment as another indirect presentation indicator of the Divine Spirit in Revelation. The narrator narrates that the Divine Spirit exists and works in the two realms in Revelation: the heavenly realm and the earthly realm. As shown in Table 3.3, the Seven Spirits are depicted "in front of the throne" of God in 1:4 and 4:5 and "sent out into all the earth" in 5:6. The Spirit is also depicted as doing something both in heaven (14:13) and on earth (2:7, 11, 17, 29; 3:6, 13, 22; 11:11; 22:17). The two cases of the Spirit in the expression, "in the Spirit" are explicitly described to act both in heaven (4:2) and on earth (1:10). Another two cases are implicitly depicted to act both in heaven (21:10) and on earth (17:3). In this case the high mountain, that is, the New Jerusalem represents heaven and the wilderness can be understood to be a place on earth.

It is notable that the narrator indicates not just the location of the Divine Spirit, but also the direction of the Divine Spirit. In 5:6, the

Character Presentation of the Holy Spirit in Revelation

narrator narrates the movement of the Seven Spirits from the throne of God to all the earth. This implies that all the authority and power of the Divine Spirit who works on earth comes from the heavenly throne. On the other hand, the Seven Spirits can be identified with the Spirit. The narrator depicts that Jesus, who has the Seven Spirits in 3:1, commands the churches to pay attention to what the Spirit says to them. The narrator does not use the name of the Seven Spirits in the Revelation narrative anymore, but the Spirit, after the expression of "seven Spirits sent out into all the earth" (5:6b), is used. Precisely speaking, there is no report for the Seven Spirits sent into the earth to work on earth in the Revelation narrative, whereas just the Spirit is described to work on earth. Hence, readers can infer that the Spirit can be identified with the Seven Spirits sent to all the earth.

We should also note that it is important to discover the characterization of the Divine Spirit from the description of how the Divine Spirit exists and what he does both in heaven and on earth throughout the Revelation narrative. In heaven, firstly, the Divine Spirit is depicted to exist as a God-like Spirit who is closely related to God and Jesus. The narrator describes the Divine Spirit in heaven as an independent being (1:4; 4:2; 14:13; 21:10) as well as a dependent being (3:1; 4:5; 5:6). The Divine Spirit is characterized as an independent character, one of the three heavenly givers of grace and peace in 1:4, a heavenly communicator with heavenly voice in 14:13, and a guardian or guide of John in the heavenly realm in 4:2; 21:10. On the other hand, the Divine Spirit is characterized as a dependent character, as a co-worker or an apostle of God and Jesus in that He is with them and is sent to all the earth in 3:1; 4:5; 5:6. Secondly, the narrator describes that there are four sorts of ministries the Divine Spirit carries out on earth. The Divine Spirit is characterized as (1) a messenger to churches in 2:7, 11, 17, 29; 3:6, 13, 22; (2) the Spirit of spiritual revival to breathe life into churches in 11:11; (3) an evangelist or a missionary who is working with the bride, that is, church, to invite people to the marriage supper of the Lamb in 22:17; and (4) a spiritual director of the prophets and the saints, who guides or inspires them to a new spiritual experience in the fullness of the Spirit.

In short, the Divine Spirit is characterized through the environment as the omnipresent God-like Spirit who exists and works in heaven as well as on earth. He exists and works in heaven as a co-worker of God and Jesus to bestow grace and peace to the saints, as well as works as an apostle or a missionary to be sent to all the earth by God and Jesus. He is not described just to exist on earth, but to work on earth as a messenger, an inspirer of spiritual revival and triumph, an evangelist with prophetic proclamation, and a spiritual director or revelatory guide. The Divine Spirit is depicted as a connector between heaven and earth as well as a unifier between the heavenly church and the earthly church. He even plays a role as a significant mediator or a divine conductor who makes the New Jerusalem come down from heaven to the earth.

Table 3.3 Indirect Presentations of the Spirit(s) in Revelation

	Speech	Action (active/ passive)	External appearance	Environment (heaven/ earth)
The Seven Spirits (1:4)		Giver of grace and peace to the seven churches (semi-active)		The Seven Spirits who are before His throne (heaven)
The Seven Spirits (3:1)		Belong to glorified Jesus (semi-passive)		(implicitly both heaven and earth)
The Seven Spirits (4:5)		Burn (semi-passive)[55]	The seven flaming torches	In front of the throne (heaven)
The Seven Spirits (5:6)		Sent out into all the earth (passive), belong to a Lamb (Jesus-semi-passive)	Seven horns and seven eyes	Sent out into all the earth (earth)
The Spirit (2:7, 11, 17, 29; 3:6, 13, 22)	The Spirit is saying to the churches.			Jesus says to the churches=> Listen to what the Spirit is saying to the churches (earth)

55. The Greek word for "burn," καιόμεναι, is used as a passive form.

Character Presentation of the Holy Spirit in Revelation

	Speech	Action (active/ passive)	External appearance	Environment (heaven/ earth)
The Spirit of life (11:11)		The Spirit of life from God entered two dead witnesses		(earth) => ascended to heaven after resurrection
The Spirit (14:13)	The Spirit says, "Yes, they will rest from their labors, for their deeds follow them."			(heaven)
The Spirit (22:17)	The Spirit and the bride say, "come."			The Spirit is shown as a co-inviter to the coming of Jesus with the bride, the church.[56] (earth)
In the Spirit (1:10)		The Spirit plays a role to inspire John so that he may be prepared to receive the vision and voice of the glorified Jesus (semi-active)		John was in the Spirit on the Lord's day at the island of Patmos. (earth)

56. The Divine Spirit is depicted as one who is doing something for the churches on the earth as a one-way service: speaking to the churches (2–3), recovering the two witnesses (11:11), and prophesying the witness of Jesus (19:10). However, the narrator describes both the Divine Spirit and the bride, that is, the church as working together in a two-way service. With this description, the narrator attempts to encourage readers to participate in the witnessing ministry actively, awakening to the voice of the Divine Spirit. Readers must understand that churches cannot be separated from the Divine Spirit and must be united with the Divine Spirit.

	Speech	Action (active/ passive)	External appearance	Environment (heaven/ earth)
In the Spirit (4:2)		The Spirit plays a role to inspire John so that he may be prepared for entering heaven to experience the visions and voices. (semi-active)		John was immediately in the Spirit before he saw the heavenly visions. (heaven)
In the Spirit (17:3)		The Spirit plays a role to inspire John so that he may be prepared for moving to wilderness to see a woman sitting on a scarlet beast. (semi-active)		John was in the Spirit before he moved to the wilderness. (earth= wilderness)
In the Spirit (21:10)		The Spirit plays a role to inspire John so that he may be prepared for moving to the New Jerusalem to experience its glory. (semi-active)		John was in the Spirit before he moved to the great and high mountain, the holy Jerusalem. (heaven)

Analogy of the Divine Spirit in Revelation

The narrator adopts the mode of analogy to characterize the Divine Spirit in Revelation. Usually an analogy reinforces the construction of characters' traits. In other words, an analogy, as Rimmon-Kenan argues, is regarded as "a reinforcement of characterization rather than as a separate type of character-indicator," that is, by direct definition and indirect presentation.[57] Hur modified Rimmon-Kenan"s model of analogy with four factors of analogy: (1) repetition, (2) similarity, (3) contrast, and (4) comparison.[58] I shall apply these four factors of analogy to the Divine Spirit in Revelation.

Repetition and the Characterization of the Divine Spirit

Repetition is one of the most frequently used rhetorical devices in Revelation.[59] Resseguie argues about the repetition in Revelation as follows:

> Repetition forces the reader to pay close attention to particular events, persons, and pivotal moments in Revelation. Often it is used for rhetorical effects to accentuate the importance of threes, fours, or sevens. John's fondness for repetition is seen at every level in the book—from the smallest unit of words or phrases to entire scenes or series of events. Repeated words draw narrative together.[60]

I find two kinds of repetitions in view of the Divine Spirit in Revelation: (1) phraseological repetition, and (2) conceptual repetition.

PHRASEOLOGICAL REPETITION

For the phraseological repetition of the Divine Spirit, there are two kinds of repetitions: (1) "what the Spirit is saying to the Churches" (seven

---

57. Rimmon-Kenan, *Narrative Fiction*, 39, 76. She proposes three elements: analogous names, analogous landscape, and analogy between characters. She also suggests four elements of cohesion to unify categories for constructing a character: repetition, similarity, contrast, and implication (in the logical sense).

58. Hur, *Dynamic Reading*, 127–28. He classifies analogous landscape as the same category of environment, and implication as the same category of definition. He employs four factors of analogy. A repetition can be functionally classified as analogy in that it serves to reinforce the characterization just as similarity does, even though it looks like a different group from the other three.

59. Resseguie argues that "three rhetorical devices are common in this book [of Revelation]: 1) numerals, 2) repetitions, and 3) figures of speech." Resseguie, *Revalation Unsealed*, 10.

60. Ibid., 12.

times: 2:7, 11, 17, 29; 3:6, 13, 22), and (2) "in the Spirit" (four times: 1:10; 4:2; 17:3; 21:10).

What the Spirit is saying to the churches
(τί τὸ πνεῦμα λέγει ταῖς ἐκκλησίαις)

First of all, the narrator employs two rhetoric devices, that is, repetition and number, together in the phrase, "what the Spirit is saying to the churches" (τί τὸ πνεῦμα λέγει ταῖς ἐκκλησίαις). Repetitions of "seven times" are adopted to play an explicit role to draw the readers to pay attention to the fact that the Spirit is speaking to the churches.[61] Besides the sevenfold repetition pattern, the narrator intends to emphasize that the role of the Spirit is to speak to the churches, and this is done with another repetition of the same phrase, "Ὁ ἔχων οὖς ἀκουσάτω" (Let anyone who has an ear listen).

In addition, there are some implicit functions of the sevenfold repetition pattern of this phrase in relation to the Divine Spirit. Firstly, the sevenfold repetition pattern reinforces the characterization of the Spirit to take a prophetic role to communicate the divine will of God in heaven to the churches on earth. In other words, the Spirit conveys revelatory inspired oracles as well as divine orders for individual needs to the churches. The Spirit may speak not only directly to the churches, but also to the churches through the prophets or saints who are filled with the Spirit at any time and in any place. The Spirit usually speaks through the words of the prophecy inspired by the Holy Spirit through the prophets. That is why the narrator emphasizes the "word" or the "word of prophecy" or the "word of prophecy in this book" repeatedly. From this implication, readers may be encouraged to hear, read, and keep the prophecy in the Scripture. They also may be persuaded to listen to the voice of the Holy Spirit from the sermons of the preachers who are responsible to communicate the Word to the audience in the worship services. They are encouraged to pay attention to what the Spirit says to them for the needs in their

---

61. The narrator adopts fifty-five times the number formular, "seven," which describes three categories: characters (Spirits [flaming torches/horns/eyes, angels], stars, thunders); series (seals, trumpets, bowls, plagues); and symbols (golden lampstands [churches], heads [red Dragon], kings [mountains/scarlet beast/beast from the sea]). Besides the three categories—characters, series, symbols—the narrator adopts another category of seven, which is the seven repetitions of the same formular of the seven letters to the seven churches.

Character Presentation of the Holy Spirit in Revelation

own individual lives. Secondly, seven repetitions have a rhetoric effect to induce obedience of the audience or readers. In other words, readers are encouraged to obey quickly when they listen to what the Spirit says to them. Thirdly, the seven repetitions give an esoteric effect about the Spirit. In other words, the narrator attempts to exhort that the audience or readers are supposed to pay attention to the Spirit as they do to God and Jesus. Fourthly, the seven repetitions include an identification effect of the Spirit with Jesus. In other words, the Spirit is characterized to be identified with Christ Jesus. Furthermore, the Spirit is also characterized to be indistinguishable from the Spirit of prophecy.

IN THE SPIRIT (ἐν πνεύματι)

The narrator again adopts repetition with the four uses of "in the Spirit." Here, in the Spirit, the narrator again uses a double rhetorical device, that is, a numeric device and repetition. He employs a fourfold repetition pattern in relation to the Divine Spirit. What is the explicit effect of a fourfold repetition pattern with a view to the Divine Spirit? The Spirit of a fourfold repetition pattern of "in the Spirit" is characterized to work in the world, whereas the Spirit of sevenfold repetition pattern of "what the Spirit says to the Churches" is characterized to bring God's prophecy from heaven. An apocalyptic number, four, represents the world or the earth, and the Spirit of "in the Spirit" represents the inspiration of the prophets such as John or the saints on earth.[62] Furthermore, the fourfold repetition pattern of the Spirit of "in the Spirit" is represented not only to work in the whole world, but also to move individually inspired persons such as John into the heavenly court in Revelation. In other words, the Spirit inspires individuals to experience a spiritual journey in order to be transferred into heaven, that is, the spiritual realm. Readers may understand that it is the Spirit of "in the Spirit" who makes us, individual persons, experience a spiritual mystery, such as hearing heavenly voices, seeing visions, and visiting spiritual places.

In addition, the narrator adopts two repetitions in relation to "in the Spirit": ἐγενόμην ("I was," 1:10; 4:2), and ἀπήνεγκεν με ("He carried me," 17:3; 21:10). Both of them represent John, the prophet, who

---

62. To learn more about the apocalyptic number four and how it represents the world or earth, see Bauckham, *Climax of Prophecy*, 326; *Theology of the Book*, 66–67, 109.

experiences the spiritual state of being "in the Spirit." They also represent that one, like John, who is "in the Spirit," does not lose one's consciousness, but keeps one's own clear mind. In the Spirit, John interacts with an angelic being who carries him to other places.

Conceptual repetition

Conceptual repetition is a sort of repetition of the descriptions related to a character. They include the similar repetitions of a character, such as theme, place, relationship, and the exact repetitions of the descriptions related to a character, even though not the exact repetitions of a character. In Revelation, four conceptual repetitions are discovered in relation to the Divine Spirit: (1) "Presence of the Divine Spirit 'before God,'" (2) "Revelatory transmission," (3) "Belong to Jesus," and (4) "Spiritual endowment."

Presence of the Divine Spirit "before God"

The narrator indicates the location of the Seven Spirits two times as "in front of the throne" where the God Almighty is sitting in 1:4 and 4:5. What are the rhetoric effects of using this repetition with the Seven Spirits? Firstly, readers are forced to recognize that the Seven Spirits do not originate from the earth, but are rooted in heaven, and that they are also holy enough to exist in front of the throne of God. Secondly, careful readers may recognize that the Seven Spirits are together with a great multitude of saints and prophets who are dead because of persecutions in 7:9; 20:12, that is, among the 144,000 sealed ones who sing a new song in 14:3 in front of the throne of God. Actually, the phrase, "in front of the throne" is employed ten times in the whole Revelation narrative. Two of them, which are the golden altar in 8:3 and something like a sea of glass or like crystal in 4:6, are depicted not as characters, but as things. Another two related to twenty-four elders in 4:10 and all angels in 7:11 just indicate the places where their crowns are cast and their faces were fallen down. Just six uses are related to characters: two times for the Seven Spirits in 1:4, 4:5; four times for a great multitude in 7:9, 15; the number 144,000 in 14:3; and the dead in 20:12. The narrator attempts to identify a great multitude in 7:9, with 144,000 in 14:3, and the dead in 20:12. He depicts that both a great multitude in 7:9 and 144,000 in 14:3 come from the same origin of all the earth, that is, every nation, all tribes, all nations, and all languages. They are described to be holy: robed in white in 7:9, virgins and not having defiled themselves with women in 14:4, and not lying and blameless in 14:5. He describes that both a great multitude in 7:9 and the dead in 20:12 are identified through the expression, "they who have come out of the great ordeal" in 7:14. Hence, the Seven Spirits, who are with the faithful saints and prophets in front of the throne in heaven, can be identified with the Spirit who is working with the bride which represents the faithful saints and prophets on earth in 22:17. Furthermore, the Seven Spirits can be understood to be identified with the Spirit of life from God in 11:11, who is sent to breathe into the two dead witnesses, to resurrect them and to enable them to ascend up to heaven in order to stand in front of the throne of God. Thus the narrator employs a repetition about the location of the Seven Spirits to reinforce the direct and indirect definitions of the Divine Spirit in Revelation.

Revelatory Transmission

Besides the repetition pattern of the location of the Seven Spirits, the narrator employs repetitive revelatory transmission narratives to reinforce the direct and indirect definitions of the Divine Spirit in Revelation. In other words, using repetition, the narrator intends to focus on the fact that the Divine Spirit is deeply involved in the revelatory transmission process. Even though the Divine Spirit does not appear in the list of the revelatory transmission process in 1:1–2, the narrator depicts that the Divine Spirit relates to all the participants in the revelatory transmission process: God, Jesus, the angel, John, churches, and the world of nonbelievers. For God, the Seven Spirits are described to relate to God with such expressions as "who are before God's throne" in 1:4 and the Seven Spirits "of God" in 3:1; 4:5; 5:6. For Jesus, the Seven Spirits are depicted to relate to Jesus with such expressions as "ὁ ἔχων τὰ ἑπτὰ πνεύματα" (who has the Seven Spirits) in 3:1; and "a Lamb as it had been slain, having seven horns and seven eyes, which are the Seven Spirits of God" in 5:6. Seven letters of Jesus to the seven churches also reflect that the Spirit relates to Jesus through the seven repetitions of "what the Spirit says to the Churches." With regard to the angel, the narrator does not describe the relationship of the Divine Spirit to the angel succinctly whereas he does when describing how the angel relates to God and Jesus. However, he narrates it in several ways in Revelation so that readers can catch it clearly. First of all, careful readers may figure out the possible cooperation between the angel of the church and the Spirit from the narrative of the seven letters. The first part of each of the seven letters starts with the expression, "to the angel of the church of . . . write," whereas the last part of each of them starts with the sentence, "let anyone who has an ear listen to what the Spirit is saying to the churches." If the angel of local churches receives the letter from Jesus to them and the Spirit speaks to the churches, a sort of cooperation between the Spirit and the angel in communicating Jesus' messages to the churches can easily be imagined. In this cooperation, the narrator attempts to focus more on the role of the Spirit rather than the angel in the revelatory transmission process. In other words, the narrator employs the Spirit as a significant agent in the transmission process of revelation. Secondly, the narrator depicts the relationship between the Spirit and the angel to Jesus with the expression of Jesus as one "who has the Seven Spirits of God and the seven stars" (3:1) which represent the angels of the seven churches in 1:20. Thirdly, the narrator also depicts the relationship between the Spirit and the angel to God with two expressions: "all angels fell on their faces before the throne and worshipped God" (7:11), and "seven angels who stand before God" (8:2). In other words, the location of both the Divine Spirit and angels is described to be the same in front of God. Fourthly, the narrator also depicts the relationship between the Spirit and the angel to John with the repeated expression, "he [one of seven angels who had the seven bowls] carried me away in the spirit" (καὶ ἀπήνεγκέν με ἐν πνεύματι) in 17:3 and 21:10. For John, the narrator presents the relationship between the Divine Spirit and John with the four uses of "in the Spirit." For the churches, the narrator shows the relationship between the Spirit and the churches with the sevenfold repetition pattern of "what the Spirit says to the churches." In addition, the narrator presents a close relationship of the two with the expression of "the Spirit and the bride say, 'Come'" in 22:17. For nonbelievers', the Spirit is described as inviting them to come. Thus, readers understand that the Divine Spirit is involved not only in each participant of the revelation process, but also in the whole process of the revelatory transmission through the repetition of revelation transmission narratives. Audiences and readers may understand that the narrator deliberately intends to illuminate the reason why the Divine Spirit is not included as one of the participants of the revelation process in 1:1.

Character Presentation of the Holy Spirit in Revelation

BELONG TO JESUS

The narrator provides a repetition by indicating that Jesus "has" (*e;cwn*) the Seven Spirits in 3:1 and 5:6. What are the literary effects of this repetition in the Revelation narrative? First of all, the narrator intends to emphasize the close relationship of the Divine Spirit to Jesus through this repetition. Secondly, he intends to highlight through this repetition the supremacy of Jesus in that even the Seven Spirits "of God" are owned by Jesus and must be submissive to him. Thirdly, the narrator intends to present an implicit picture of working together among God, Jesus, and the Divine Spirit, who are called later to be the Holy Trinity. Fourthly, the narrator implicitly intends to present not only the separation of the Divine Spirit from angels, that is, the seven stars, but also the cooperation of the Divine Spirit with angels. In 1:16, the narrator depicts that Jesus owns only the seven stars. In 3:1, both the Seven Spirits of God and the seven stars are described as being owned together by Jesus. In 5:6, only the Seven Spirits are depicted as being owned by Jesus. Thus, the Divine Spirit is portrayed to be cooperating with Jesus, submissive to Jesus, and independent of the angel by the expression of the Divine Spirit's being owned by Jesus.

Then, what is the narrator's implicit purpose of using the word "ἔχων" (has) as related to Jesus? When the narrator employs ἔχων in relation to Jesus, I find that the objects usually play roles of tools or as cooperators in the Revelation narrative. The role of tool is necessary to describe the appearance of Jesus and Jesus' ministry when the narrator presents that Jesus ἔχων (has): a sharp two-edged sword in 1:16, eyes like a flame of fire in 2:18, key of David in 3:7, golden crown in 14:14, and a name that no one knows in 19:12. In other words, they are characterized as person-unlike. On the other hand, it takes the role of cooperators to represent helpers of Jesus when the narrator presents that Jesus ἔχων (has) the seven stars in 1:16; 3:1 and the Seven Spirits in 3:1. In other words, they are characterized as person-like. However, seven horns and seven eyes, which are the Seven Spirits of God in 5:6, are characterized as both person-unlike and person-like. Thus the Divine Spirit can be inferred to be both person-like and person-unlike by the expression of the Divine Spirit's being owned by Jesus who is person-like and person-unlike.

A Dynamic Reading of the Holy Spirit in Revelation

Spiritual Endowment

Another repetition in relation to the Divine Spirit is found in the concept of spiritual endowment in the Revelation narrative: I (John) was in the Spirit (1:10; 4:2; 17:3; 21:10), the Seven Spirits were sent into all the earth (5:6), and the two witnesses are breathed with the Spirit of life from God (11:11). The Divine Spirit was endowed into John before he experienced the spiritual visions and the spiritual journeys. Spiritual endowment happens personally in this case for the purpose of the revelatory transmission process. However, the general spiritual endowments are found in 5:6. The Seven Spirits are sent not into an individual person or into Christian communities, but into all the earth generally. In other words, the Divine Spirit does not work only for the Christian communities or individual Christians, but also for all the earth. In another sense, the Divine Spirit is not only involved in the salvation history, but also involved in the whole world history as well as in the natural grace. Another spiritual endowment is found in 11:11. It can be called the ecclesiastic spiritual endowment in this case. The two witnesses, who represent all of the witnessing churches, were endowed or filled with the Spirit of life from God to be revived from death and to ascend into heaven. Thus, the Divine Spirit is characterized as being related to the whole world as well as to the Christian communities. The Divine Spirit is depicted as being related to individual persons as well as to groups or communities. With the repetition of spiritual endowment, the narrator attempts to support or reinforce the direct and indirect definitions of the Divine Spirit.

Table 3.4 Repetitions of the Divine Spirit in Revelation

Phraseological Repetition	Conceptual Repetition			
	Presence before God	Revelatory Transmission	Belong to Jesus	Spiritual Endowment
τί τὸ πνεῦμα λέγει ταῖς ἐκκλησίαις (What the Spirit is saying to the churches 2:7, 11, 17, 29; 3:6, 13, 22) => 7 times	ἐνώπιον τοῦ θρόνου (In front of the throne 1:4; 4:5) 10 times => The Seven Spirits 2 times	Revelation process (1:1): implicit role of the Spirit	Jesus has the Seven Spirits (3:1)	John => I was in the Spirit
		Jesus with the Spirit (3:1) => John in the Spirit 1:10–3:22		
ἐν πνεύματι (in the Spirit 1:10, 4:2, 17:3, 21:10) => 4 times		John in the Spirit => the seven churches (1:4; 2:1–3:22)	Jesus having the Seven Spirits (5:6)	The Seven Spirits were sent into all the earth => implicit influence
		Spirit => churches: Spirit says to the churches (2:7, 11, 17, 29; 3:6, 13, 22)		
Ἐγενόμην ἐν πνεύματι (I was in the Spirit: 1:10, 4:2) => 2 times		The angel => John: open the scroll (10:8–11) => all inhabitants: many peoples and nations and languages and kings (10:11)		The two witnesses => Spirit of life from God enter into them
Ἀπήνεγκέν με ἐν πνεύματι (he carried me in the Spirit: 17:3, 21:10) => 2 times		The two witnesses => the peoples and tribes and languages and nations (11:9–13)		
		The testimony of Jesus is the Spirit of prophecy (19:10)		
		The Spirit and the bride say, "come" (22:17)		

Similarity and Comparison and the Characterization of the Divine Spirit

Besides repetition, similarity and comparison are employed as well to reinforce direct and indirect definition of the Divine Spirit in Revelation. The narrator adopts five kinds of expression in relation to the Divine Spirit: (1) The Spirit, (2) the Seven Spirits, (3) in the Spirit, (4), the Spirit of Prophecy, and (5) the Spirit of life from God. We can find both similarities and differences among them. For similarity, all five have connection through one common theme in Revelation, that is, the witness to Jesus. The Spirit is depicted as speaking to the seven churches with the words of Jesus in Revelation 2 and 3. The Spirit also invites people who are thirsty and need the water of life to come as a witness to Jesus in 22:17. The Spirit of prophecy is related to the testimony of Jesus in 19:10. The Seven Spirits belong to Jesus in 3:1; 5:6. Careful readers can infer that they are sent out into all the earth in 5:6 as witnesses to Jesus since they belong to Jesus. The Spirit inspires John to be prepared for being a witness to Jesus through the words of Jesus and visions about Jesus. The Spirit of life from God breathes into the two witnesses who were dead due to the witness to Jesus in 11:11. Thus, readers or audiences can assume that the Divine Spirit has the same identity since there is a common role of witness to Jesus among the four kinds of Spirit.

However, some differences can be found among them as well. The Seven Spirits are depicted to exist in heaven, whereas the Spirit (of prophecy) is depicted to exist on the earth, even if they are sent out into all the earth from heaven. The Seven Spirits, the Spirit of life from God, and the Spirit "in the Spirit" are portrayed as person-unlike, whereas the Spirit and the Spirit of prophecy are depicted as person-like. Thus, all five expressions can be understood by the readers or audiences to be both identical and different.

Contrast and the Characterization of the Divine Spirit

Besides repetition, similarity, and comparison, the narrator adopts another analogical method, that is, contrast, to reinforce the direct and indirect definitions of the Divine Spirit. The Divine Spirit is contrasted to the demonic spirits in Revelation.

The contrasts are found in two words: "spirits" and "spirit." For spirit, the Divine Spirit is contrasted to every foul spirit in Rev 18:2: "He called out with a mighty voice, 'Fallen, fallen is Babylon the great! It has become a dwelling place of demons, a haunt of every foul spirit, a haunt of every foul bird, a haunt of every foul and hateful beast.'" Some contrasts between the Divine Spirit and foul spirits can be found in this verse. Firstly, the Divine Spirit is contrasted to "foul" spirits. The direct definition of the evil spirit is "foul," "demonic," and "hateful," whereas the Spirit is "holy," "prophetic," and "lovely."[63] Secondly, the foul spirit is related to the destruction or falling of Babylon as the great whore, whereas the Spirit is related to the construction of the New Jerusalem, that is, the church as the bride of Jesus in 22:17.

For spirits, the Divine Spirits are contrasted to foul spirits in 16:13–14: "and I saw three foul spirits like frogs coming from the mouth of the Dragon, from the mouth of the beast, and from the mouth of the false prophet. These are demonic spirits, performing signs, who go abroad to the kings of the whole world, to assemble them for battle on the great day of God the Almighty." Several contrasts between the Divine Spirits and foul spirits can be found here. Firstly, "seven" Spirits are contrasted to "three foul" spirits. As we see, there is another divine number besides seven in apocalyptic literature. The narrator attempts to illuminate that the three spirits are imitating the Divine Spirits; however, they are "foul" spirits. In other words, three spirits are deceiving spirits. Secondly, the Seven Spirits "of God" are contrasted to three foul spirits "coming from the mouth of the Dragon, the beast and the false prophet." In other words, they are satanic spirits consumed with deceit and false prophecy, as they work among kings. Thirdly, the Seven Spirits, which are the seven flaming torches (4:5) and the seven horns and the seven eyes (5:6), are contrasted to three "demonic" spirits "like frogs" (16:13). In short, with literary contrast to foul spirit(s), the narrator intends to emphasize that the Divine Spirit is the Holy Spirit of God and that the Divine Spirit is contrasted against foul and satanic spirit(s).

In addition, the Divine Spirits are contrasted to spirits of the prophets in 22:6: "And he said to me, 'These words are trustworthy and true, for

---

63. The Spirit is defined in Revelation as the Spirit who speaks to the churches with the words of Jesus. The Spirit is depicted to be holy since Jesus is also depicted to be holy in 3:7. The Spirit is prophetic since the Spirit is portrayed as the Spirit of prophecy in 19:10. The Spirit is beneficent since the Spirit is described to invite those who are thirsty to take the water of life without price in 22:17.

the Lord, the God of the spirits of the prophets, has sent his angel to show his servants what must soon take place.'" The narrator depicts the Divine Spirit as being separated from the human spirits. However, the narrator also intends implicitly to relate the Divine Spirits to the human spirits by employing the word, "spirits," and not using "souls." In other words, the narrator attempts to present that the Divine Spirits are working with the spirits of prophets since God of the spirits of prophets cannot be separated from the Seven Spirits of God. In short, with the literary contrast to the spirits of prophets, the Divine Spirits are portrayed not only to be separated from human spirits, but also to be united to the spirits of prophets as the Spirit of prophecy.

Thus, Table 3.5 represents the summary of the contrast between the Divine Spirit and other spirit(s). Literary contrast concerned with the Divine Spirit contributes to the identity of the Divine Spirit as the narrator has intended.

Table 3.5 Contrast between the Divine Spirit and Other Spirit(s) in Revelation

The Divine Spirit		Direct Definitions	Indirect Presentations	Similarity	Comparison
Spirits	The Seven Spirits	Seven/ of God	No speech/Action–semi-active, semi-passive, passive/ Appearance–flaming torches, horns, eyes/ Environment–heaven		

Character Presentation of the Holy Spirit in Revelation

The Divine Spirit		Direct Definitions	Indirect Presentations	Similarity	Comparison
	Foul spirits	Three/foul /from the Dragon/ from beast/ from false prophet/ demonic	No Speech/Action–3 active actions: performing signs; going abroad to the whole world kings; assembling them for battle on the great day of God Almighty/ Appearance–frog-like/ environment–earth 16:13: And I saw three foul spirits like frogs coming from the mouth of the Dragon, from the mouth of the beast, and from the mouth of the false prophet 16:14: These are demonic spirits, performing signs, who go abroad to the kings of the whole world, to assemble them for battle on the great day of God the Almighty.		
	Spirits of prophets	Of prophets	No speech/No Action/No Appearance/ Environment–heaven 22:6 And he said to me, "These words are trustworthy and true, for the Lord, the God of the spirits of the prophets, has sent his angel to show his servants what must soon take place."		

The Divine Spirit		Direct Definitions	Indirect Presentations	Similarity	Comparison
Spirit	The Divine Spirit	Spirit of prophecy (19:10)	No Speech/ No Action/ No Appearance/ Environment–earth		The Spirit and the bride in the New Jerusalem (22:17)
	Foul spirit	foul spirit	No Speech/No Action/ No Appearance/ Environment–earth 18:2 He called out with a mighty voice, "Fallen, fallen is Babylon the great! It has become a dwelling place of demons, a haunt of every foul spirit, a haunt of every foul bird, a haunt of every foul and hateful beast.	Demon, foul bird, foul and hateful beast (18:2)	Babylon the great=> the place of foul spirit (18:2)

The Divine Spirit in Revelation as a Character

As shown in the character presentation of the Divine Spirit in Revelation, the Divine Spirit can be regarded as a character since the Divine Spirit is depicted as "person-like." For example, the narrator tells us that the Divine Spirit blesses (1:4), and speaks (2:7, 11, 17, 29; 3:6, 13, 22; 14:13; 22:17). This implies that the Divine Spirit is an active character(s) who takes part in events in the episodes of Revelation and interacts or conflicts with other characters within the plot or structure of Revelation. The Spirit interacts with earthly local churches: sometimes encouraging them, sometimes confronting them in relation to their sins, but ultimately guiding them to the way of what Jesus wants them to be and do as persons in their communities. The Spirit works together with the bride, the church, and invites nonbelievers to have a relationship with Jesus and to enjoy His grace (22:17). On the other hand, the Divine Spirit has some characteristics that common people cannot share. The Divine Spirit has the character trait of "person-unlikeness." To exemplify, the Divine

Spirits have an enigmatic appearance such as the seven flaming torches (4:5) and seven horns and seven eyes (5:6). The Divine Spirit makes two dead witnesses come alive (11:11) and knows what shall happen after the death of the saints (14:13).

Conclusion

In this chapter we have analyzed the Divine Spirit as a character in Revelation, employing narrative theories of character and character presentation. In summary, the characterization of the Divine Spirit through character-presentation is shown in Table 3.6.

Table 3.6 Summary of Characterization of the Divine Spirit According to Character Presentation

Character presentation of the Divine Spirit			Characterization of the Divine Spirit	Related character(s)	Related verse(s)
Direct presentation (Definition)	Adjective	Seven	(1) Relationship to God => Divine "Holy" Spirit => Holiness.	Jesus and God	1:4
			(2) Relationship to Jesus => "God's" Divine Spirit = > Godliness.	Jesus	3:1
			(3) The Holy perfect fire of the Spirit in heavenly throne => Fullness and Perfection.	God	4:5
			(4) Powerful watcher and the scroll transmitter in the whole world => Wholeness.	The Lamb	5:6
		Of God	Holy God-like Spirit. Differentiated not only from God, but also from the seven angels, four living creatures, twenty-four elders/ Spirit of creation=> Person-unlikeness, Holiness.	God	1:4; 3:1; 4:8

A Dynamic Reading of the Holy Spirit in Revelation

Character presentation of the Divine Spirit			Characterization of the Divine Spirit	Related character(s)	Related verse(s)
		Of prophecy	The Divine Spirit (1) inspiring the Word of prophecy, (2) equipping believers to become witnesses with prophetic imagination, (3) being sent to make nonbelievers become converts of Jesus in all the earth => involved in the whole process of revelation transmission.	Jesus	19:10a
		Of life from God	Godly (Holy) Spirit of resurrection, restoration and revival.	God	11:11
	Other kind of noun	Testimony of Jesus	Spirit of worship (19:9–10) based on the Word of God and spiritual warfare (14:1–12).	Jesus	14:1–12; 19:10b
Indirect presentation	Speech	Speaking actor	A Reliable Witness to eternal blessings for the saints (14:13); A Spiritual Director or Wonderful Counselor to strengthen the faith of the saints (14:12–13); An Evangelist and mission Mobilizer (22:17); An Ongoing Speaker to the Churches (2–3): A Co-worker with Jesus => An Enigmatic Divine Character who holds both person-likeness and God-likeness.	Jesus, heavenly voice,	14:12–13; 22:17; chaps. 2–3

Character Presentation of the Holy Spirit in Revelation

Character presentation of the Divine Spirit			Characterization of the Divine Spirit	Related character(s)	Related verse(s)
	Action	The Divine Spirit as acting	The Omniscient Spirit paying attention to the Churches, especially spiritual warfare between the two witnesses (saints or churches) and the beast => Church-centered Spirit	God	11:11
		The Divine Spirit as acted upon	God and the Lamb-centered Spirit => God-likeness.		5:6
		The Divine Spirit as semi-acting	The Divine Spirit controlling the saints; A Divine Benefactor => Enigmatic God-like impersonal force.		1:4, 10; 4:2; 17:3; 21:10; 19:10
		The Divine Spirit as semi-acted upon	The Divine Spirit belongs to Jesus and is somewhat controlled by Jesus and is working with God; The Divine Spirit is working somewhat passively with God who has initiative over the Divine Spirit.	Jesus; God	3:1; 4:5; 5:6
	External appearance	Seven burning fire torches	The Divine Spirit is depicted as fire that is related to judgment of God; prayer of the saints; power of God; the messianic war; praise and worship.	God	4:5; 8:3, 5; 16:17; 15:2

A Dynamic Reading of the Holy Spirit in Revelation

Character presentation of the Divine Spirit			Characterization of the Divine Spirit	Related character(s)	Related verse(s)
		Seven horns and seven eyes	The Omnipotent and Omniscient Spirit who rules over all creatures both in heaven and on earth.	Jesus	5:6
	Environment	Heaven (before the throne/ heavenly vision)	The Seven Spirits sent to all the earth from the heavenly throne are identified with the Spirit who is speaking to the earthly churches. The Divine Spirit is depicted as God-like Spirit who is both an independent being and a dependent worker with Jesus and God; a heavenly communicator with heavenly voice; a guide of John in the heavenly realm.		1:4; 3:1; 4:2; 5:6b; 14:13; 21:10
		Earth (all the earth/ the seven churches/ Island of Patmos)	A messenger or missionary to earthly churches; Spiritual revivalist to breathe life to Churches; an evangelist and mission mobilizer; Spiritual Director for the prophets and saints; connector between heaven and earth; unifier between heavenly Church and earthly churches.		2:7, 11, 17; 3:6, 13, 22; 11:11; 22:17
Analogy	Repetition-Phraseological	What the Spirit is saying to the Churches	Prophetic Spirit speaking to the Churches through preachers and prophets as a revelation conveyer.		2:7, 11, 17; 3:6, 13, 22

Character Presentation of the Holy Spirit in Revelation

Character presentation of the Divine Spirit			Characterization of the Divine Spirit	Related character(s)	Related verse(s)
		In the Spirit	Guardian of the personal spiritual journey and experience with clear mind.		1:10; 4:2; 17:3; 21:10
	Repetition-Conceptual	Presence before God	Originated from heaven; The Seven Spirits are identified with the Spirit working with the Bride, the Church as well as the Spirit of life from God.		11:11; 22:17
		Revelatory transmission	Involved in the whole process of revelatory transmission with God, Jesus, the angel, John, Churches and the world.		1:1, 20; 3:1; 7:11; 8:2; 22:17
		Belong to Jesus	work with the angels; differentiate from angels; submissive to Jesus; working together with Jesus.		1:16; 3:1; 5:6
		Spiritual endowment	Involved in the Spiritual endowment for not only the Christian community with spiritual revival, but also the whole world history with natural grace.		5:6; 11:11
	Similarity and Comparison		Five expressions of the Divine Spirit such as the Seven Spirits; in the Spirit; the Spirit; the Spirit of prophecy; the Spirit of life from God, have the same identity to witness to Jesus as well as the different role.		3:1; 5:6; 19:10; 22:17

A Dynamic Reading of the Holy Spirit in Revelation

Character presentation of the Divine Spirit			Characterization of the Divine Spirit	Related character(s)	Related verse(s)
	Contrast-spirits	The Seven Spirits/ foul spirits/ spirits of prophets	The Seven Spirits are separated from the foul spirits as well as the human spirits, so that they may be called to be "divine holy" Spirits.		16:13–14; 22:6
	Contrast-spirit	The Divine Spirit/ foul spirit	The Spirit is emphasized to be holy, prophetic and lovely, so that the Spirit may be called the "holy" Spirit.		18:2; 19:10; 22:17

We may find that each character-presentation shows its own characterizations about the Divine Spirit. Table 3.6 shows that there are some characterizations that are common and repeated in each character-presentation. In short, the characterization of the Divine Spirit can be summarized with eighteen points of the identity of the Divine Spirit, such as: (1) the "Holy" God-like Spirit "with fullness and perfection," (2) differentiated from angels and heavenly beings, (3) powerful watcher over the whole world, (4) involved in the whole process of revelation transmission, (5) speaking to the churches through preachers and prophets, (6) sent to revive the churches spiritually by the expression of giving resurrection to the two witnesses, (7) Spirit of worship based upon the word of God, (8) Spirit of spiritual warfare, (9) reliable witness to eternal blessings for the sincere saints, (10) wonderful counselor to strengthen the faith of the saints, (11) spiritual director to guide the personal spiritual journey, (12) evangelist, (13) mission mobilizer, (14) enigmatic divine character with both God-likeness and person-likeness, (15) omniscient Spirit paying attention to the churches, (16) omnipotent Spirit ruling over all creatures both in heaven and on earth with salvational and natural grace, (17) omnipresent Spirit presenting in both the heavenly realm and the earthly realm, and (18) having the same identity among all descriptions of the Divine Spirit with different characteristics.

As shown in Table 3.6, the following three aspects can be highlighted by summarizing the presentation of the Divine Spirit in Revelation: (1) the Divine Spirit in Revelation is characterized as the "holy" Spirit;

(2) this "holy" Spirit is frequently presented in close link with God, Jesus, and His witnesses, and is also separated from heavenly beings including angel(s); and (3) the role of the Divine Spirit is presented mostly as the prophetic Spirit.

The implications of the direct definitions of the Divine Spirit are supported by the indirect presentation of the Divine Spirit. The Divine Spirit is described to as one who speaks or acts in directing or guiding the churches, that is, the witnesses of Jesus to testify to Jesus in the whole world as a spiritual director or guide.

The repeated effects of the Spirit are also presented as similar to the direct and indirect definitions of the Divine Spirit. Most importantly, five expressions of the Divine Spirit are presented to be identical by comparison. However, the Divine Spirit is presented as an enigmatic divine character with two dialectic paradigms: person-likeness and person-unlikeness. It is noted that person-likeness is mainly related to the Spirit and the Spirit of prophecy, whereas person-unlikeness to the Seven Spirits, in the spirit, and the Spirit of life from God. In addition, the Seven Spirits are usually located in the heavenly realm, whereas the Spirit and the Spirit of prophecy in the earthly realm. By contrast, the Divine Spirit is presented to be the "holy" Spirit(s), which is contrasted to the "foul" spirit(s).

So far, I have explored the characterization of the Divine Spirit through character-presentation. In the following chapter, I shall observe the characterization of the Divine Spirit through the plot and structure of Revelation.

4

Plot and the Holy Spirit in Revelation

Introduction

IN CHAPTER 3, THE character presentation of the Divine Spirit in Revelation was observed and discussed. In this chapter, I shall further explore the Divine Spirit in Revelation as a character by first exploring the narrative function of the Spirit in terms of the plot of Revelation.[1] To do this, previous studies of the plot of Revelation shall be discussed. I shall attempt to define the literary term "plot" and to suggest what I believe to be "the plot of Revelation." After defining the plot of Revelation, plot-functional characterization of the Divine Spirit shall be presented according to the plot of Revelation.

---

1. The relationship between the plot and the structure of Revelation shall be discussed later in this chapter, under the section, "Characterization of the Holy Spirit According to the New Plot of Revelation." For the narrative function of the Spirit, the plot is separated from the characterization of the Spirit in the immediate context. The former denotes the overall effect of the Spirit delineated in the process of the narrative, whereas the latter denotes the contextual results caused by the Spirit in an immediate narrative context. The latter is needed to find the plot of Revelation.

Definition of Plot

Various definitions of plot have been suggested since Aristotle defined plot as "the arrangement of the incidents."[2] Two issues concerned with the definition of plot have been emphasized: causal sequence in terms of internal literature and affective function in terms of external literature such as readers.

Quoting Egan's explanation of divergent opinions about plot and introducing the definitions of Egan and Matera,[3] Hur suggests his own definition of plot by clarifying the difference between various concepts of plot as follows:

> I note that story refers to general and broad contents in a narrative, whereas *plot refers to a narrative-flow that is engendered by causality in orderly sequence, evoking an affective or emotional response in the reader.* Hence, a plot may involve "narrative structure" or "narrative pattern" or "major themes." For my study, however, when I employ the term plot, it has a slightly different nuance or emphasis from these terms. Although these subjects often overlap, "structure" refers to formal outline, "pattern" identifies similar types among some narrative blocks, "theme' is relevant to topic or interest in a narrative, whereas "plot" refers to an orderly sequence unified by causality, which creates an emotional response in the reader. In this sense, a major theme is closely related to a plot as a sub-plot, whereas a well-organized meta-theme can be seen as a plot.[4]

I discover that the definitions of plot above seem to lack a concept of parallel-plot or multi-plot.[5] So, in the light of these definitions, I suggest

---

2. Aristotle, *Poetics*, 1450a.

3. Egan summarizes the various opinions of definitions of plot and then concludes that "a plot is a set of rules that determines and sequences events to cause a determinate affective response." Egan, "What is the Plot?," 470. Matera summarizes various critical views on plot: (1) arrangement of events in terms of causality (Forster, Scholes and Kellogg, Ricoeur and Muir), (2) time and final causality (Kermode, Crane, Ford, and Brooks), (3) emotional effect which this ending should produce in the reader (Friedman and Egan), and (4) interrelationship between discourse and story as plot-events (Chatman). Then he concludes that "we can say that although literary critics nuance their approaches to plot, they agree that it has something to do with how discourse arranges events by time and causality in order to produce a particular affective or emotional response." Matera, "Plot of Matthew's Gospel," 236.

4. Hur, *Dynamic Reading*, 183; italics in the original.

5. J. S. Bell argues for parallel-plot or multi-plot in his book, *Plot and Structure*. "Parallel plots are just that: two or more plot lines that run along the same forward

that *plot* refers to *a narrative flow or multi-narrative flows, with subplot(s), that is (are) engendered by causality in orderly sequence, evoking an emotional reaction in the reader.*

Previous Study of Plot of Revelation

Jang insists in his doctoral dissertation, "A Narratological Approach to the Structure of the Apocalypse of John," that there are eight suggestions of the plot for Revelation: linear, spiral movement, expanding scope, U shape, christological actions, multi-level, complex, multi-linear sequence, and fivefold scheme of the superstructure.[6] His study, including a fivefold scheme of superstructure, makes an undeniable contribution to the understanding of the previous plot studies of Revelation. Nevertheless, it needs to be reorganized in classifying the previous studies of plot of Revelation. Firstly, he classifies both Lindsey as a representative of radical premillennial believers and Walvoord as a representative of the dispensationalists to have linear plot concept. However, Jang does not describe the other group of interpreters like other dispensationalists who consider them to be in the conservative premillennial group, the postmillennial group, or the millennial group. Secondly, Jang also does not mention that they do not have a clear literary understanding that Revelation is a sort of narrative that has plot. Lindsey just interprets that the sequence of events in Revelation is related to history. Walvoord interprets that the judgments of seals, trumpets, and bowls are chronologically sequential. In short, neither has the concept of literary linear plot, even if they have a linear structure concept in their interpretation. Thirdly, Jang argues that recapitulationists such as Fiorenza have a spiral plot concept. However, he seems to be confused between plot and thematic interpretation. Many scholars of Revelation propose that "the organizing principle" of Revelation is "the repetition or retelling of the same events repeatedly with expanding and evolving variations."[7] After

---

path. You may have a main plot-featuring a lead character you wish to emphasize—and one or more parallel plots to go with it. Or you can equalize among the plot lines" (136). He also suggests using a subplot in the same book. "A subplot can be primarily thematic, concerned with what the Lead character needs to learn. While the outer action of the main plot is going on, causing all sorts of problems for the Lead, the thematic subplot focuses on issues that are personal and interior" (131).

6. Jang, "Narratological Approach," 121–23.
7. Resseguie, *Revelation Unsealed*, 160.

exploring the literary outline with distinct topical groupings through divisional indicators as well as reviewing various recapitulation theories, Beale concludes that "the dominant themes from 6:1—20:15 are, in order of importance, judgment, persecution and salvation/reward and that these themes are intensified as the book progresses."[8] According to the analysis of Beale, recapitulationists attempt to find a sort of broad flow of thought, which can be used in discovering a thematic structure of Revelation. Fourthly, both the expanding scope suggested by Du Preez and christological actions suggested by Du Rand are hardly to be classified as a literary plot.[9] They just present a thematic expansion of the people of God and theological movement of Christology. However, they do not propose the literary plot of Revelation. Accordingly, Jang fails to elucidate the classification of previous plot studies of Revelation in that he fails to distinguish thematic structure, that is, the macrostructure, from plot, that is, the superstructure.[10]

So in my opinion, four kinds of literary plot in Revelation can be classified from the previous studies of those who have the literary understanding of the plot of Revelation: (1) non-plot, but segmental subplot; (2) multi-level plot; (3) U-shape plot; and (4) fivefold scheme plot.

NON-PLOT, BUT SEGMENTAL SUBPLOT

A. CONTENT

Barr argues that "one should not assume that there is only one possible plot, except in the simplest of stories."[11] He concludes that "the Apocalypse is a complex story and no single reading will ever imagine all the possible connections between incidents."[12] At that point he stops trying to discover the single plot of Revelation. However, he attempts to divide Revelation as a book bound with three different story segments: letter scroll (1–3), worship scroll (4:1—11:18), and war scroll (11:19—22:21).

8. Beale, *Book of Revelation*, 144.

9. Du Preez, "Die Koms van die koninkryk," 216–18; Du Rand, *Johannine Perspective*, 310–16.

10. Van Dijk distinguishes the schematic superstructure to discover the schema or the plot of a narrative from the semantic macrostructure to find the themes of a narrative. See his *Macrostructures*, 107–15.

11. Barr, *Tales of the End*, 12.

12. Ibid.

Then, he explores the subplot from each segment. Even though he does not attempt to explore the plot of Revelation as a whole, he describes it indirectly through discovering the interrelation among three stories. Barr asserts about the first scroll that "the story of the first scroll is the story of conflict and victory in the ongoing life of the church.... A literary reading of this story sees this as the first movement of a three-part plot."[13] He connects the first scroll to the second one by asserting that the second story is prepared by the first story about "the divine messages for those who would be faithful" (Rev 1–3).[14] The second story sets up the audience to enable them to "see themselves in the role of the faithful witness."[15] He argues that the third story of war, conquest, and renewal helps the audience "grasp more clearly what it means to be faithful."[16] He adds that the third story segment explains "why it is that Jesus can instruct the churches (letter scroll) and enable the worship of God (worship scroll)" since Jesus has conquered over evil powers in battle.[17] In short, Barr does not propose a clear plot of Revelation, whereas clear concentric structure is presented.[18]

B. Evaluation

Barr contributes to the understanding that the single plot of Revelation is hard to find since Revelation is composed with three different scrolls of letter, worship, and war. However, he seems to be too pessimistic about finding the plot of Revelation, even if he attempts to do it indirectly.

Multi-level plot

A. Content

M. E. Boring proposes a fresh attempt to find the multi-level plot of Revelation.[19] He argues that the narrative of Revelation has a plot to express

13. Ibid., 53–54.
14. Ibid., 100.
15. Ibid.
16. Ibid.
17. Ibid., 149.
18. Concentric structure shall be discussed in chapter 5. It represents a chiastic structure in which literary concepts or ideas are placed in a special symmetric order or pattern to emphasize them.
19. Boring, *Narrative Christology*, 702–23.

Plot and the Holy Spirit in Revelation

the idea of Christ to be fulfilled in the events of history. In other words, the idea of Christ becomes a certain plot: the "problem" of unfulfilled task, and "the action which resolves the problem; and the happy ending."[20] In his discussion of the narrative Christology of Revelation, Boring suggests four level narrations in which four different plots can be found: John's and the Churches' story, the heavenly Christ's and God's story, the world's story, and the narrative christological story.[21]

B. Evaluation

Boring makes a contribution in his effort to find four level narrations in Revelation. However, if causality is an essential element for plot, the multi-level narration cannot be classified as plot of Revelation since causality cannot be found among them.

U-shape plot

A. Content

Resseguie proposes that Revelation has a U-shaped plot that begins with a stable condition (ch. 1, 4, 5), moves downward into an unstable condition (ch. 6–19), and moves upward to a new stable condition (ch. 20–22).[22] He insists that chapters 2–3 parallel the whole plot of Revelation, since chapters 2–3 have a plot of stability, instability, and new stability as chapters 4–22 have the same plot: stability (ch. 4–5), instability (ch. 6–19), and new stability (ch. 20–22).[23] U-shape plot comes out of his definition of plot that must include two elements: sequential events with stable condition, unstable condition, and new stable condition; and causality.[24] Besides two essential elements, he adopts six other necessary elements to understand the plot of Revelation: conflict, suspense, surprise, defamiliarization, primary effect, and recent effect.[25] He argues that the scene of perfect order and coherence that governs the universe with an "endless display

20. Ibid., 702.
21. Ibid., 704.
22. Resseguie, *Revelation Unsealed*, 166–92.
23. Ibid., 168–74.
24. Ibid., 23–24.
25. Ibid., 26.

of worship and praise" in chapters 4 and 5 establishes the "overwhelming primary effect," which cannot be overturned by the "recency effect of gloom and doom" found in the subsequent chapters.[26] Suspense is used in chapters 6 and 8. Conflict is used in chapters 9–19. Defamiliarization is used in describing both the risen Lord and the disgusting beasts. With these plotting techniques, readers are to be surprised. He explains the U-shape plot chapter by chapter with plot elements.

B. Evaluation

We cannot deny that the U shape makes a good contribution to understanding the plot of Revelation. In these terms it is quite easy to discover the key story of Revelation. The model is also easy to understand since it is simple. However, some weaknesses also can be found. Firstly, the U shape of chapters 2–3 cannot be explained with this model, even if Resseguie argues that it parallels the whole plot. Secondly, it is hard to explain why the sealing part of chapter 7 is placed in the instability section. Thirdly, the U-shape plot looks too simple to describe the complicated text of Revelation.

Fivefold scheme plot

A. Content

Jang employs the fivefold scheme model of Van Dijk as a plot of Revelation. According to the fivefold scheme model of Van Dijk, the narrative plot of Revelation can be classified with five parts: setting (1:1—4:11), complication (5:1—11:19), resolution (12:1—16:21), evaluation (17:1—22:5), and coda/moral (22:6–21).[27] Jang insists in his doctoral writing that Van Dijk's fivefold scheme model "appears to be preferable to any other scheme"[28] such as Freytag's five-act-play scheme for the plot of Revelation.

---

26. Ibid., 175–76.
27. Jang, "Narratological Approach," 125.
28. Ibid.

Plot and the Holy Spirit in Revelation

B. Evaluation

Jang makes a valuable contribution toward helping us to understand more clearly the plot of Revelation with the fivefold scheme plot. This plot overcomes the weaknesses of other suggested models, including non-plot, multi-plot, and U-shape plot. However, a significant flaw can be discovered in Jang's fivefold scheme. He makes a mistake to apply Van Dijk's model to the plot of Revelation. Van Dijk does not include moral/coda in the plot as we see in his diagram.[29]

Diagram 4.1 Van Dijk's Fivefold Scheme Plot

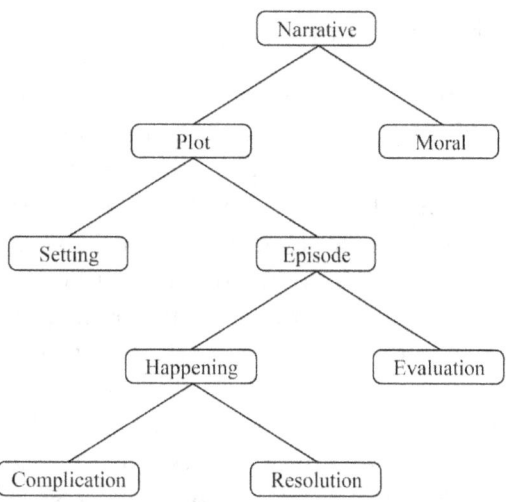

Actually, Van Dijk divides the narrative into two different parts: plot and moral. He proposes that a plot is composed of four components: setting, complication, resolution, and evaluation. He excludes moral from plot. Nevertheless, Jang employs moral/coda as a stage of the plot of Revelation. It is clear that Jang failed to apply Van Dijk's model in his study of plot. Furthermore, I think that he failed in choosing not to separate the introduction (1:1–8) from the setting. In my opinion, the moral as well as the introduction may be included in plot as plot components.

---

29. Van Dijk, *Macrostructures*, 116.

Evaluation of the Previous Study of the Plot of Revelation

We have already argued that there are not only contributions, but also weaknesses among four previous plot models for Revelation. Hence, another attempt to discover an advanced model of the plot of Revelation is needed. Thus, I shall attempt to define the plot and offer a proposal to correct the weaknesses of the fivefold scheme model before considering the characterization of the Holy Spirit according to the plot of Revelation.

Sixfold and Four-Level Scheme Plot: The New Scheme Plot of Revelation

I suggest that there are four location levels in the Revelation narrative: (1) heaven, (2) earth, (3) abyss, and (4) the lake of fire. Each level has its own categories of plot even though some are omitted. However, each level has the same introduction and conclusion. That is why I propose a sixfold and four-level scheme plot for the Revelation narrative.

On one hand, I attempt to transform Van Dijk's fivefold scheme in two parts into a sixfold scheme. Firstly, the introduction statement is separated from the setting, whereas Van Dijk insists that "the first typical category of narrative is setting"[30] since the introduction statement (1:1–8) is shown before the setting (1:9—4:11) in the Revelation narrative. Secondly, the moral (22:6–21) will be classified as the last part of plot, whereas Van Dijk separates the moral from the plot of a narrative since the moral in Revelation can be classified as conclusion that parallels with the introduction. Nevertheless, the recursive formation rule and transformation rules of Van Dijk's model can still be employed in Revelation.[31] Thus, I propose a sixfold categorization for plot: (1) introduction (1:1–8),

---

30. Ibid., 113. Van Dijk argues that "setting in general feature descriptions of the original situation, the time and the place of the various episodes, a description of the main character(s) involved in these episodes, and possibly further background information about the social or historical context of the events" (ibid.). All these things start from Rev 1:9.

31. Van Dijk, *Macrostructures*, 115. The categories of setting, complication, resolution, and evaluation can be partially recursive (recursive formation rule). Certain categories are to be deleted or change place (transformation rule).

Plot and the Holy Spirit in Revelation

(2) setting (1:9—4:11), (3) complication (5:1—11:19), (4) resolution (12:1—16:21), (5) evaluation (17:1—22:5), and (6) moral (22:6–21).[32]

On the other hand, the four-level scheme is based on Garrow's four location levels of Revelation. Garrow argues that there are four location levels in the Revelation narrative. According to him, the location of the lake of fire must be a different place from inhabited universe, that is, there is a three-part universe: heaven; earth; Death and Hades.[33] A three-part universe "is inhabited by a concentric cast of characters."[34] I find that it is useful to identify the plot of the Revelation narrative when a sixfold categories and four-level scheme are united. The introduction and conclusion are the same for each four-location level. The sixfold and four-level scheme can be shown with a diagram as follows.[35]

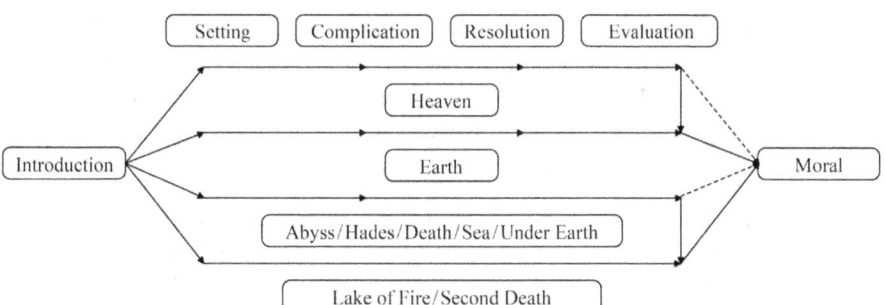

Diagram 4.2 The Sixfold and Four-Level Scheme Plot

---

32. The standards of making classification among categories shall be discussed in each category section.

33. Garrow, *Revelation*, 103. Garrow insists that the "nether world" of abyss, hades, death, sea, and under the earth "represent different expressions of the same shadowy location."

34. Ibid., 103. Garrow argues that the lake of fire is "clearly separate from Hades/Abyss since characters are taken from Hades /Abyss and thrown into the lake of fire (20:10, 15)."

35. This diagram takes some hints from the diagram of Jang, "Naratological Approach," 131. However, his diagram does not show both abyss level and lake of fire level, but just heaven level and earth level. In the evaluation, even though New Jerusalem comes down to the earth and abyss (or Death and Hades) and is put into the lake of fire, heaven and abyss do not disappear. The dotted lines illustrate this in the diagram. However, Jang's model does not consider the causality of the plot of Revelation. The heads of the arrows show level descriptions along the stages. There is no description of abyss in the resolution stage, nor the lake of fire in either the complication or resolution stage. Arrow marks cannot be found in the model.

Even though there are four levels from the setting to the evaluation, this is not a multi-plot, but a single-plot since there is a single introduction and a single moral. For the level of lake of fire, the complication and the resolution stages are deleted in the Revelation narrative. For the Death and Hades level, the resolution stage is deleted, whereas each level of both earth and heaven has setting, complication, resolution, and evaluation. Now we shall observe the sixfold and four-level scheme plot.

Introduction (1:1–8)[36]

Different from common "canonical ordering" of a narrative,[37] Revelation starts from special introduction of the title, the beatitude, the literary characteristics of Revelation as apocalypse, prophecy and letter, the descriptions of main characters of narrative such as Jesus, God, the Divine Spirit, angels, and John.[38] Nevertheless, Revelation follows the common canonical order such as main character description and some attention markers. Especially, attention markers are remarkably employed in the introduction. The introduction is composed of six attention markers.[39] Van Dijk argues as follows:

<small>36. Introduction and moral are not included in the components of plot according to Van Dijk, *Macrostructures*, 115. However, they are included intentionally with two purposes. Firstly, they need to be described to show the relationships to the plot components such as setting, complication, resolution, and evaluation. Secondly, this section will be shared with the next chapter of the structure of Revelation since it represents a part of structure of Revelation.

37. According to Van Dijk, the general description of the first part of a narrative is about the original situation, the time and place, the main character(s), and further background information of social and historical context of the events and attention markers. Van Dijk, *Macrostructures*, 113–14. However, Revelation does not start with general descriptions in the introduction. They are described in the second part of Revelation. Quoting Van Dijk, Jang also argues that the preparatory expressions preceding the narrative proper, such as title and attention marker are not included in the narrative proper. Van Dijk, *Macrostructures*, 114, quoted in Jang, "Narratological Approach," 125. That is why 1:1–8 should be separated from the following categories.

38. Even if main characters are described in the introduction, one specific main character, John, is focused on in the second part of setting.

39. Aune divides the introduction into five segments: revelation of Jesus (1:1–2), beatitude (v. 3), epistolary prescript (vv. 4–5c), doxology (vv. 5d–6), and two prophetic oracles (vv. 7–8). Aune, *Revelation 1–5*, 7–51. I prefer to separate the two prophetic oracles into two different parts for a few reasons. Firstly, they are different in regards to literary theme, even if similar in regard to prophetic form. Secondly, the last one is related not only to verse 7, but also to verses 1–6. Thus I propose that introduction has six segments.</small>

Stories however also have all kinds of preparatory expressions preceding them that function within the communicative interaction as *attention markers*: Hey, listen . . . ; do you know what happened to me yesterday? . . . ; Guess what. . . . We do not count them among the proper narrative categories because they have a more general communicative function, which also *holds for other kinds of discourse markers* such as titles in written discourse.[40]

They can be identified with six thematic groups such as revelation process (1:1-2),[41] beatitude (1:3),[42] blessing from Trinity through letter form, (1:4-5a),[43] worship to Jesus (1:5b-6),[44] eschatological expectation (1:7),[45] and self-revelation of God Almighty (1:8).[46] As Van Dijk argues, these

40. Van Dijk, *Macrostructures*, 114-15; emphasis mine.

41. The process of revelation from God to the servants of God via Jesus, the angel and John (1:1-2) is employed as an attention marker for the audience or readers. If God the Almighty, who is and who was and who is to come, and the Alpha and the Omega, gives this revelation of Jesus Christ, the audience or readers must be attentive to it. This attention marker of the revelation process is linked with the following five thematic groups of the attention marker in Rev 1:3-8.

42. Beatitude passage (1:3) is also employed as an attention marker of the Revelation narrative. When the audience (or readers) hears (or reads) the beatitude that is related to the revelation of Jesus, they must be more attentive since blessing is related to the revelation of Jesus, that is, the prophecy. The means of obtaining blessing is through reading, hearing, and keeping the word of prophecy.

43. Blessing from Trinity through letter form (1:4-5a) is also employed as an attention marker. The audience must be attentive to the one who is the source of the blessing related to the revelation of Jesus. The third attention marker focuses on Trinity's aspect of the blessing, whereas the second one focuses on the human responsibility of the blessing.

44. Worship to Jesus (1:5b-6) is also employed as an attention marker. The audience must be attentive to the fact that doxology is to be given not to three ultimate beings, but just to Jesus. The audience, who is used to the concept of Jewish worship whereby they only worship God, must be surprised at this kind of suggestion to worship Jesus as is stated in the introduction stage. Worship to Jesus appears repeatedly along the following categories in the Revelation narrative: setting stage (1:17), complication stage (5:11-14), and resolution stage (14:2-4).

45. Eschatological expectation of Jesus' coming and lamentation of all tribes (1:7) is also employed as an attention marker. Look (*VIdou.*), as the demonstrative particle, is used 26 times in Revelation with the two functions: to give strong emphasis "indicating the validation of statement it introduces and can be translated 'indeed, certainly,'" and "to draw attention to that which it introduces and can be translated 'look, listen, pay attention.'"

46. Self-predication of God as the Alpha and the Omega; Who is and Who was and Who is to come; the Almighty (1:8) is also employed as an attention marker. The

attention markers function to combine the communicative interaction along the whole narrative of Revelation. We find great value in exploring the communicative function of attention markers in the Revelation narrative.

To sum up, the six literary attention markers of the introduction have some specific roles. Their first role is to put all literary categories of Revelation together. In another sense, they unite the whole segments of the Revelation narrative with a single unity in view of the theological themes. Secondly, there is an internal unity among them. In other words, the six attention markers have a close relationship with each other. All six literary attention markers become a set as a whole in the introduction. The meaning of the set can be described like this: the readers will be blessed through keeping the Revelation delivered by God, Jesus, and the Seven Spirits since they will come again in the eschatological day as the sources of the blessings. Thirdly, besides thematic unity, the introduction plays a role of uniting the structure of the Revelation narrative. Especially, the introduction is paralleled structurally with the moral to make a literary parallelism.

Four Levels in the Setting, Complication, Resolution, and Evaluation Stages

The Level of Heaven

Heavenly court is depicted as a totally stable state in the setting stage. There is no tension or conflict to break its stability since the opposite forces never exist in the heavenly world. There is a unity of praising and worshipping God among the living creatures and the twenty-four elders. Heavenly situation is well-ordered. One seated on the throne rules according to His will. The Seven Spirits of God and sea of glass are before the throne in Rev 4:5. There is no description of time in the heavenly world since God the Almighty who is and who was and who is to come is an eternal one who transcends time. That is why four living creatures praise him day and night without ceasing.

However, the state turns into being unstable since the Lamb takes the scroll and opens the seven seals in the complication stage. Four living

---

attention of the audience must be moved from the coming of Jesus to the sovereign God due to this sudden prophetical self-revelation of God in 1:8.

creatures and twenty-four elders start to worship and praise the Lamb (5:8–10). Myriads of myriads of angels start to sing (5:11–12). Every creature in heaven and on earth and under the sea and in the sea starts to sing (5:13).

In the resolution stage, the first scene of heaven shows that a human-like participant, a male child who is to rule all the nations with a rod of iron (12:5), is ready to be born by an apocalyptic woman as a human who may resolve the cosmic conflict. The second scene shows that a great red Dragon is ready to devour the child. The situation of heaven represents a climax of the cosmic conflict. However, the climaxing conflict is described as being resolved. The child is born and snatched in order to be taken to God without being devoured by the Dragon. On the one hand, the Dragon not only fails to kill the child, but also is defeated with his angels by Michael and his angels (12:7–9), and also by the blood of the Lamb (12:11a). Finally, the Dragon is thrown down to earth from heaven (12:7–9). On the other hand, the Lamb and the redeemed of 144,000 from the earth (7:4–8) are standing on Mount Zion in heaven (14:1–5). They are the sealed of 144,000 on the earth in 7:4–8. In 14:1–5, and they are portrayed to stand before the throne and the four living creatures and the elders. This represents that the conflict on the earth has been resolved. In heaven, a voice says, "blessed are the dead who from now on die in the Lord." Last judgment with the seven bowls is described in detail in chapters 15–16. We find it very useful to explain how the whole cosmic conflict in heaven is resolved.

A great multitude in heaven evaluates not only the judgment of God to be true and just, and the salvation, glory, and power of God to be praised, but also the saints to be worthy to be a bride in the marriage of the Lamb in 19:1–9. The narrator evaluates that the heavenly messianic armies and the rider of the white horse, whose name is called Faithful and True, word of God, triumph over the enemies in the messianic war in 19:11–16. The New Jerusalem, that is, the bride, is evaluated not only by the voice of the throne to be God's presence and comfort, but also by God to make her new and become his child from the nations and kings of the earth in 21:1–27. The saints are evaluated to produce its fruit each month and to reign and heal the nations in 22:1–5. The saints are evaluated to reign forever and to live with God and the Lamb as their light in 22:4–5.

A Dynamic Reading of the Holy Spirit in Revelation

The Level of Earth

As for original situation in the setting, John explains that his original situation is to write his letter-narrative to his church community members in 1:9–10. The contemporary church members of John share the same experience of persecution when they keep the word of God and give their testimony to Jesus.[47] However, they may be able to experience the kingdom of God in their lives and ministries even in the persecuted situations.[48]

From the unstable state of the churches, the appearance of the Lamb makes changes the situation of both the churches and their opponents. For the saints, there are two possible changes in their situations. In the one hand, the Churches become more stable by the protection (ch. 7) and the empowering to witness (ch. 10–11), whereas opponents such as Babylon and satanic power become unstable, taking the process of degradation (ch. 6, 8, 9). The servants of God, who live on the earth, are protected by marking a seal on their foreheads (7:1–8). The prayers of all the saints are answered on the earth (8:5). On the other hand, the Churches may be more unstable since they are given their missions to prophesy

---

47. One of the negative situations of the earthy churches is persecution. Persecutions may come from not only outside of churches politically or socially, but also inside the churches spiritually or physically. Several kinds of attacks of the churches are described in the seven letters in chapters 2–3: false apostles, losing their first love to Jesus, the heretical teaching of the Nicolaitans, the slander of Jews, affliction, economic poverty, the killing of Antipas as a martyr, the teaching of both Balaam and Jezebel leading to fornication, the false teaching of the deep things of Satan, the spiritual sleeping, the trial "coming on the whole world to test the inhabitants of the earth" (3:10b), lukewarmness, spiritual blindness, spiritual poverty, and spiritual nakedness. On the other hand, some provocateurs inducing the attacks against the earthly churches are also depicted in chapters 2–3: false prophets or false teachers, satanic powers including those of the devil (2:10, 24), political power of anti-Church (2:10), and the spiritual and ethical vulnerability of the saints.

48. There are some positive situations of the earthly churches. Above all, many have positive attitudes or spiritualities. They can be hard working and growing in love. They have endurance, spiritual awareness to identify the false apostles, faithful witness, and faith. They can be of service, have patience, and keep the words of Jesus, including the nondenial of the name of Jesus, even though they have little power. Some supporters of the earthly churches are depicted as well. It is Jesus himself who comes to the earth to give guidance to them, even though he is risen, glorified, and seated in the throne of heaven. Another supporter of Jesus is the Spirit who guides the seven churches by speaking to them. Both Jesus and the Spirit not only guide and instruct them as a shepherd with the promises for heavenly setting, but also correct and discipline them as a warrior with warning.

Plot and the Holy Spirit in Revelation

with the witness of Jesus (10:11). Their powerful testimony causes them to make war against the beast (11:7–10). Nevertheless, the Churches are described prophetically to be stable because of three prophetical events of victory, such as the measurement of the temple and the altar and those who worship there (11:1), giving the authority to prophesy to the two witnesses (11:3–6), and the resurrection of the two witnesses through the Spirit of life of God (11:11). Even though ultimate victory is prophetically proclaimed, many conflicts and problems still exist among the Churches in the earth without resolution.

We are told that the resolution in heaven directly agitates the earth through the movement of members. Firstly, the woman, who gave birth to a male child, comes down to the earth from heaven and stays in the wilderness, fleeing and being nourished. Secondly, the Dragon, who accuses the saints day and night before God (12:10c), called ancient serpent, the devil and Satan, the deceiver of the whole world (12:9), and his angels are thrown down from heaven to the earth (12:9). The devil comes down to the earth with great wrath, pursuing the woman and making war against those who keep the commandments of God and hold the testimony of Jesus (12:12, 17). The agitation is getting worse not only because of the appearance of the two beasts on the earth from the sea and the earth, but also because the Dragon gives to them his great power, throne, and authority (13:1–18).

However, the increased conflict or agitation is resolved in 14:6—16:21. The resolution starts with the proclamation of three angels. The first angel proclaims an eternal gospel to those who live on the earth—to every nation and tribe and language and people. The first words or content of this gospel are to fear God and give Him glory and worship Him (14:7a, 7c). The second words or content of this gospel is that the time of the judgment of God has come (14:7b). The second angel proclaims the destruction of Babylon the great since she has made all nations drink of the wine of the wrath of her fornication (14:8). The third angel proclaims the judgment of those who worship the beast and its image and receive a mark on their forehead or hands (14:9). One like the Son of Man harvests and another angel judges with a sharp sickle (14:14–20). The conflicts are all resolved with the seven bowls of God's wrath, which are poured out in the whole earth (16:1–21). Thus, at the first stage in chapters 12–13, the resolution on the earth is not so successful. However, it is successful in the second stage in chapters 14–16.

An angel evaluates the identities of Babylon not only spiritually, but also politically and economically in 18:2–3. The heavenly voice evaluates that she deserves to be punished and the saints have to come out of her in 18:4–8. The war between the rider on the white horse and his army and the beast and kings with their armies is evaluated and the beast and the false prophet are then captured and thrown into the lake of fire and the rest are killed in 19:17–21. The devil, who is in the earth, is evaluated to be put into the bottomless pit and then into the lake of fire after being released for a while in 20:1–10.

It is notable that the movement of the New Jerusalem, the bride, from heaven to earth, is described in the evaluation stage. This is significant for two reasons. Firstly, the narrator is focusing on the earth, not heaven since the prophetic words should be accomplished on the earth to build the New Jerusalem as a bride. Secondly, however, the New Jerusalem comes out of heaven, not earth. All sources have to be supported from heaven. That is why the hearer is requested to depend humbly on heaven.

The Level of Abyss/Death and Hades

Actually there is no detailed description of the original situation, time and place, and social or historical context. However, "Death and Hades" in 1:18 are introduced not personified, but spatially.[49] They are portrayed to have some doors that need keys. Jesus is characterized as a ruler of Death and Hades as well as the main character in Death and Hades. The self-proclamation of Jesus as a key bearer of Death and Hades has a significant meaning: that He rules over the gods or goddesses, such as the goddess Hekate who is asserted by Aune to govern Death and Hades among the contemporary people of John.[50] After the resurrection and ascension of Jesus, He becomes the ruler of Death and Hades, even though He was imprisoned in Death and Hades during His death. There seems to be no conflict or tension described in Death and Hades since Jesus rules over them in the setting. In other words, they can be understood as a stable place in 1:18. However, some descriptions of the conflict in Death

---

49. Aune, *Revelation 1–5*, 103. Aune rightly argues that Death and Hades must be understood spatially since they are objective genitive, not possessive genitive.

50. Ibid., 103–5. For important regional divinities including Hekate related to Death and Hades, see 104–5.

Plot and the Holy Spirit in Revelation

and Hades are expected in the following categories, such as the death and resurrection of Jesus who was imprisoned in Death and Hades and came out of them in the resolution stage), the beast from the abyss, and those who die in the evaluation stage).

From the stable state in the setting, every creature under the earth starts to praise God and the Lamb since the Lamb takes the scroll and opens the seven seals (5:13). A star, an angel, falls down to the earth from heaven and gets the key to the shaft of the bottomless pit, and then opens it. When the shaft is opened, smoke and locusts come up on the earth. The king of the locusts is the angel of the bottomless pit named Abaddon or Apollyon. They are commanded by Jesus, the one who rules over Death and Hades with the key (1:18), not to damage even trees and green grasses, but to harm only those who do not have the seal of God on their forehead (9:4–5). Furthermore, the beast that comes from the bottomless pit is allowed to make war against the saints and kill them in the last days (11:7).[51] Thus, in the complication, the bottomless pit or under the earth (Death and Hades) must become unstable because of the appearance of the Lamb. There are many kinds of members in Death and Hades, such as Abaddon, Jesus, and the beast. Each has its own mission, which may be another factor that causes instability in the bottomless pit, Death and Hades.

In short, each part of the three-level universe, that is, heaven, earth, and under the earth or bottomless pit, has a kind of interaction, even though each has something blocking it. An angel, for example, comes down from heaven to earth and then opens the door of the bottomless pit. Locusts come out of the bottomless pit to the earth. With this kind of circulation among them, the appearance of the Lamb breaks out the universal complication or conflict and causes in the whole universe to be unstable. This complication is "increasingly serious until a final action by the Lamb" in chapters 12–16.[52]

The narrator personifies not only Death and Hades, but also the Sea.[53] They are evaluated as persons who will die in the end times. For

---

51. Aune argues that 11:7 may parallel 13:1 even though only 11:7 has an article. He also insists that "it might be assumed that the beast in Rev 17 is identified by the author with the one mentioned in 11:7; 13:1–10." Aune, *Revelation 6–16*, 616. He rightly argues again that "his war against the two witnesses is narrated not as an event that has already occurred but rather as a prophecy that will occur in the future" (ibid.).

52. Jang, "Narratological Approach," 134.

53. Aune, *Revelation 17–22*, 1102–3. Aune argues that "Death and Hades are often

Death and Hades, their destruction is described clearly with the phrase, "were thrown into the lake of fire." However the Sea's destruction is not portrayed clearly, but readers can suppose that it disappears from the description of new heaven and new earth by the description of the phrase of "the sea was no more" (Rev 21:1c).

Even though both Death and Hades and Sea are personified, the narrator also attempts to describe both as places in which the dead are kept. However, finally they are evaluated to give up the dead.

In addition to Death and Hades and Sea, the narrator employs another expression to describe the deadly place, abyss, that is, the bottomless pit. Aune argues that the abyss is "sometimes synonymous with the underworld, which is the abode of the dead" in the Old Testament and Middle East literature.[54] However, in my opinion, the narrator intends to separate the abyss from Death and Hades and Sea in Revelation. The first refers to the prison of the locusts, the beast and the Dragon, whereas the latter refers to the place of the dead.[55]

Furthermore, the narrator depicts that the abyss has the shaft to be opened by the key and has a connection to the earth. The narrator portrays more concretely that the angel of a star opens the shaft of the abyss to free smoke and locusts (9:2–3), the beast (11:7), and the Dragon (20:3) to the earth for a while. In the evaluation stage, concerning Death and Hades and the abyss, the beast is depicted as being destroyed, whereas the Dragon, who is thrown and locked and sealed into the bottomless pit, will be let out from abyss for a while.[56]

It is noteworthy that another movement can be found from the abyss to the lake of fire as the movement of the New Jerusalem is described from heaven to the earth. The beast (19:20), the false prophet (19:20), the devil (20:10), Death and Hades (20:14), and those whose names are not found written in the book of life (20:15) are depicted to move from the abyss to the lake of fire.

---

equated and the pair are personified four times in Revelation" (1103). Aune insists that "ancient coastal societies were conscious of two abodes of the dead" (1102): the sea and the land below which the realm of Hades was located.

54. Aune, *Revelation 6–16*, 526.

55. Malina argues that the abyss referred to in Rev 9:1 is the celestial abyss which is in contrast to the terrestial abyss. Malina, *Genre and Message*, 142–43. However, Aune does not agree with the opinion of Malina. Aune, *Revelation 6–16*, 526.

56. Of course, in the same evaluation stage, the Dragon is depicted as being thrown into the lake of fire in Rev 20:7–10.

The Level of Lake of Fire

Garrow argues that the lake of fire is "clearly separate from Hades/Abyss since characters are taken from Hades/Abyss and thrown into the lake of fire."[57] In other words, second death represents the ultimate judgment, which is to be put into the lake of fire (20:14). In the setting, there is no description of the lake of fire, but of second death in 2:11. The second death, that is, the lake of fire, is described as a place where those who do not conquer will be harmed. In 2:11, the final judgment of the beasts, devil (Satan), and Death and Hades to be thrown into the lake of fire, has not yet been presented; only the judgment of the unbelieving persons is described. Even though there is no detailed description of second death in 2:11, we can imagine that there is no conflict or tension in the lake of fire. In other words, the lake of fire must be stable.

The narrator employs the lake of fire to evaluate the destiny of all evil ones in the evaluation stage: the beast (19:20); the false prophet (19:20); the devil (20:10); Death and Hades (20:14); those whose names are not found written in the book of life (20:15); the cowardly, the faithless, the polluted, the murderers, the fornicators, the sorcerers, the idolaters, and all liars (21:8).

It is remarkable that the narrator emphasizes their being alive in the lake of fire; they have not been killed nor have they disappeared. In 19:20, the narrator depicts that both the beast and the false prophet were thrown "alive" into the lake of fire. In 20:10, the narrator portrays that the devil will be in the lake of fire "forever and ever." However, the fate of the dead is not described clearly as to whether they are "alive" or not in the lake of fire. Nevertheless, it is not so difficult to understand that they are alive in the lake of fire in that those who are thrown into the lake of fire are already depicted as being alive in 19:20 and 20:10.

On the other hand, the narrator intentionally emphasizes the torment of the evil ones by the description of the lake of fire with the added words, "with sulfur" (19:20; 20:10), "tormented day and night" (20:10), and "the lake that burns with fire and sulfur" (21:8).

In short, both the earth and the lake of fire are focused as the final places in the evaluation stage. The life and work of all creatures on earth will be the measure for their eternal life and their eternal judgment. That is why they have to hear the prophetic messages in Revelation. With this,

---

57. Garrow, *Revelation*, 103.

A Dynamic Reading of the Holy Spirit in Revelation

the evaluation stage finishes its role by preparing all members of the audience to receive what is written in the moral stage in 22:6–21.

Moral (22:7–22)

Moral commands for further actions are identified in Rev 22:7–22 for the hearer in three ways: direct narrative commands, requirements from the narrative characters, and comparing the moral with the introduction.[58] These commands can be overlapped or repeated so that readers may understand and practice them.

Direct Commands for Further Actions in the Narrative

In the moral state, two kinds of further actions are required to of the hearer or the audience: desirable actions and undesirable actions. These actions are given more explicitly than those from the characters. The hearers are requested to perform these desirable actions: to keep the words of the prophecy of this book (22:7), to worship only God (22:9), to witness the words of the prophecy (22:10), to do right and be holy (22:11), to wash their robes or deeds (22:14), and to take the water of life (22:17). The desirable actions are required in a more positive way as compared to the undesirable ones, except for the action, which is more of a command, "do not seal up the words of prophecy of this book" (22:10).

Undesirable actions are given in the direct way of warnings. There are two warnings and both are related to the words of prophecy. Both adding and taking away from the words of the prophecy in this book are designated as undesirable actions that will bring the punishment from God directly (22:18–19). In addition, undesirable actions are also given in the indirect way. Any worshipping acts to any other object but God himself, even to the glorious angel, are sternly prohibited with the phrase, "You must not do that!" (22:9a). All kinds of sealing acts upon the words

---

58. The general pragmatic function of narratives, finally, appears in the well-known category of coda or moral. Such a moral draws a conclusion so to speak from the events for further actions, both of the hearer and of the speaker (e.g., I'll never take him on a vacation again! Next time I'll stay home). Morals are, as we see, not only explicit in fables or parables but also occur normally in everyday stories, especially when they are told to inform somebody about the possible consequence of doing something. Van Dijk, *Macrostructures*, 115.

Plot and the Holy Spirit in Revelation

of the prophecy in this book are forbidden (22:10). In other words, any attitude or tendency to be lazy in witnessing the words of prophecy must be banned. Furthermore, all acts to love and practice falsehood are depicted to be fatally dangerous since practitioners will have no right to take the tree of life and to enter the New Jerusalem (22:15). In short, these further actions of hearers are also intensified by the speaking of the narrative characters.

Requirements from the Narrative Characters

The narrator employs some reliable characters such as the angel, Jesus, the narrator, and the Spirit and the bride to enlighten the further actions of the audience. Firstly, an angel, who plays a role as a guide for the visions John sees, is employed to proclaim the trustworthiness and truthfulness of the words (22:6a) as well as the source of them, that is, God of the spirits of prophets (22:6b). The angel also informs the significance of keeping the words through introducing his identity (22:9a). Moreover, the angel is employed to emphasize that the essential worship, which represents for worshipping only God, cannot be separate from keeping the trustworthy and true words (22:9b). Secondly, Jesus is employed to assert the importance of keeping the words of prophecy (22:7) in the work of everyone (22:12). The importance of everyone working to keep the words of prophecy is intensified not only with the description of the encouragement of reward from Jesus himself (22:12), but also with the description of the identity of Jesus as the Alpha and the Omega, the first and the last, the sender of the testimony for the churches, the beginning and the end (22:13), the root and the descendent of David, and the bright morning Star (22:16). Thirdly, the narrator is also employed to claim the impact of both "doing" and "being" in the life of the hearer (22:11). The narrator divides each of them into two contradictory aspects. For every "doing," there are only two choices, between "evil" and "right." For every "being," there are only two choices, between "filthy" and "holy" (22:11). The narrator relates the righteous and the holy (22:11) to those who wash their robes, whereas the evildoer and the filthy (22:11) to those who love and practice falsehood (22:14–15). The impact of the first group in doing right and being holy is described both to have the right to the tree of life and to enter the city of the New Jerusalem by the gates (22:14). The impact of the latter group in doing evil and being filthy brings upon them the description that they are "the dogs and sorcerers and fornicators and murderers and idolaters" (22:15a). Fourthly, the Spirit and the bride are also employed to invite every hearer who is thirsty to come and take the water of life (22:17). They are working together in this invitation with the narrator who invites the hearer, the thirster, and the wisher in 22:17b. In short, with these kinds of descriptions, the readers must understand the messages of prophecy in Revelation more clearly. In addition to them, another technique to make the messages of Revelation more clear is found in the moral stage. This can be discovered from the comparison between the moral and the introduction.

The Messages through the Parallel between the Moral and the Introduction

The narrator attempts to communicate some messages through the parallel structure of the moral to the introduction. First of all, the revelation, namely, the words of prophecy, is outstandingly focused in the moral stage. Especially the revelation process is commonly described from God to his servants through his angel in both stages. However, the description of the revelation process in the moral is different from the one in the introduction. Jesus and John are omitted in the moral (22:6), whereas the explanation of God as God "of the spirit of prophets" is added.[59] With this, readers understand that the main message is closely related to the revelation or the words of prophecy. Secondly, the nature of revelation as "true and trustworthy," is added in the moral. This plays a role of persuading readers to pay attention to the words of prophecy in Revelation. Thirdly, only keeping the words of prophecy is emphasized in the moral, whereas reading, hearing, and keeping what is written are described in the introduction. Moreover, the true worship is related to keeping the words of prophecy (22:9). This shows that Revelation has the typical moral, in which further action of readers is focused. Fourthly, proclaiming (not sealing up) the words of prophecy is emphasized in the moral in that it is connected with an alert phrase, "for the time is near" (22:10), whereas this phrase is connected with the reading, hearing, and keeping phrase in the introduction (1:3). From this we can conclude that witnessing to the words of prophecy is required to be another further action of read-

---

59. Even if they are omitted in 22:6, Jesus is actually described in 22:16 as well as in John in 22:8.

ers. Fifthly, the eschatological reward (22:12) as well as self-revelation of Jesus as the Alpha and the Omega, the first and the last, the beginning and the end, reinforces further actions of readers in keeping and witnessing the words of prophecy. Sixthly, the narrator emphasizes not only the deeds, but also the good news of Christ with the gospel phrase, "wash one's robes" (22:14) with the blood of the Lamb (7:14). Even though further actions of the readers are encouraged, the Revelation narrative also emphasizes faith in the blood of the Lamb. It seems that the narrator attempts to create a balance between the faith and the deed in that two verses, 22:7 and 22:14, are paralleled with the same beatitude passage. Seventhly, besides keeping and witnessing to the revelation of prophecy, making any changes to the revelation itself is strictly forbidden by the description of judgement against those who change it (22:18–19). This warning is justified because the nature of the words is trustworthy and true (22:6). Finally, the description of the identity of Jesus as the root and the descendant of David, the bright morning star, who sent His angel with this testimony for the churches (22:16) supports the significance of keeping and witnessing the revelation of Jesus as well as indicates that it is the churches who keep and witness to it. In addition, the first-person narration of Jesus noting his eschatological coming two times ("I am coming" in 22:7, 12) reinforces the literary effect for readers to act according to the revelation of Jesus. In short, it is quite clear that the narrator emphasizes the further acts of the readers related to the revelation of Jesus with using the parallel of the moral to the introduction.

Causality of the Plot of Revelation

Until now, I provided the "multi-narrative flow" of a sixfold and four-level scheme for the plot of Revelation and applied it to the whole narrative of Revelation. Now in this section, I shall further explore the causality of the plot of Revelation in that *plot refers to "a narrative flow or multi-narrative flows," with subplot(s), that is (are) engendered by "causality" in orderly sequence, evoking an emotional reaction in the reader,* according to Hur.[60] What is the causality in the plot of Revelation? It seems to be clear that Revelation has a causality of "witnessing to the word of prophecy" if we observe both the introduction and the moral stage.[61] How can we find the

60. Hur, *Dynamic Reading*, 183; italics in the original.
61. Moral is paralleled with introduction to unite the whole narrative by offering

causality of the plot of Revelation? According to J. S. Bell, the causality of the plot must be crucial to the readers as well as the saints in their eternal wellbeing.[62] The witnessing to the word of prophecy is significant for the readers or saints since the promises of the blessing are proposed in the beatitude passages. According to the beatitude passages, the witnessing to the word of prophecy cannot be separate from keeping the word of prophecy (1:3; 22:7), washing the linen of life (19:8), awakening (16:15), and even being persecuted or killed (14:13). Those who want to witness to the word of prophecy have to keep the word of prophecy, awakening spiritually, and purifying themselves at the expense of their lives in advance. And then they will preach the word of prophecy to others on the earth. The main purpose of "witnessing to the word of prophecy" is the conversion of all nations.[63] This is why Bauckham rightly claims that the central message of prophecy of Revelation is the conversion of all nations.[64]

Besides the seven beatitudes, the narrator applies the causality of the plot of Revelation to a sixfold and four-level scheme to evoke the emotional reaction of readers. Now I shall explore how the causality of witnessing to the word of prophecy is applied in the Revelation narrative. In the setting stage, the "identification" and the "inner conflicts" of the seven churches (Revelation 2–3) are presented to show the present state of the seven churches.[65] They are compared with the heavenly worship group including heavenly beings in Revelation 4. With this comparison, we are told how the seven earthly churches are ready to witness to the word of prophecy. They are commanded to be changed by both Jesus and the Spirit. Their change can be experienced with two directions: "to get something" (first love, faithfulness until death, repentance, waking up, walking with Jesus, dressing in white, holding fast to what you have, being earnest), and "to get away from something"[66] (teaching of Balaam,

---

some moral commands for further actions for the hearer as well as from the narrative characters. The key issue of the commands in both stages is associated with witnessing to the word of prophecy.

62. For this, see Bell, *Plot and Structure*, 223. Bell employs the word, "objective" instead of causality.

63. Bauckham rightly argues that the "conversion of the nations" is "at the centre of the prophetic message of Revelation." Bauckham, *Climax of Prophecy*, 238.

64. Ibid.

65. Bell, *Plot and Structure*, 238.

66. Ibid. Bell argues, "The objective is what gives the Lead (or Character) a reason for being in the story. There are two types of objectives: to get something (information,

Plot and the Holy Spirit in Revelation

Nicolaitans, and the deep things of Satan; lukewarm attitude). According to their changes, the heavenly rewards are promised in Revelation 2–4. In short, the seven churches and readers are required by both Jesus and the Spirit to be changed from their complacent and stable state to the witness of the word of prophecy in the setting stage.

In the complication stage, unstable states are evoked both in the heavenly realm and in the earthly realm when the Lamb of God opens the seven seals of the scroll (Revelation 5). When the Lamb of God opens the scroll, heavenly beings start to worship in the heavenly realm together. In the earthly realm, two quite different phenomena happen: upon the opening of the scroll, all the earth shall be punished (Revelation 6; 8–9), whereas all the saints who are sealed on their foreheads shall be protected from the universal punishment (Revelation 7). Two things emphasized in the complication stage are the activity of the prophet John (Revelation 10) and the two witnesses (Revelation 11). John is commanded not only to take and eat the scroll, but also to prophesy to "many peoples and nations and languages and kings" (10:11). The two witnesses, who represent the witnessing churches, are described as prophesying with authority as Moses and Elijah did on the earth. However, when they have finished their testimony on the earth, the beast from the bottomless pit makes war against them (11:7). In the end, the beast conquers and kills them (11:7). The inhabitants of the earth celebrate the death of the two witnesses (11:10). But the Spirit of life from God enters the two dead witnesses (11:11a) and they are raised and ascend to heaven (11:11b, 12). Finally, people give glory to the God of heaven (11:13). "The kingdom of the world has become the kingdom of our Lord and of his Messiah, and he will reign forever and ever" (11:15b). Even "God's temple in heaven was opened, and the ark of his covenant was seen within his temple" (11:19). The accomplished witness to the prophecy results in this final victory even in the context of spiritual attacks.

In short, the complication stage shows that there is a kind of spiritual warfare between the beast from the bottomless pit and the two witnesses on earth in the witnessing to the word of prophecy. In other words, the witness to the word of prophecy causes a sort of spiritual conflict between the two witnesses and the beast. As the complication stage in literature usually happens, according to Van Dijk, the complication

---

love, etc.) or to get away from something (the law, a killer, etc.). It must be crucial to the Lead's well-being" (ibid.).

events in Revelation also are "undesired or counter to the goals of the participant(s)," the two witnesses.[67] The two witnesses are killed by the beast. The people of the world come to be fearful after the ascension of the two witnesses. That is why readers may usually expect that "the resolution will mention those actions that attempt the reestablishment of the original situation or the creation of a new situation in which further normal functioning is possible."[68] Thus the audience is persuaded to wait for the further resolution stories.

In the resolution stage, it should be noted that at least two things are depicted to show how the complication is resolved in view of the witness to the prophecy. Firstly, it is shown who is involved in the spiritual warfare for the witness to the prophecy as participants. There appear to be six participant groups: the woman and her offspring (the 144,000; those who conquered the beast), the Child (the Lamb), Michael and his angels, the Dragon (Satan) and his angels, two beasts, and demonic spirits. Most of participants are involved in the witness to the prophecy. The Child can be identified with Jesus, a faithful witness (Rev 1:5) and the Lamb who takes the Scroll from God Almighty (Rev 5:7) since He is portrayed as one who is to rule all nations with a rod of iron (Rev 12:5). The Dragon is also involved in interrupting the witness to the prophecy. The Dragon is hostile toward all three witnessing subjects: Child, Michael, and the woman. The Dragon even tries to kill the newborn Child on earth. The Dragon and his angels fight against Michael and his angels. The Dragon persecutes the woman and her offspring. Two beasts are also involved in interrupting the witness to the prophecy. The beast from the sea is portrayed to be like Christ Jesus who was resurrected from the dead: "the beast that had been wounded by the sword and yet lived" (Rev 13:14b). The beast from the earth is portrayed to be like a prophet or a priest who will deceive all people on earth to worship the first beast. Both of them play a role to destroy the work of witness done by the two witnesses and to mislead all the people on earth into false worship. Demonic spirits are portrayed to be like the Seven Spirits of God to support three evil subjects, that is, the Dragon, the first beast, and the false prophet (the second beast) (Rev 16:13–14), to prepare for the battle of the great day of God Almighty.

Secondly, it is shown how to increase the conflict and to resolve the conflict. The conflict seems to be increased in Revelation 12–13 through

---

67. Van Dijk, *Macrostructures*, 114.
68. Ibid.

Plot and the Holy Spirit in Revelation

the attack of evil against the good, whereas the conflict is resolved in Revelation 14–16 through both the judgment against evil and the harvest for the good. However, even in the increasing conflict, the evil attacks seem to be less successful. In other words, there are two different aspects to resolve the conflict. One is that the evil powers are not successful in attacking the good ones. The other is that the evil ones are judged by the Lamb and God Almighty. The attempt of the Dragon to kill the Child, who opens the seal of the word of God, fails. After the child ascends into heaven, the Dragon attacks the woman and her offspring since the Dragon was cast out of heaven through the fight with Michael and his angels. But it fails as well. Two beasts seem to prevail over not only the nonbeliever, but also the saints whose names are written in the book of life by the weapon of violence and deception. The purpose of the attacks of two beasts is to make all people worship the beast. In another sense, the true worship caused by the witness to the prophecy is the target to be destroyed from the ministry of two beasts. However, the prevailing violence of the beast from the sea must be open to failure because of the patience and the faith of the saints (13:10). The prevailing deception of the beast from the earth must be open to failure also because of the wisdom (13:18).

In Revelation 14–16, it is written clearly that the vulnerable triumphs of the dragon and two beasts on earth turn out not only to be a complete failure due to the judgment against the evil and those who follow the evil, but also to be the final triumph of the Lamb and the 144,000 who have the name of God. The latter is described in Rev 14:1–5, whereas the former is described in Rev 14:6—16:21. The triumph of the Lamb and the 144,000 is depicted to be deeply related to the witness of prophecy. The Lamb who opens the seven seals of the scroll is portrayed to stand on the heavenly Zion, which represents the place where the word of God was given to the people of God in the desert. The 144,000 are portrayed as those who keep the word of prophecy: "It is these who have not defiled themselves with women, for they are virgins; these follow the Lamb wherever he goes. They have been redeemed from humankind as first fruits for God and the Lamb, and in their mouth no lie was found; they are blameless" (Rev 14:4–5). In another sense, they are called those who worship in truth according to the word of God.

There are two main themes throughout the whole passage in Revelation 14–16: salvation and judgment. Both result from the witness to the prophecy. In Rev 14:6–20, both the eschatological salvation and judgment through the gospel were proclaimed by three angels in the mid-heaven, before the final judgment happens in Rev 15–16. In other words, it can be shown that the gospel is related to the witness of prophecy which proclaims not only the salvation, but also the judgment. The content of the gospel is, "Fear God and give him glory, for the hour of his judgment has come; and worship him who made heaven and earth, the sea and the springs of water" (14:7). The first angel focuses on worshipping God with fear, which is the same with the message of the two witnesses. The second angel and the third angel are portrayed to be involved in the judgment (14:17–20).

Rev 15 explores how those who had conquered the beast and its image and name had been equipped to defeat the beast as well as where the final judgment is to be ready. The former is explained with the song of Moses and the Lamb: "Great and amazing are your deeds, The Lord God the Almighty! Just and true are your ways, King of the nations! The Lord, who will not fear and glorify your name? For you alone are holy. All nations will come and worship before you, for your judgments have been revealed" (Rev 15:3–4). In other words, all nations will worship God through the witness to the prophecy. The latter is also explained to be related to the temple of the tent of witness. This shows that the judgment is based on the words of the prophecy, which are usually given from the tent of witness. Rev 16 shows who or what will be judged. There are two groups to be judged. One is the natural sphere: the earth, the sea, the rivers, and the sun. The other is the throne of the beast, the place of the Dragon and Babylon. In short, the complication is resolved in relation to the witness to the prophecy in this stage.

In the evaluation stage, both the judgment and the salvation in the resolution stage are evaluated and brought to conclusion with more detailed descriptions than in the resolution stage: the judgment of the great harlot, Babylon (17:1—19:10), the two beasts (19:11–21) and the Dragon (20:1–10); and the New Jerusalem for the saved. It should be noted that the judgment of the great harlot is caused by her drunkenness with the blood of the saints and with the blood of the martyrs of Jesus (17:6). The place where the great harlot dwells is called a desert that shows the place where the evil powers persecute the church (woman and her offspring in Rev 12) who keeps and witnesses to the word of God. The beast on which the great harlot sits is portrayed as having the full names of blasphemy

Plot and the Holy Spirit in Revelation

(17:3c). In other words, the beast speaks blasphemies against God and the saints with back reference to Rev 13:6: "It opened its mouth to utter blasphemies against God, blaspheming his name and his dwelling, that is, those who dwell in heaven." Then the judgment against the beasts and the Dragon is described in Rev 19–20. In the middle of the judgment of Babylon the great, the people of God are protected, given the description, "Come out of her, my people, so that you do not take part in her sins, and so that you do not share in her plagues" (18:4b). This judgment is explained to be given as God's avengement for the sake of the saints, apostles, and prophets in saying, "Rejoice over her, O heaven, you saints and apostles and prophets! For God has given judgment for you against her" (18:20).

In the following section, the messianic feast, that is, the marriage supper of the Lamb is prepared for those who worship God because of the testimony of Jesus through the Spirit of prophecy (19:10). The New Jerusalem is identified with the bride, the Lamb's wife, that is, the Church of Christ Jesus (21:9b). The New Jerusalem represents how blessed those who witness to the word of God and to the testimony of Jesus are. The church, as the two witnesses, will experience the glory and light of God and his presence since God the Almighty and the Lamb are its temple (21:22). The church as a bride of the Lamb will be adorned with the beauty and purity of jewels (21:18–21), and clothed with the fine, bright, and clean linen, which represents the righteous acts of the saints (19:8). All the people of God both in the Old Testament period (twelve tribes) and the New Testament period (twelve apostles) are included as the members of the New Jerusalem (21:10–14). All the nations of those who are saved and the kings of the earth will enter it (21:24). Their lives will be restored with the tree of life and the river of life just as human beings experienced in the garden of Eden (22:1–5). They shall reign forever and ever (22:5). In short, through the description of Babylon and the New Jerusalem, the readers are offered the opportunity to evaluate between the judgment and the rewards. They are supposed evaluate and then choose whether they belong to Babylon or the New Jerusalem. They are ready to hear and obey what will be commanded in the moral stage.

In the moral stage, as discussed before, the direct commands to witness to the word of prophecy are given to the readers with the eternal rewards.

Definition of the New Plot of Revelation

Thus, if we define *plot* as referring to *a narrative flow or to multi-narrative flows, with subplot(s), that is (are) engendered by causality in orderly sequence, evoking an emotional reaction in the reader,* how can we define the plot of Revelation? My claim is that *the plot of Revelation is the way of witness to the word of prophecy for the conversion of all nations, opposed by the evil powers and engendered by Jesus and his witnesses through the guidance of the Holy Spirit in accordance with God's will, given promise of the rewards for the witnesses as well as of the judgment against the evil ones in the four levels of space: heaven, earth, abyss, and the lake of fire along the sixfold and four-level scheme.*

Characterization of the Holy Spirit According to the New Plot of Revelation

In this section, I shall examine how the Divine Spirit can be characterized in the light of the whole plot of Revelation. As mentioned, the plot of Revelation is expressed and developed through its references to four levels or spheres: heaven; earth; abyss, Hades and Death and under the earth; and lake of fire. And, it has a sixfold scheme: introduction, setting, complication, resolution, evaluation, and moral (conclusion). The causal aspect of the plot of Revelation is related to the keeping and witnessing to the words of prophecy through the guidance of the Divine Spirit. In other words, the Divine Spirit is characterized as leading the readers to keep and witness to the words of prophecy in both direct and indirect ways. Thus, the characterization of the Divine Spirit in the plot of Revelation can be outlined as follows:

1. Introduction (Rev 1:1–8): The Divine Spirit prepares for the words of prophecy through the revelation process.

2. Setting (Rev 1:9—4:11): The Divine Spirit speaks to the seven churches through John the prophet.

3. Complication (Rev 5:1—11:19): The Divine Spirit makes all the universe unstable through the Lamb of God with the opening of the seven seals of the scroll as well as through the two witnesses with the powerful prophecy.

Plot and the Holy Spirit in Revelation

4. Resolution (Rev 12:1—16: 21): The Divine Spirit resolves the unstable state through the Lamb.
5. Evaluation (Rev 17:1—22: 5): The Divine Spirit guides both the messianic war and the messianic feast through the Lamb of God.
6. Moral (Rev 22:6-21): The Divine Spirit directs the tasks of the saints in the age of the messianic war.

Introduction (Rev 1:1-8): The Divine Spirit Prepares for the Words of Prophecy through the Revelation Process

Unlike the letters of Paul, Revelation proposes the Divine Spirit, that is, the Seven Spirits, as a divine character who, along with God and Jesus, provides grace and peace to the seven churches in Asia.[69] This can be a clue to understand how significantly the role of the Divine Spirit is emphasized in Revelation. By describing "the Seven Spirits as before God's throne," the narrator attempts to make sure readers understand that the Seven Spirits have a very important position in sharing the blessing for the saints. In the introduction section (Rev 1:1-8), I shall now examine how the Divine Spirit is characterized with respect to the literary aspect.

First of all, the Divine Spirit is explicitly characterized as one of the sources of blessing. In another sense, the Divine Spirit is characterized as occupying the same position as God and Jesus. The Divine Spirit is characterized explicitly in the second attention marker of the introduction. Secondly, the Divine Spirit seems to be characterized implicitly as being involved in the revelation process (Rev 1:1-2) in that the Divine Spirit is depicted as being related closely to God who gave the revelation to Jesus who transmitted it to his servants through his angel and John. Thirdly, the Divine Spirit seems to be characterized implicitly as bestowing the blessing for the saints, in that the Divine Spirit is involved in the process of their keeping the words of prophecy. Fourthly, in the light of the close relationship of the Divine Spirit to Jesus, one could consider that the Divine Spirit is characterized implicitly to be involved in the process of salvation for the saints to be freed from their sins and to become priests and a kingdom through Jesus. Before the main story begins, the narrator attempts to show that many have already become servants of Jesus

---

69. All of Paul's letters describe the source of grace and peace as God and Jesus except Colossians, which refers only to God in Col 1:2b.

including John, who will be given a mission for the testimony of Jesus. It can hardly be acceptable if we exclude the role of the Divine Spirit who is the source of the blessing for the saints in the salvation history.

In short, the Divine Spirit is characterized both openly and implicitly as preparing the servants of Jesus such as John for testifying to the word of God in the introduction. Since the Divine Spirit blesses the servants of Jesus before the throne of God, they could receive grace and peace in Jesus, that is, freedom from their sins by Jesus' blood, and becoming priests and a kingdom to serve God. In other words, by the efforts of the Divine Spirit, the servants of Jesus including John are ready to testify to the words of prophecy in the introduction. They are ready to keep what is written in the words of prophecy since the Divine Spirit blessed them.

Setting (Rev 1:9—4:11): The Divine Spirit Speaks to the Seven Churches from the Throne of Heaven through John the Prophet Who is in the Spirit

The activity of the Divine Spirit is depicted more dynamically and explicitly in the setting stage than in the introduction. The identity of the Divine Spirit is portrayed as the seven flaming torches in the setting (Rev 4:5), whereas as the Seven Spirits "who are before God's throne" in the introduction (Rev 1:3). The Divine Spirit is described as active in making the main character, John, be in the Spirit in Rev 1:10; 4:2. From this we can infer that the Divine Spirit has intentionally prepared John for testifying to the word of God and to the testimony of Jesus through filling John with the Spirit. Since John was in the Spirit, he was ready to hear the heavenly voice and to see the heavenly vision from the glorified Jesus in Rev 1:12–20. With the help of the Divine Spirit, John could take a journey into the heavenly realm in Rev 4. Thus, in the Spirit, John could be not only a prophet who testifies to the word of God and Jesus, but also a witness who testifies to the glory of the risen Jesus (1:12–16) and the heavenly throne (4:1–11). Furthermore, the Divine Spirit acts more explicitly in speaking to the seven churches directly with the words of Jesus in Revelation 2–3. The Divine Spirit speaks to the seven churches for the purpose of equipping them for witness to the word of God and Jesus in this world. The Divine Spirit and Jesus know and show both the state and the situation of all churches, especially, both the weakness and the strength of each church. The Divine Spirit is portrayed implicitly as

Plot and the Holy Spirit in Revelation

joining in spiritual warfare by asking the saints or churches to "conquer" seven times over the seven churches. Besides showing the earthly setting, the Divine Spirit plays a significant role in that he shows the heavenly setting through the spiritual journey of the Spirit-filled prophet, John. From the journey of John, the Divine Spirit shows not only the position of the Seven Spirits as "in front of the throne," but also the substance of the Seven Spirits as "the seven flaming torches" (Rev 4:5). The Divine Spirit is portrayed as a character who continues to speak to the churches on the earth here and now.

Complication (Rev 5:1—11:19): The Divine Spirit Makes All the Universe Unstable through the Lamb of God with the Opening of the Seven Seals of the Scroll as well as through the Two Witnesses with the Powerful Prophecy

In the complication stage, two explicit characterizations of the Divine Spirit are explored. On the one hand, the Divine Spirit is characterized as working with the Lamb of God in opening the seven seals of the scroll: "seven horns and seven eyes" who are sent out into all the earth, in Rev 5:6. One can discover that the narrator attempts to characterize the Divine Spirit in a few ways. Firstly, the Divine Spirit is characterized as working with the Scroll (the word of God) since he is described when Jesus is about to open the seven seals of the scroll. Secondly, by characterizing the Seven Spirits as the Divine Spirit sent out from the heavenly throne by the Lamb of God to all the earth, the narrator implies that the Divine Spirit is working in the whole world with heavenly authority. In another sense, the Divine Spirit is characterized as working among all the churches in the world as well as in all the world history of the world. Thirdly, all the earth is classified with a more detailed category: "every tribe and language and people and nation" in Rev 5:9. Thus, the Divine Spirit is characterized as the Holy Spirit who is working with Jesus for the salvation of every tribe and language and people and nation in the world.[70] Furthermore, the Divine Spirit speaks in the churches with the

---

70. In Rev 5:6, Jesus is portrayed as being slain at the same time as he is depicted as having the Divine Spirit. This is parallel with Rev 5:9 by the use of the same phrase, "to be slain," which is added in connection with the purpose of Jesus' death to ransom the saints from every tribe and language and people and nation. In this connection, readers can consider that the Divine Spirit works with Jesus for the redemption of the saints.

word of God and applies the Scroll to world history. Thirdly, by characterizing the Divine Spirit as seven horns sent to the world, the narrator implies that the Divine Spirit is responsible for joining the powerful ministry of Jesus Christ to conquer or destroy or judge the evil powers in Revelation. Moreover, the Divine Spirit as seven horns is characterized as empowering the two witnesses, that is, the churches in the world to carry out powerful witness ministries like Moses and Elijah (11:5–6). This shows by means of a retrospective literary effect the reason why the seven churches are asked to conquer in the world in the setting stage. Fourthly, by characterizing the Divine Spirit as seven eyes sent to the world, the narrator implies that the Divine Spirit knows all the affairs of the earthly churches as well as world affairs throughout world history. This shows, by means of a retrospective literary effect, the reason why all the situations of the seven churches as well as their worldly situations are known through the Divine Spirit by Jesus in the setting stage.

On the other hand, the Divine Spirit is characterized explicitly as giving life to two dead witnesses with the Spirit of life of God in Rev 11:11. One can explore that the narrator attempts to characterize the Divine Spirit in a few ways in relation to the two witnesses. Firstly, the Divine Spirit is implicitly related to the one who gives the two witnesses authority to prophesy since the Divine Spirit is characterized to work with the Scroll together with Jesus in chapter 5. Secondly, the Divine Spirit is implicitly related to the powerful ministry of the two witnesses on the earth to finish their missions (11:7a) in that the Divine Spirit is sent to the earth from heaven. Thirdly, the Divine Spirit is implicitly related to spiritual warfare between the two witnesses and the beast from the bottomless pit who conquers and kills them. Fourthly, the Divine Spirit is explicitly characterized as involved in the resurrection of the two witnesses by entering them as the breath of life of God. Fifthly, the Divine Spirit is implicitly characterized as involved in the ascension of the two witnesses up to heaven. Sixthly, the Divine Spirit is implicitly characterized as above in making the people of the earth give glory to the God of heaven (11:13).

Besides two explicit characterizations, more implicit characterizations of the Divine Spirit can be discovered. Firstly, the Divine Spirit is characterized as making John understand how significant both the Scroll and the seal opening are. How can we trace it? By exploring the gap effect on the readers of the gap in the narrative of Rev 5:1–5. A mighty angel asks John who he thinks is worthy to open the seals of the scroll. Then, John seeks to find a worthy one anywhere in the universe. However, he fails. Then, John begins to weep bitterly and readers are not given any detailed description of what transpires in John's heart. At that time, one of the elders informs him who the worthy one is. In this case, readers are asked to fill the gap concerning what happened in John's inner heart. We can raise the question of who makes John weep and how John is challenged. It is clear that neither a mighty angel nor any heavenly elder can be the answer since they are described as outsider characters toward John in this narrative. The answer is not so hard to find since John is depicted as still being in the Spirit and so can see and hear the visions in heaven. As far as we consider the cumulative effects in the narrative, John is still in the Spirit in Rev 5:1–5 since he was in the Spirit when he was transmigrated to the heavenly realm in Rev 4:2. Thus, it is the Divine Spirit who still speaks and guides John on the heavenly journey as both insider and outsider character in the narrative of Revelation.[71] In short, the Divine Spirit is characterized not only as controlling and guiding the prophet, John, but also as making him understand the significance of opening the word of God. The Divine Spirit can also be characterized as controlling and guiding the churches through John because John is asked to send what he sees and hears to the seven churches. Above all, the Divine Spirit is characterized as illuminating the content of the scroll, for not only the prophet John, but also the churches. Secondly, in Rev 5:6, Jesus is portrayed as slain when Jesus is depicted as having the Divine Spirit. This is parallel with Rev 5:9 by means of the use of the same phrase, "to be slain," which is added in relation to the purpose of Jesus' death to ransom the saints from every tribe and language and people and nation. In this connection, readers can consider that the Divine Spirit works with Jesus for the redemption of the saints.

In short, the Divine Spirit is characterized as involved in the messianic war as well as in the whole process of the redemption of the people of God in this unstable world.

---

71. I mean the insider character is the one who works in the inner heart of the narrative character. The outsider character is defined as the one who works outside the inner heart of the narrative character.

Resolution (Rev 12:1—16:21): The Divine Spirit Resolves the Unstable State through the Lamb

In the Resolution stage there is only one explicit characterization of the Divine Spirit to be explored and it is in Rev 14:13. When John, who is in the Spirit, hears a voice from heaven saying, "Write this: Blessed are the dead who from now on die in the Lord," the Spirit responds with the answer, "Yes" and gives the reason why they are blessed. In this, some characterizations of the Divine Spirit are discovered.

First of all, the Divine Spirit is characterized as the one who knows what John experienced in the vision and can confirm what the voice asserts. In other words, the narrator attempts to show that the Divine Spirit is portrayed as with and within the prophet, John. This reminds readers of the passages that describe John as being in the Spirit in Rev 1:10 and Rev 4:2. Readers can apply this knowledge to help them understand that the Divine Spirit is at work in the events on earth that the portents correspond with, even though the Divine Spirit does not appear. With John, the Divine Spirit is characterized as an implicit witness of some visions: the process of the birth of a child, the attack of the Dragon against the child, the ascension of the child to the throne of God, the heavenly war between Michael and the Dragon, the war of the Dragon against those who keep the commandments of God and hold the testimony of Jesus, the attack of the two beasts against the saints, the victory of the Lamb and 144,000, and the final judgment of the Lamb. Moreover, the Divine Spirit is characterized as a recipient of heavenly voices: a loud voice that proclaims the coming of salvation, power, the kingdom of God and the authority of his messiah (Christ) and that declares the throwing down of the accuser, the way to conquer the accuser by the blood of the Lamb and the word of the testimony of the saints as well as their bravery which does not fear death (Rev 12:10–12); the song of the Lamb, which sings that all nations will come and worship before God the Almighty (Rev 15:3–4); and the voices of the angel of water and the altar to declare that the judgments of God are true and just (Rev 16:5–7).

Secondly, the Divine Spirit is characterized as having a profound concern for the life of the saints and a desire for John to have confidence about these facts. Especially the Divine Spirit is considerate of the eternal life of the saints after their death. The Divine Spirit knows that the saints will be able to take rest from their labor on the earth. Furthermore, the Divine Spirit informs them that they will get rewards on the basis of their deeds on earth. Thus, it is not hard for readers to understand that the Divine Spirit has a concern for the life of the saints on earth and attempts to take part in their lives on earth via communication with John so that they may be blessed forever. The Divine Spirit speaks of the labor of the saints since the Divine Spirit sees how they have to experience the spiritual warfare including martyrdom from evil powers. The Divine Spirit is a comforter and guide in their labor. The Divine Spirit, who has been with the saints in their spiritual warfare, proclaims that the death of the saints will lead them to rest and that they will get rewards according to their deeds. In short, the Divine Spirit reveals himself as a character in 14:13 because he has a deep concern for the eternal hope of the saints, even though he does not usually appear in this stage of the narrative.

Thirdly, the Divine Spirit is characterized as having an interaction with a heavenly voice. When the heavenly voice speaks, "Write this: Blessed are the dead who from now on die in the Lord," the Spirit responds, "Yes, they will rest from their labors, for their deeds follow them" (14:13). It can be noted that the Divine Spirit is concerned with writing heavenly revelation since the voice from heaven is characterized as responsible for writing revelations. Not only in 14:13, but also in 10:4, the voice from heaven says to John, "Seal up what the seven thunders have said, and do not write it down." When the Spirit of life from God comes into the two witnesses in 11:11, the voice from heaven says to them, "come up here." Thus, we can consider that the Divine Spirit is characterized as a co-worker with the voice from heaven.

Evaluation (Rev 17:1—22:5): The Divine Spirit Guides Both the Messianic War and the Messianic Feast through the Lamb of God

Van Dijk insists that the evaluation stage usually represents the emotional and intellectual response of the characters in the episodes. Revelation has the same characteristic in its evaluation stage, even though it seems to have what is not a big role. The narrator indicates that the main character, John, "was greatly amazed" in 17:6b when he saw the great whore. Moreover, the narrator confirms to the readers John's emotional state when the angel asks why he is so amazed (17:7). Another usage of an emotional expression can be found in 17:8: "The inhabitants of the earth will be amazed when they see the beast." The emotional word "amazed" is used three times just in 17:6–8.[72] In chapters 18 and 19, various other emotional expressions can be explored. Several people groups express their own emotional responses, that is, "weep and mourn" (18:11) and "rejoice" (18:20), about the destruction of Babylon. Even in chapters 19 and 20, which do not include any emotional expression by characters, it is not so hard for readers to understand that John must be amazed when he sees that the first and second beasts and the Dragon were thrown into the lake of fire. In Rev 21:1—22:5, readers will not find it difficult to understand that John is amazed when the New Jerusalem, that is, the bride, is presented to him.

Neither is it difficult for readers to explore evidence that the Divine Spirit has been working in the emotional responses of the characters in the evaluation stage. First of all, when John was amazed at the great whore in the desert in chapter 17, John was in the Spirit and was taken to the desert by the Divine Spirit. Secondly, when John saw the destruction of Babylon and heard the various emotional responses from different people groups in chapter 18, he was in the Spirit. Thirdly, when John saw the punishment of the first beast and the second beast and the Dragon in chapters 19 and 20, John was in the Spirit. Fourthly, when John was taken to the great mountain in the Spirit, he could see the New Jerusalem, the bride of the Lamb in 21:1—22:5. In short, the whole emotional expression can be said to be related to the Divine Spirit. In another sense, the Divine Spirit has been working in the whole evaluation stage. If so, what is written of the characterization of the Divine Spirit in the evaluation stage?

The Divine Spirit is clearly presented as a character three times in the evaluation stage. In 17:3 and 21:10, the Divine Spirit is portrayed as a character who inspires John to be guided by an angel to the desert to see the destruction of Babylon and to the great mountain to see the New Jerusalem. The Divine Spirit functions as a person-like guide to move a character, John, from one place to another. In this, the Divine Spirit is depicted as an active character. The Divine Spirit functions as a prophet-like character who is responsible for all kinds of prophecy. In addition, the Divine Spirit is portrayed as a Spirit who gives a testimony to Jesus.

---

72. Actually the emotional word, "amazed" is also used in 13:3 and 15:3. However, they do not represent the main character's emotions. Revelation 13:3 says that the whole world is amazed by the beast, while 15:3 indicates that the deeds of the Lord are amazing.

The Divine Spirit is depicted as a God-like character who inspires the power of testimony in the prophets who testify to Jesus.

It is notable that the Divine Spirit is described as one who is involved in the messianic war and messianic feast, in the evaluation stage. The messianic war is closely related to the messianic feast since the messianic feast can be the result of victory in the messianic war. The messianic war is described in chapter 16 as war at Harmagedon (16:16). The process and result of the messianic war are depicted in chapter 17. The evil powers that control the beast and the united kings makes war against the Lamb (17:13–14). However, the Lamb and His "chosen and faithful" army conquer them since "he is the Lord of lords and King of kings" (17:14). The great whore is portrayed as going to be killed by kings (17:16). Chapter 19 depicts how the Lamb, a rider of a white horse, conquers the evil powers. Chapter 20 depicts how the evil powers will be punished. Revelation 21:1—22:5 figures how the followers of the Lamb will enjoy the messianic feast in the New Jerusalem. John is able to see the messianic war and the messianic feast unfold with guidance of the Divine Spirit (17:3; 21:10). The weapon of the messianic army can be construed as the testimony of Jesus, that is, the Spirit of prophecy in 19:10, in that the rider of the white horse is named "The Word of God" in 19:13 and "Faithful and True" in 19:11. Evidence can be persuasive that the Divine Spirit is involved in the messianic war and the messianic feast.

In short, the Divine Spirit is portrayed figuratively as one who guides both the whole salvation history for the people of God and the whole punishment process for the evil powers including their followers. The evaluation stage shows how the Divine Spirit is involved in the process of both the destruction of Babylon and the establishment of the New Jerusalem. The Divine Spirit has a significant role in the messianic war and the messianic feast as a "testimony of Jesus." The Divine Spirit of prophecy inspires the followers of the Lamb with the testimony of Jesus. The testimony of Jesus through the Holy Spirit can be the key both to the bringing of the New Jerusalem and to the destruction of Babylon in the messianic war. The testimony of the Divine Spirit can be the key both to the calling of the bride of the Lamb and to the killing of the great whore.

Moral (Rev 22:6–21): The Divine Spirit Directs the Tasks of the Saints in the Age of the Messianic War

What is the characterization of the Divine Spirit in 22:6–21?

First of all, in contrast to the introduction (1:1–8), the Divine Spirit is characterized as very active in calling the people into the New Jerusalem to be the bride of the Lamb. In 1:1–8, the Seven Spirits are just described as before the throne of God. However, the Spirit is working together with the bride to call the thirsty to get the water of life in 22:17. We can discover the progressive shift of the position of the Divine Spirit from the heavenly realm in the introduction to the earthly realm in the moral. In the introduction, the Divine Spirit is described as positioned on the heavenly throne. In the setting, the Divine Spirit is depicted as positioned both in heaven and in earth. The Divine Spirit is working with Jesus in heaven while the Divine Spirit is speaking to the earthly seven churches using the words of Jesus. In the complication, the Divine Spirit is moving to both heaven and earth. The Divine Spirit is working with the Lamb of God as seven eyes and seven flames in heaven, whereas the Divine Spirit is inspiring the two witnesses on earth. The Divine Spirit is portrayed as being sent from heaven to earth. In the resolution, the Divine Spirit is portrayed as working for the resolution of the conflicts both in heaven and on earth. The Divine Spirit is working in heavenly conflict between two heavenly powers, whereas the Divine Spirit is working on earthly conflicts between the woman and her descendents, and the evil powers including the Dragon and the beasts. In the evaluation, the position of the Divine Spirit is focused on earth rather than heaven. The Divine Spirit is working in the process of both the destruction of Babylon and the coming of the New Jerusalem on the earth. The Divine Spirit is inspiring the prophets and saints with the Spirit of prophecy. In the moral, the Divine Spirit is depicted as working with the bride on earth. There is no description of the heavenly position of the Divine Spirit any more in the moral. In short, the Divine Spirit is characterized as being responsible for doing mission work on earth by calling people to be the bride of the Lamb.

Secondly, the Divine Spirit is characterized as working with other characters such as Jesus, the angel, and the bride. We can see how the Divine Spirit is working with other characters in 22:6–21. Firstly, the Divine Spirit is characterized as a co-worker with Jesus to motivate the saints to keep the words of prophecy. When Jesus declares his second coming, readers must be attentive to keep the words of prophecy in 22:7 since they are blessed for doing so. Keeping the words of prophecy is described as being equivalent to purification in the people's daily lives with the connecting word, "blessed" in both 22:7 and 22:14. It is not hard for the readers to understand that the Divine Spirit takes a significant role in making sure the saints are blessed, that is, purified by keeping the words. The Divine Spirit must help them to be alert to the second coming of Jesus so that they may receive the rewards from Jesus (22:12). Secondly, the Divine Spirit is characterized as a co-worker with the angel. Jesus says in 22:16 that he sent his angel to bring his words to the churches through John. What is the content of prophecy or revelation given by the angel? It is related to what must take place soon (22:6). Moreover, the angel emphasizes the true worship to God alone (22:9). The angel identifies the prophet with one who keeps the word of the prophecy. The angel indicates a close relationship between the true worship of God and keeping the word of the prophecy (22:9). The angel also commands John not to "seal up the words of the prophecy of this book" (22:10). In other words, John, as a representative of the prophets and the churches, has a responsibility to proclaim the words of the prophecy. The angel informs John of the eschatological reason for preaching the words of the prophecy: "for the time is near" (22:10). The angel emphasizes holiness and righteousness (22:11). How can we know that the Divine Spirit is working together with the angel? The messages that the angel declares are quite similar to what the Spirit of prophecy focuses on, such as giving testimony by proclaiming the need for purity and holiness through keeping the words of prophecy. Both the angel and the Divine Spirit take the eschatological second coming of Jesus seriously. The angel reminds the prophet that "the time is near." Thus, the readers must understand that the Divine Spirit is working together with the angel. Thirdly, the Divine Spirit is characterized as a co-worker with the bride (22:17). They hear together what Jesus speaks. They have the same hope or desire for the second coming of Jesus. They speak together for Jesus to come. They work just as one body functionally. However, the narrator differentiates two entities with two different names: the Spirit and the bride (22:17). With this expression, readers can understand that they have their own identities even though they are working just like one body. Moreover, the Divine Spirit is working for the bride so that she may be purified and keep the word of prophecy.

In short, the characterization of the Divine Spirit in the moral can be summarized as follows.

1. The Divine Spirit is characterized as a co-worker with Jesus, the angel, and the bride.
2. The Divine Spirit is characterized as one who is involved in all the process of the coming down of the New Jerusalem from heaven to earth.
3. The Divine Spirit is characterized as one who intervenes in all the process of molding the bride to be a true worshipper of God and the holy one who does good.
4. The Divine Spirit is characterized as one who intervenes in all the process of witness to Jesus through unsealing the revelation of Jesus.
5. The Divine Spirit is characterized as one who intervenes in all the process of protecting the revelation of Jesus.
6. The Divine Spirit is characterized as one who employs prophetic imagination to prepare all the saints for the second coming of Jesus.

Summary

So far I have explored how the Divine Spirit is characterized along the sixfold and four-level scheme plot of Revelation. Now I will summarize what has been explored with a table. Then I will find some characteristics of the characterization of the Divine Spirit along the plot line of Revelation.

CHARACTERIZATION OF THE DIVINE SPIRIT ACCORDING TO THE PLOT OF REVELATION

The characterization of the Divine Spirit according to the plot of Revelation can be summarized as follows.

Table 4.1 The Characterization of the Divine Spirit According to the Plot f Revelation

Introduction 1:1–8	Setting 1:9—4:11	Complication 5:1—11:19	Resolution 12:1—16:21	Evaluation 17:1—22:5	Moral 22:6–21
God-like Provider of Divine blessing	God-like Inspirer of the servant with fullness	God-like Co-worker with Jesus in opening the scroll	God-like Witness of the visions of John	Person-like guide in the heavenly journey	God-like Inviter for the messianic feast to anyone who wants
God-like Guide in revelation process	Angel-like Guide to heavenly journey	God-like Descended almighty and omniscient Divine Messenger	God-like Comforter in the labor of the saints with the hope of rest	Prophet-like messenger	Co-worker with Jesus
God-like Co-worker (savior) with Jesus to be freed from their sins and to be a kingdom and priests.	Angel-like Equipper of the prophet for seeing the heavenly vision and hearing the heavenly voice	God-like Participant and messenger in the Church history and world history with God's word	Angel-like Guide in the spiritual warfare	God-like inspirer for the testimony of Jesus to the prophets	Earthly person-like mission inviter with the bride (church)
Angel-like Reinforcer for the saints to keep the words	God-like Orator to the earthly churches	God-like Equipper of the earthly churches in the spiritual warfare	Angel-like Communicator with the heavenly voice	Guide of the messianic war and the messianic feast	Angel-like co-worker with the angel
Person-like Mission Equipper for the servants of God to testify to the word of God	God-like Omniscient of the earthly churches	God-like raiser of the two dead witnesses (Churches)			

173

A Dynamic Reading of the Holy Spirit in Revelation

Introduction 1:1–8	Setting 1:9—4:11	Complication 5:1—11:19	Resolution 12:1—16:21	Evaluation 17:1—22:5	Moral 22:6–21
	God-like Encourager for the spiritual warfare	God-like Helper of the churches in ascension			
	God-like Heavenly Flaming torches (fires)	Person-like Mission agent to encourage the earthly people to glorify God.			
		Angel-like Illuminator of the significance of the scroll for the prophets and churches			

Characteristics of characterizing the Divine Spirit in the plot of Revelation

The characteristics of the characterization of the Divine Spirit are summarized as follows:

1. The characterization of the Divine Spirit is presented both explicitly and implicitly.

2. The characterization of the Divine Spirit is presented as an independent as well as a co-working character.

3. The characterization of the Divine Spirit does not present the direct self-identification of the Divine Spirit, but shows the indirect self-identification of the Divine Spirit.

4. The characterization of the Divine Spirit is one who moves from the heavenly real to the earthly realm. Note that the direction the Divine Spirit moves is the same as with the direction of the New Jerusalem.

5. The characterization of the Divine Spirit is classified into three types: God-like Divine Spirit, angel-like Divine Spirit, and person-like Divine Spirit.
6. The characterization of the Divine Spirit is one who focuses on the works on all the earth, whereas the works of the Divine Spirit in heaven are hardly to be found. The Divine Spirit is portrayed to work as a divine mission worker.
7. The characterization of the Divine Spirit is one who works with the word of God, that is, the scroll. In other words, the Divine Spirit is portrayed as a prophetic Spirit.
8. The characterization of the Divine Spirit is one who works for the conversion of all nations.
9. The characterization of the Divine Spirit is one who has a profound concern for the eternal lives of the saints.

5

Structure and the Holy Spirit in Revelation

Introduction

IN THE LAST CHAPTER, I presented the Holy Spirit as a narrative character by focusing on the narrative plot of Revelation, using the fourfold scheme of Van Dijk. Continuing this aim, I shall now alter the focus by examining the semio-narrative structure offered by Jang, which covers the syntactic, semantic, and pragmatic structure of Revelation.[1] So, firstly, I shall examine previous attempts to identify the structure of Revelation. Then, I shall extend this analysis by adopting a new narrative approach. I shall conclude by explaining the characterization of the Divine Spirit according to the structure of Revelation.

Retrospect: Previous Studies of the Structure of Revelation

The studies of the structure of Revelation have received considerable attention among Revelation scholars; however, a consensus can hardly be found. As Kempson insists, the previous studies of the structure of

---

1. Jang employs Patte's category of semio-narrative structure in his dissertation, "Narratological Approach," 66–222.

Revelation depend on the "presuppositions" of the interpreter.[2] Among various proposals to the structure of Revelation, the categorizing principle of Kempson has been one of the most helpful in classifying structures of Revelation.[3] He classifies all interpreters who propose their own structures of Revelation into two groups: those who follow external approaches and those who choose internal approaches. The first group employs some external factors outside the text of Revelation such as Greek drama, Imperial games, or early Christian paschal liturgy, to determine the structure of Revelation.[4] The second group exploits some internal factors within the text of Revelation such as key phrases (e.g., "and I saw" or "in the Spirit"), key verse (e.g., Rev 1:19), the number seven, etc., to discover the structure of Revelation.[5]

Christopher R. Smith, who insists that Ezekial and 4 Ezra's structures form models for Revelation, expands Kempson's classification.[6] He also argues that E. S. Fiorenza and Austin Farrer belong to the first group. Fiorenza's chiastic structure, for example, appeals to the concentric design of the Pauline letters. Farrer similarly appeals to Jewish cultural patterns such as the sacred week, ritual ceremonies, and signs of the Zodiac. Smith adds to these categories by suggesting that the structure of Revelation can only be found by combining the external and internal approaches. In other words, the structure of Revelation can only be traced by combining the quest for external influences with the "indicated

---

2. Kempson, "Theology in The Revelation," 39. He argues, "In each instance, the final structure will only be as strong as the presuppositions on which it is based."

3. Jang, "Narratological Approach," 10. Kempsom proposes the structure of Revelation as: Prologue (1:1–8); Vision 1 (1:9—3:22); Vision 2 (4:1—16:21) A. Introduction: Revealing Heaven's Purpose (4:2—5:14) B. The Scroll unsealed (7 seals 6:1—8:1) C. The Scroll heralded and summarized (7 trumpets 8:2—11:19) D. The Scroll opened and executed (Woman and Dragon 12:1—14:20, The seven bowls of God's wrath 15:1—16:21); Vision 3 (17:1—21:8) A. The Harlot and the Beast (17:3-18) B. The dirge over Babylon (18:1—19:10) C. The Final Victory (19:11—21:8); Vision 4 (21:9—22:5); Epilogue 22:6-21. Kempson, "Theology in The Revelation," 72.

4. Kempson, "Theology in The Revelation," 45.

5. Ibid., 72.

6. Smith also proposes the structure of Revelation according to the phrase, "in the Spirit": Prologue (1:1—8); In the Spirit on Patmos (1:9—3:22); In the Spirit in Heaven: A. Heavenly Journey (4:1—9:21 and 11:14-19) B. Transition (10:1–11) C. Historical vision (11:1-13, 12:1—16:21, and 19:11—21:8); In the Spirit in the Wilderness—Babylon vision (17:1—19:10); In Sprit on the Mountaintop—Jerusalem Vision (21:9—22:9); Epilogue 22:10—22:21. Smith, "Structure of the Book," 381.

authorial intent," which is internal to the text.[7] Thus, Smith proposes a "unified field approach" using both approaches.

Further, Jang expands both approaches with five and six subdivisions respectively. He categorizes external approaches into five kinds, those based on prior literature (Ezekiel—Glasson,[8] Old Testament—Swete[9]); those based on ritual pattern (ancient paschal liturgy—Shepherd,[10] ritual elements—Fiorenza,[11] Imperial games—Stauffer[12]); approaches based on drama (Greco—Roman drama form—Bowman,[13] Greek drama form—Fiorenza[14]); those based on symbolism (three key Jewish symbols: the week, the Jewish liturgical and festival calendar, and the signs of Zodiac—Farrer[15]); and those based on structuralism (Fiorenza, Gager[16]). Jang also identifies six internal approaches: septenary approaches (many); content approach (Swete[17]); phrase approach (In the Spirit—Tenney[18]); recapitulation approaches (Yabro Collins, Lambrecht, and Giblin[19]); concentric approach (ABCDC'B'A'—Fiorenza[20]); and the transposition approach

---

7. Ibid., 377.

8. Glasson, *Revelation of John*, 12–13.

9. Swete, *Commentary on Revelation*,1–50.

10. Shepherd proposes the following structure: Scrutinies 1–3; Vigil 4–6; The Initiation 7; Synaxis 8; Prayer 8:3–5; Law 8–9; Prophets 10–11; Gospel 12–15, 16–18; Psalmody 19; Eucharist 19–22. M. Shepherd, *Paschal Liturgy*, 48–64, 77–84.

11. Fiorenza, "Composition and Structure," 353.

12. Stauffer, *Christ and the Caesars*, 174–91.

13. Bowman, *Drama of the Book*, 15, 450.

14. Fiorenza, "Composition and Structure," 354.

15. Farrer, *Rebirth of Images*; and *Revelation of St. John the Divine*.

16. Fiorenza, "Composition and Structure," 346–50; Gager, *Kingdom and Community*, 52.

17. The structure proposed by Swete: Prologue and greeting 1:1–8; Part 1: A. Vision of Christ in the midst of the churches 1:9—3:22 B. Vision of Christ in heaven 4:1—5:14 C. Preparations for the end; Part 2: A. Vision of the mother of Christ and her enemies 12:1—13:18 B. Preparations for the end C. Vision of the bride of Christ 21:1—22:5; Epilogue and Benediction 22:6–21. Swete, *Commentary on Revelation*, 1–50.

18. The structure proposed by Tenney: Prologue-Christ communicating 1:1–8 Vision 1—Christ in the Church 1:9—3:22 Vision 2—Christ in the cosmos 4:1—16:21 Vision 3— Christ in conquest 17:10—21:8 Vision 4—Christ in consummation 21:9—22:5 Epilogue—Christ challenging 22:6–21. Tenney, *Interpreting Revelation*, 32–41.

19. Yabro Collins, *Combat Myth*, 32–34; Lambrecht, "Structuation of Revelation"; Giblin, "Literary Coherence," 81–95.

20. Fiorenza, "Composition and Structure," 344–66.

(Charles[21]). Jang concludes that while none of these approaches is "wholly adequate," they sometimes overlap and serve to "yield good results" by corroborating other approaches.[22]

However, I find that these approaches result in similar problems. Firstly, there is no consensus on literary genre since the interpreters disagree about which external or internal factor most significantly shapes the structure of Revelation. As for internal factors, it is hard to define authorial intent when the existence of one or more real authors is itself a question. Secondly, even having identified the literary genre, the perspective of the real readers or real audiences co-determines the meaning of the structure. Such important variables thus remain undetermined. A new and more comprehensive approach is therefore needed to identify the structure of Revelation. As was pointed out in chapter 1, the narrative approach may be an alternative way to discover the structure of Revelation since it can overcome the limits of present approaches.[23]

Scholars use the narrative approach to identify the framework of Revelation, disclosing at the same time, much external reference. For example, in a way typical of apocalyptic narrative, Revelation contains embedded historical facts that belong to its contemporary horizon. Revelation thus reveals both the early Christian community's confession and experience, and its literary and cultural background. Secondly, the narrative approach can reveal to interpreters otherwise unrecognizable elements of the text, such as its real author and real readers or audience, as well as what is recognizable, such as the implied author and implied reader or the implied audience.[24] Thirdly, the narrative approach is sensitive to the literary artistry engineered to affect reader response. Fourthly, the narrative approach uses the storytelling method. Storytelling has been "the most important traditional method" to deliver divine words to Christian communities.[25] Thus, the narrative approach can be understood as a comprehensive method to establish the structure of Revelation as a whole.

---

21. Charles, *Critical and Exegetical Commentary*.

22. Jang, "Narratological Approach," 26.

23. The narrative approach may overcome the problems caused by both the real authors and the real readers (audiences) by using the implied author and the implied readers (audiences).

24. Mckenzie and Haynes, *To Each Its Own Meaning*, 171.

25. Jang, "Narratological Approach," 28.

Since modern narrative criticism emerged in Mimesis (Auerbach 1953), many scholars have used the narrative approach to analyze the Gospels: Rhoads and Michie, Best, Culpepper, Kingsbury, and Tannehill.[26] Since J. J. Collins defined apocalypse as a "genre of revelatory literature with a *narrative* framework," many Revelation scholars have used the narrative approach to analyze Revelation and its structure.[27] Garrow, for example, focuses on finding the story of Revelation before locating this story in the contextual history of the text. Then he explores the interpretation of the story, that is, "what must soon take place." He particularly seeks the storytelling passages by reviewing the content of the little scroll. He then relates "foreshadowings of the scroll's contents" to the direct revelations of the contents of the scroll in the other parts of the text.[28] While Garrow does not claim to uncover the whole structure of Revelation, he does lay out a compelling version of Revelation's story.

David L. Barr presents the first narrative commentary of Revelation under the title, *Tales of the End: A Narrative Commentary on the Book of Revelation*. He divides the main part of the text into three scrolls: The letter scroll; The worship scroll; The war scroll. He proposes a new narrative approach to Revelation.[29] However, he fails to provide a convincing structure of Revelation as a whole.

James L. Resseguie presents another narrative commentary of Revelation under the title, *Revelation Unsealed: A Narrative Critical Approach to John's Apocalypse*. He identifies the literary elements of the narrative using such features as numbers, repetition, figurative language, setting, character, plot, and the reader. He proposes not only the U-shaped plot structure of Revelation—stable condition (1, 4–5); instabilities (6–19); new stable condition (20–22)—but also theological themes such as the church, evil, God, worship, salvation, Christ, and the future.[30] However, he fails to provide an adequate structure for the whole of Revelation since

---

26. Rhoads and Michie, *Mark as Story*; Best, *Mark*; Culpepper, *Anatomy of the Fourth Gospel*; Kingsbury, *Matthew as Story*; Tannehill, *Narrative Unity*.

27. J. J. Collins defines that the "Apocalypse is a genre of revelatory literature with a narrative framework, in which a revelation is mediated by an otherworldly being to a human recipient, disclosing a transcendent reality which is both temporal, insofar as it envisages eschatological salvation, and spatial, insofar as it involves another, supernatural world." J. J. Collins, "Introduction," 9.

28. Garrow, *Revelation*, 5–65.

29. Barr, *Tales of the End*, 25–129.

30. Resseguie, *Revelation Unsealed*, 160–91.

he does not employ literary tools to discover the other aspects in the structure of Revelation besides the U-shape structure.

In short, almost all Revelation scholars who offer narrative analyses fail to provide every aspect in the structure of Revelation, including even a syntactic structure. In what follows, I shall highlight a new narrative approach to discover the various aspects in the structure of Revelation. This new narrative approach to define the structure of Revelation is possible due to the apocalyptic studies in which the storytelling or the narrative has been a key issue toward understanding the apocalyptic stories.

Prospect: A New Narrative Approach to the Structure of Revelation

The publication of the SBL Apocalypse group's genre project in *Semeia* 14 (1979) has accelerated apocalyptic studies—with fruitful results. Thus, Hartman argues with respect to apocalyptic literature that, in addition to the form and the content, "function" should be an important topic. He proposed three types of function: the literary function (how the text works); the message (what the author wants to deliver to the readers); and the social function (the relation between the text and its social setting).[31] Hellholm used the text-linguistic method for genre research. He believes that two steps are needed to identify the structure of the apocalypse. Step one is to divide the text into hierarchically arranged communication levels such as the sender and receiver, the author and reader, and between characters. Step two is to divide the text into hierarchical text-sequences identified with some markers such as changes in the world, and episode markers presenting changes in time and place, etc.[32] Offering a different analysis, Boring argues that Revelation has four different levels of narrativity.[33] Du Rand, like Resseguie, offers a semantic focus on the theology of Revelation.[34]

Jang, however, in his doctoral thesis, "A Narratological Approach to the Structure of the Apocalypse of John," challenges previous narrative approaches. Using Patte's category of semio-narrative structure, he

---

31. Hartman, "Survey of the Problem," 339.
32. Hellholm, "Problem of Apocalyptic Genre," 47–54.
33. Boring, "Narrative Christology in the Apocalypse."
34. Du Rand, "Your Kingdom Come."

proposes a three-dimensional approach to Revelation's structure, namely, syntactic-structure, semantic-structure, pragmatic-structure. He says,

> Using the narrative theory, my study aims to establish an appropriate syntactic-structure according to its narrative elements, to identify the theological semantic-structure, and then to seek the pragmatic-structure of the Apocalypse, by enquiring into narrative strategies (in the literary context or the external context) to persuade or correct or transform the readers/hearers.[35]

In addition, he explores the syntactic-structure using two more detailed levels: the narrative-syntactic (surface-level) structure and the fundamental-syntactic (deep-level) structure. His contribution is the second of these—an unprecedented attempt to discover the fundamental-syntactic structure through an actantial model. He also explores the semantic structure with two more detailed categories: the narrative-semantic structure (theme-oriented concentric structure) and the fundamental-semantic structure (macrostructure). Based on the argument of Hartman, he also explores the pragmatic (functional) structure to discover how the theology of the author can be delivered rhetorically in the readers' social settings.

Another contribution of Jang's study is to explore the narrative-syntactic structure by delimiting the narrative units. He asserts,

> By using Patte's ideas for identifying discourse units, we can apply some criteria for identifying narrative units as follows: (1) A change of theme at the beginning and after the end of a passage will be a strong indication that we have a complete narrative unit, since each has a specific theme[36]. . . . (2) In a narrative, changes of character(s) or setting (space and/or time) bring about a change of event (scene) accompanying the change of theme. By finding such changes, one can easily identify narrative units[37]. . . . (3) Inverted parallelisms exist between the beginning and the end of each complete narrative unit. . . . (4) In case there are no inverted parallelisms between the beginning and the end of a section that should form a discrete narrative unit, we can use the similar criterion known as "inclusion," which refers to a repetition of features at the beginning and end of a unit. . . . (5) For the definition of the basic narrative unit, the following

---

35. Jang, "Narratological Approach," 2.
36. Patte, *Structural Exegesis*, 15, quoted in Jang, "Narratological Approach," 85–86.
37. Patte, *Structural Exegesis*, 16, quoted in Jang, "Narratological Approach," 85.

Structure and the Holy Spirit in Revelation

elements of narration also is worth considering, because the size of the basic narrative unit varies from just one verse to a whole chapter. There are *mimesis* (showing) and *diegesis* (telling) as two describing ways in the narrative theory.[38]

After partial units are fixed through the delimitation process, basic units are discovered according to the five criteria mentioned above. After basic narrative units are found, higher level units can be found through integrating basic units. Thus, Jang proposes that Revelation has five levels of syntactical narrative unit. Unit level one is the basic narrative unit, unit level two is found through grouping adjacent basic units, and unit level three is replaced with the plot of Revelation through the global integration of basic units. Unit level four is divided by coming into and out of the visionary world and epistolary form. The whole is presented in three parts: Introduction (1:1–8), Body (1:9—22:5), End (22:6–21). Unit level five is the whole narrative text of Revelation.

One more contribution from his study is to propose the fundamental-syntactic structure of Revelation, applying the actantial model, one of the structuralist approaches, to the whole narrative.[39] While criticizing the model proposed by Fiorenza,[40] he suggests a new actantial model of Revelation as follows[41]:

Diagram 5.1 Jang's Actantial Model of Revelation

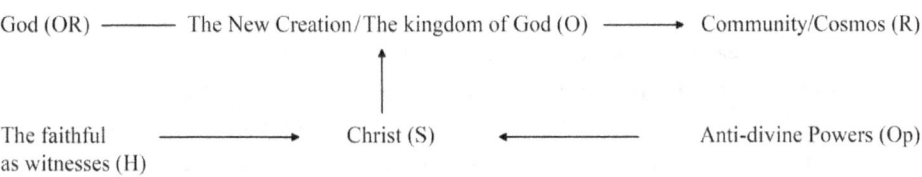

38. Jang, "Narratological Approach," 85–87.

39. Jang introduces the basic ideas of structuralism and the three models of structuralism, that is, The Functional Model, The Binary Model, and The Actantial Model. After he evaluates the weaknesses of each model, Jang applies the actantial model to analyze the fundamental-syntactic structure of Revelation. This actantial model represents that God has a willingness to make all things new or to build the kingdom of God for the community or the cosmos. The task shall be practiced by Christ who is supported by the faithful and is attacked by the anti-divine power. See Jang, "Narratological Approach," 154–61.

40. Fiorenza, *Book of Revelation*, 174.

41. Jang, "Narratological Approach," 158.

In addition, he explores the functional structure of Revelation to discover how the Revelation narrative serves to change the perception of the audience or readers. Jang asserts that the reversal narrative strategy is used in the Revelation narrative to transform the audience's view, both in the literary context and in the socio-rhetorical situational context.[42] With this narrative rhetoric of reversal, the implied author challenges the readers or audiences to resist the anti-divine power, to keep the word of God and worship only God, and to be faithful witnesses on earth.

Thus, he concludes in his abstract,

> This study could modestly be said to articulate the following results: (1) The syntactic structure of the Apocalypse, as an integral unit, shows movement from an unstable state to a stable condition, which means that God's sovereignty will be established on earth—"Thy will be done on earth as it is in heaven." (2) The semantic structure shows that the Apocalypse revolves around the activity of Jesus Christ, who is the cohering theological-element of the structure of the book. (3) The functional structure shows that the Apocalypse rhetorically requests the faithful to witness to God's word until the end of the world and the wayward to repent because the time is near.[43]

His study of the structure makes an important contribution to the understanding of the structure of Revelation, suggesting valuable insights into its theology. Nevertheless, his writing's method and its application to the structure of Revelation need to be corrected and supplemented for a few reasons. Firstly, Jang's division and naming are not appropriate in many parts of his model. Readers can be misled about the narrative-syntactic structure of Revelation. Secondly, his actantial model is also too simple. It cannot represent the fundamental semantic structure of Revelation appropriately. The whole actantial model needs to be considered as well as the partial actantial model. Thirdly, Jang's pragmatic structure does not include literary context. It cannot represent the rhetorical effects as a whole. The rhetorical effects to transform and strengthen the readers cannot be presented. As follows, I shall suggest my own structure of Revelation.

---

42. The reversal narrative strategy indicates how the narrative is designed to transform the readers while they proceed to read the story. The author must employ some reversal strategies such as conflicts or changes among characters in the narrative.

43. Ibid., 91–92.

Narrative-Syntactic Structure of Revelation and the Characterization of the Divine Spirit

NARRATIVE-SYNTACTIC STRUCTURE OF REVELATION

I shall attempt to identify the narrative-syntactic structure of Revelation by correcting Jang's model.[44] His analysis of the basic units of the Revelation narratives needs to be corrected from the mistakes in classification of unit level (UL) and in naming some units. The revisions can be summarized with a chart in Table 5.1.

Table 5.1 Comparison Between the Syntactic-Structure of Revelation in Jang's and H. Y. Lee's Models

Verses	Jang's proposed syntactic-structure of Revelation (Jang's Model)	My proposed syntactic-structure of Revelation (Lee's Model)
1:1—22:21	UL5 The whole text as a narrative	UL5 The whole text as a narrative
1:1–8	UL4 Introduction	UL4 Introduction
1:1–8	UL3 Introduction to the story	UL3 Introduction to the story
1:1–3	UL3 Prologue	UL2 Prologue
1:1a	a. Title	UL1 Title: The Revelation of Christ
1:1b–2	b. The witness	UL1 The process of Revelation
1:3	c. Those who keep the prophecy	UL1 The beatitude for the reader and those who hear and keep the prophecy
1:4–8	UL3 Epistolary prescript	UL2 Epistolary prescript
1:4–8	d. The communicators as the main characters	
1:4–6		UL1 Sender and receiver of the letter and the sources of grace and peace: God; The Seven Spirits; Jesus

---

44. In this study, the structure of Revelation shall be presented by critically revising Jang's model since the purpose of this study is not just to discover the structure of Revelation, but also to understand the role of the Divine Spirit in Revelation.

Verses	Jang's proposed syntactic-structure of Revelation (Jang's Model)	My proposed syntactic-structure of Revelation (Lee's Model)
1:7–8		UL1 The proclamation of Jesus' return and the identity of God Almighty: Alpha and Omega
1:9—22:5	UL4 Body	UL4 Body
1:9—4:11	UL3 Setting of the story	UL3 Setting of the story: The heavenly setting and the earthly setting
1:9–20	UL1 Leading into the visions	UL2 Transferring the setting from heaven to earth: Command of Jesus Christ to write
1:9–16		UL1 Epiphany in the Spirit and the appearance of the glorified Jesus
1:17–20		UL1 Response to epiphany and self-identity of the glorified Jesus
2:1—3:22	UL2 The earthly setting: Messages to the churches	UL2 The earthly setting: Messages to the churches
2:1–7	UL1 To the church in Ephesus	UL1 To the church in Ephesus
2:8–11	UL1 To the church in Smyrna	UL1 To the church in Smyrna
2:12–17	UL1 To the church in Pergamum	UL1 To the church in Pergamum
2:18–29	UL1 To the church in Thyatira	UL1 To the church in Thyatira
3:1–6	UL1 To the church in Sardis	UL1 To the church in Sardis
3:7–13	UL1 To the church in Philadelphia	UL1 To the church in Philadelphia
3:14–22	UL1 To the church in Laodicea	UL1 To the church in Laodicea
4:1–11	UL2 The heavenly setting: God ruling all the events	UL2 The heavenly setting: God ruling all the events
4:1–11	UL1 Vision of the throne and heavenly being	
4:1–2		UL1 Transporting into heavenly court in the Spirit

Structure and the Holy Spirit in Revelation

Verses	Jang's proposed syntactic-structure of Revelation (Jang's Model)	My proposed syntactic-structure of Revelation (Lee's Model)
4:3–7		UL1 The description of the heavenly ones
4:8–11		UL1 The worship of the heavenly beings to God Almighty
5:1—11:19	UL3 Complication: Opening the Scroll	UL3 Complication: The Judgment of the Lamb with seals and the two witnesses with prophecy and the avenge of the beast against the two witnesses
5:1—6:17	UL2 The seven seals (including 8:1)	UL2 The judgment of the Lamb against the unsealed with six seals
5:1–14	UL1 Heavenly liturgy for opening the seven seals	
5:1–5		UL1 Sealed Scroll and the Lion of the tribe of Judah
5:6–14		UL1 Heavenly liturgy for opening the seven seals
6:1–2	UL1 The first seal: Conquest	UL1 The first seal: Conquest
6:3–4	UL1 The second seal: Take peace from the earth	UL1 The second seal: Take peace from the earth
6:5–6	UL1 The third seal: A bad harvest	UL1 The third seal: A bad harvest
6:7–8	UL1 The fourth seal: A fourth of the earth killed	UL1 The fourth seal: A fourth of the earth killed
6:9–11	UL1 The fifth seal: Cry of the martyrs	UL1 The fifth seal: Cry of the martyrs
6:12–17	UL1 The sixth seal: The great day	UL1 The sixth seal: The great day
7:1–17	UL2 Interruption: Sealing of the 144,000 and Identifying a great multitude in white robes	UL2 The protection for the 144,000 sealed on earth and the worship of a great multitude in heaven
7:1–8	UL1 Sealing the servants of God	UL1 Sealing the servants of God

187

Verses	Jang's proposed syntactic-structure of Revelation (Jang's Model)	My proposed syntactic-structure of Revelation (Lee's Model)
7:9–17	UL1 Praising God and the Lamb in heaven	UL1 Praising God and the Lamb in heaven
8:1	UL2 The seven seals continued	
8:1	UL1 The seventh seal: Silence in heaven	
8:2—9:21	UL2 Seven trumpets	
8:1—9:21		UL2 Increasing judgment with the seventh seal and the six trumpets
8:2–6	UL1 Heavenly liturgy for seven trumpets	
8:1–6		UL1 The seventh seal and heavenly liturgy for seven trumpets
8:7	UL1 The first trumpet: A third of earth burned up	UL1 The first trumpet: A third of earth burned up
8:8–9	UL1 The second trumpet: A third of the sea harmed	UL1 The second trumpet: A third of the sea harmed
8:10–11	UL1 The third trumpet: A third of the waters turned bitter	UL1 The third trumpet: A third of the waters turned bitter
8:12	UL1 The fourth trumpet: A third of the heavenly bodies turned dark	UL1 The fourth trumpet: A third of the heavenly bodies turned dark
8:13—9:12a	UL1 The fifth trumpet: Locusts from the abyss	UL1 The fifth trumpet: Locusts from the abyss
9:12b–21	UL1 The sixth trumpet: massacre of mankind "a third of mankind" and no repentance by the rest of mankind	UL1 The sixth trumpet: Massacre of mankind "a third of mankind" and no repentance by the rest of mankind
10:1—11:13	UL2 Interruption of trumpet plagues: Last chance for prophecy and repentance	UL2 Complication between the two witnesses and the beast from the bottomless pit
10:1–11	UL1 "No more delay" and John again to prophesy	

Structure and the Holy Spirit in Revelation

Verses	Jang's proposed syntactic-structure of Revelation (Jang's Model)	My proposed syntactic-structure of Revelation (Lee's Model)
10:1–7		UL1 seventh trumpet: Prophecy of the angel about the fulfillment of God's mystery, that is, "no more delay"
10:8–11		UL1 The prophet to be commanded to eat the scroll and to prophesy again as a witness
11:1–13	UL1 The nations to trample over the holy city for 42 months and the two witnesses to prophesy for the same period	
11:1–10		UL1 The authority of the two witnesses and the killing power of the beast from the bottomless pit over the two witnesses
11:11–13		UL1 The resurrection and ascension of the two witnesses and the repentance of the rest
11:14–19	UL2 Seven trumpets continued (8:2—11:19)	UL2 Advent of Kingdom of God and Messiah with seventh trumpet
11:14–15		UL1 Proclamation of the heavenly voices about the Kingdom of Messiah
11:16–18		UL1 Proclamation of 24 elders about God's judgment and reward in the Kingdom of God
11:19		UL1 Temple opened and the ark of God's covenant seen
12:1—16:21	UL3 Resolution-bringing the complication to a settlement: The origin of the conflict, the redeemed from the conflict and the wrath of God	UL3 Resolution: The Lamb and His followers as the conquerors against the evil powers and their followers and as the earthly subjects of resolution and The God Almighty as the heavenly origin of resolution

A Dynamic Reading of the Holy Spirit in Revelation

Verses	Jang's proposed syntactic-structure of Revelation (Jang's Model)	My proposed syntactic-structure of Revelation (Lee's Model)
12:1—14:20	UL3 A mystic backdrop around the conflict and the prophetic expectation	
12:1–17	UL2 An introduction to the resolution: The origin of the conflict between the church and the evil beings	UL2 The appearance of Resolution character, Son of Man, and the Dragon's attack against Jesus and woman
12:1–6	UL1 The birth of Jesus	UL1 The ascension of resolution character, Jesus under the Dragon's attack
12:7–12	UL1 The death of Jesus on the cross[45]	UL1 The withdrawal of the Dragon and his angels through the war in heaven between them and Michael and his angels[46]
12:13–17	UL1 The church era	UL1 God's protection for woman and her descendents under the Dragon's attack
13:1–18	UL2 Beasts making war on the faithful at the end of time to kill the saints, as a parody of Jesus "on the great day"	UL2 The saints' needs of endurance and faith and wisdom under the attacks of two beasts as resolution factors
13:1–10	UL1 A beast from the sea	UL1 The saints' needs of endurance and faith under the attack of a beast from the sea
13:11–18	UL1 Another beast from the earth	UL1 The saints' needs of wisdom under the attack of a beast from the earth

45. Actually the narrator of Revelation seems to omit the event of the death and resurrection of Jesus in the text of 12:1–6 intentionally. After the description of the birth of Jesus, the ascension of Jesus is directly portrayed. In this aspect, Jang must have made a mistake to give a subject of "The death of Jesus on the cross" in 12:7–12. If it should be written, it is supposed to be placed in 12:1–6.

46. The withdrawal of the Dragon and his angels can be due to the ascension of Jesus. The withdrawal of the Dragon and his angels can also be the reason why they attack the woman and her descendents in 12:13–17.

Structure and the Holy Spirit in Revelation

Verses	Jang's proposed syntactic-structure of Revelation (Jang's Model)	My proposed syntactic-structure of Revelation (Lee's Model)
14:1–20	UL2 Harvesting at the end day	UL2 Resolution accomplished on earth: Judgment and harvest by the Lamb and 144,000 with witness and prophecy
14:1–5	UL1 the Lamb and the 144,000	UL1 The Lamb and 144,000 as subjects of heavenly triumph
14:6–13	UL1 Eternal gospel	UL1 The endurance and faith, even to the death, needed in proclaiming gospel and the prophecy about the judgments against Babylon and the worshipper of the beast
14:14–20	UL1 Symbolic action concerning harvesting at the end of time	UL1 One like the Son of Man resolves the complication with harvest and judgment
15:1—16:21	UL3 The actual resolving action	UL2 Resolution accomplished from heaven with the seven bowls of God's wrath
15:1—16:21	UL2 Seven bowls as the last wrath of God	
15:1—16:1	UL1 Heavenly liturgy for the seven bowls: Inauguration (15:1), praising and conferment (15:2-8), and commending (16:1)	
15:1–4		UL1 Worship song of Moses and the Lamb for God Almighty
15:5–8		UL1 Tent of witness in heaven opened as an origin of the seven bowls with God's wrath
16:1		UL1 The inauguration of the seven bowls of God's wrath poured on earth
16:2	UL1 The first bowl: Foul and evil sores	UL1 The first bowl: Against the worshippers of the beast with its mark on the earth

Verses	Jang's proposed syntactic-structure of Revelation (Jang's Model)	My proposed syntactic-structure of Revelation (Lee's Model)
16:3	UL1 The second bowl: The sea turned into blood	UL1 The second bowl: Against the sea and its inhabitants
16:4–7	UL1 The third bowl	UL1 The third bowl: Against the rivers and the springs of water; the blood of the saints and prophets as the reason why God's judgment against them is true and just
16:8–9	UL1 The fourth bowl	UL1 The fourth bowl: Against the people with the fierce heat of the sun; their curse against the name of God and their refusal to repent
16:10–11	UL1 The fifth bowl	UL1 The fifth bowl: Against the beast's throne and people; their curse against the God of heaven and their refusal to repent
16:12–16	UL1 The sixth bowl	UL1 The sixth bowl: Against the river Euphrates; the demonic spirits coming from the Dragon, the beast and the false prophet assemble the kings at Harmagedon for battle on the great day of God the Almighty
16:17–21	UL1 The seventh bowl (The completion of God's wrath)	UL1 The seventh bowl: Against the air; the completion of God's wrath with the voice of the throne and temple, "it's done" with the greatest earthquake and fearful hailstone; the great city, Babylon is split and the cities of the nations and every island and mountains disappear
17:1—22:5	UL3 Evaluation: The full report and its confirmation of God's salvation and judgment	UL3 Evaluation: The mental and emotional reaction of characters about God's judgment and salvation

Structure and the Holy Spirit in Revelation

Verses	Jang's proposed syntactic-structure of Revelation (Jang's Model)	My proposed syntactic-structure of Revelation (Lee's Model)
17:1—19:21	UL2 The fall of Babylon	UL2 The responses about judgment against the beast (Babylon/Great whore) and the false prophet
17:1–18	UL1 The judgment of the great harlot	
17:1–6		UL1 The proclamation of the judgment of the great whore and explanation why she is punished
17:7–8		UL1 The amazement of both John about woman and the inhabitants of the earth about the beast with 7 heads and 10 horns
17:9–14		UL1 The defeat in war of the beast and 7 heads as 7 kings and 10 horns as 10 kings by the Lamb and His followers
17:15–18		UL1 The destruction of the whore by the beast and 10 horns with the intervention of God into their hearts
18:1–24	UL1 Announcement of "the fall of Babylon"	
18:1–8		UL1 The announcement of the fall of Babylon and its reasons for the people of God
18:9–19		UL1 The response of kings and merchants and shipmasters, seafarers, sailors, sea traders about the fall of Babylon
18:20–24		UL1 The judgment for the saints and apostles and prophets against Babylon, the whore because of their blood

Verses	Jang's proposed syntactic-structure of Revelation (Jang's Model)	My proposed syntactic-structure of Revelation (Lee's Model)
19:1–10	UL1 Announcement of God's salvation and judgment	
19:1–3		UL1 The righteousness and eternity of the judgment of God
19:4–10		UL1 Heavenly worship to God for the marriage of the Lamb with the saints who hold the testimony of Jesus and the righteous deeds
19:11–16	UL1 A rider on a white horse and his armies' campaign	UL1 The portrayal of the rider on a white horse as "Faithful and True," "The Word of God," "King of kings and The Lord of lords"
19:17–21	UL1 Victory over their enemies	UL1 The defeat in war and judgment of the beast and the false prophet into the lake of fire by the rider on the white horse and his army
20:1–6	UL2 The victory over the Dragon and "the first resurrection"	
20:1–15		UL2 The judgment against the Dragon (Satan/ancient serpent) and those whose names were not found in the Lamb's book of life
20:1–3	UL1 Satan sealed for a thousand years	UL1 The Dragon captured and sealed for a thousand years
20:4–6	UL1 Satan's reign for a thousand years and "the first resurrection"	UL1 The priests of God and Christ reign with Christ for a thousand years as the first resurrection group
20:7–15	UL2 The judgment over the Dragon and "the second death"	

Verses	Jang's proposed syntactic-structure of Revelation (Jang's Model)	My proposed syntactic-structure of Revelation (Lee's Model)
20:7–10	UL1 The final judgment of the Dragon after the millennium	UL1 The defeat in war and judgment of the Dragon into the lake of fire by heavenly fire
20:11–15	UL1 The final judgment of those whose names were not found written in the book of life and "the second death"	UL1 The judgment of those whose names were not found in the Lamb's book of life into the lake of fire and the rewards for the saints according to their works
21:1—22:5	UL2 Paradise regained: The holy city, Jerusalem	UL2 The advent of the New Jerusalem from heaven on earth
21:1–8	UL1 Introduction of the holy city	UL1 The qualification to be the members of the New Jerusalem as new creation: Those who conquer
21:9–27	UL1 The outside features of the holy city, Jerusalem	
21:9–14		UL1 The New Jerusalem's glory and wall with 12 gates (the names of 12 tribes of Israelites) and 12 foundations (the names of 12 apostles of the Lamb)
21:15–21		UL1 The length and width and height of the New Jerusalem and its wall, the materials of the New Jerusalem (gold) and its wall (jasper) and foundations (12 jewels), gates (12 single pearls)
21:22–27		UL1 God and the Lamb as the temple and light of the New Jerusalem and the openness of the New Jerusalem to the nations and kings and people and the qualification to enter the New Jerusalem: Those written in the Lamb's book of life

Verses	Jang's proposed syntactic-structure of Revelation (Jang's Model)	My proposed syntactic-structure of Revelation (Lee's Model)
22:1–5	UL1 The inside features of the holy city, Jerusalem	UL1 The river and tree of life with its fruits and leaves and the life of the servants of the Lamb in the New Jerusalem
22:6–21	UL4 Ending	UL4 Ending
22:6–21	UL3 Coda/Moral	UL3 Coda/Moral: Epilogue
22:6–17	UL3 Epilogue with moral: the communicator	
22:18–21	UL3 Epistolary postscript with moral	
22:6–7		UL2 The authentication of the book of Revelation
22:6		UL1 The trustworthiness of the revelation of Jesus Christ
22:7		UL1 The beatitude for those who keep the prophecy
22:8–11		UL2 The commands of the angel
22:8–9		UL1 Worship only God
22:10		UL1 Do not seal the prophecy
22:11		UL1 Choose righteousness or evil
22:12–16		UL2 The sayings of Jesus Christ
22:12		UL1 Coming soon with His reward according to one's work
22:13		UL1 The identity of the one coming: Alpha and Omega; the first and the last; the beginning and the end
22:14–15		UL1 Blessing to those who wash their robes and warning to those who are outside of the New Jerusalem

Verses	Jang's proposed syntactic-structure of Revelation (Jang's Model)	My proposed syntactic-structure of Revelation (Lee's Model)
22:16		UL1 Further identity of Jesus as a sender of Revelation: the root and the descendant of David; the bright morning star
22:17–21		UL2 Final sayings and Epistolary postscript
22:17		UL1 Calling of the Spirit and the bride for everyone to come
22:18–19		UL1 Finalization of the text of Revelation and warning against changing the prophecy of the book
22:20		UL1 Jesus again proclaims His coming, and offers a plea for His return
22:21		UL1 Concludes with benediction

In the UL3 resolution part, Jang names Rev 12:1—16:21 and 12:1—14:20 as the same level UL3, which would be unreasonable. The topic of UL3 also needs to be edited as UL3 Resolution: The Lamb and His followers as the conquerors against the evil powers and their followers and as the earthly subjects of resolution and The God Almighty as the heavenly origin of resolution. Van Dijk mentions that a resolution part will explain "those actions that attempt the reestablishment of the original situation or the creation of a new situation in which further normal functioning is possible."[47] Following Van Dijk, I offer two topics focused on the resolution characters.

Van Dijk asserts that an evaluation part describes, "the global mental or emotional reaction of the narrator participant with respect to the narrated episode: whether it was nice, awful, funny, etc."[48] According to Van Dijk, I attempt to give the topics in the evaluation focused on the mental or emotional reaction of characters. UL3 Evaluation: The mental and emotional reaction of characters about God's judgment and

---

47. Van Dijk, *Macrostructures*, 114.
48. Ibid., 115.

salvation (17:1—22:5). UL2 The responses about judgment against the beast (Babylon/great whore) and the false prophet (17:1—19:21); UL1 The proclamation of the judgment of the great whore and explanation why she is punished (17:1-6); UL1 The amazement of both John about woman and the inhabitants of the earth about the beast with 7 heads and 10 horns (17:7-8); UL1 The defeat in war of the beast and 7 heads as 7 kings and 10 horns as 10 kings by the Lamb and His followers (17:9-14); UL1 The destruction of the whore by the beast and 10 horns with the intervention of God into their hearts (17:15-18); UL1 The announcement of the fall of Babylon and the reasons for it are given to the people of God so they will not make the same mistakes (18:1-8); UL1 The response of kings and merchants and shipmasters, seafarers, sailors, sea traders about the fall of Babylon (18:9-19); UL1 The judgment for the saints and apostles and prophets against Babylon, the whore because of their blood (18:20-24); UL1 The righteousness and eternity of the judgment of God (19:1-3); UL1 Heavenly worship to God for the marriage of the Lamb with the saints who hold the testimony of Jesus and the righteous deeds (19:4-10); UL1 The portrayal of the rider on a white horse as "Faithful and True," "The Word of God," "King of kings and The Lord of lords" (19:11-16); UL1 The defeat in war and judgment of the beast and the false prophet into the lake of fire by the rider on the white horse and his army (19:17-21); UL2 The judgment against the Dragon (Satan/ancient serpent) and those whose name were not found in the Lamb's book of life (20:1-15); UL1 The Dragon captured and sealed for a thousand years (20:1-3); UL1 The priests of God and Christ reign with Christ for a thousand years as the first resurrection group (20:4-6); UL1 The defeat in war and judgment of the Dragon into the lake of fire by heavenly fire (20:7-10); UL1 The judgment of those whose names were not found in the Lamb's book of life with the lake of fire and the rewards for the saints according to their works (20:11-15); UL2 The advent of the New Jerusalem from heaven on earth (21:1—22:5); UL1 The qualification to be the members of the New Jerusalem as the new creation: Those who conquer (21:1-8); UL1 The New Jerusalem's glory and wall with 12 gates (the names of 12 tribes of Israelites) and 12 foundations (the names of 12 apostles of the Lamb) (21:9-14); UL1 The length and width and height of the New Jerusalem and its wall, the materials of the New Jerusalem (gold) and its wall (jasper) and foundations (12 jewels), gates (12 single pearls) (21:15-21); UL1 God and the Lamb as the temple and light of the

Structure and the Holy Spirit in Revelation

New Jerusalem and the openness of the New Jerusalem to the nations and kings and people and the qualification to enter the New Jerusalem: Those written in the Lamb's book of life (21:22–27); UL1 The river and tree of life with its fruits and leaves and the life of the servants of the Lamb in the New Jerusalem (22:1–5).

The coda/moral (22:6–21) will be classified as UL4 Ending and UL3 Coda/Moral: epilogue. I attempt to classify in more detail since there are many kinds of levels and different parts as follows: UL2 The authentication of the book of Revelation (22:6–7); UL1 The trustworthiness of the revelation of Jesus Christ (22:6); UL1 The beatitude for those who keep the prophecy (22:7); UL2 The commands of the angel (22:8–11); UL1 Worship only God (22:8–9); UL1 Do not seal the prophecy (22:10); UL1 Choose righteousness or evil (22:11); UL2 The sayings of Jesus Christ (22:12–16); UL1 Coming soon with His reward according to one's work (22:12); UL1 The identity of the one coming: Alpha and Omega; the first and the last; the beginning and the end (22:13); UL1 Blessing to those who wash their robes and warning to those who are outside of the New Jerusalem (22:14–15); UL1 Further identity of Jesus as a sender of Revelation: the root and the descendant of David; the bright morning star (22:16); UL2 Final sayings and Epistolary postscript (22:17–21); UL1 Calling of the Spirit and the bride for everyone to come (22:17); UL1 Finalization of the text of Revelation and warning against changing the prophecy of the book (22:18–19); UL1 Another proclamation by Jesus of coming again and the plea for His return (22:20); UL1 Concluding with benediction (22:21).

According to my analysis of the basic units of Revelation, what can be understood as the narrative-syntactic structure of Revelation, is shown in Table 5.2.

A Dynamic Reading of the Holy Spirit in Revelation

Table 5.2 Narrative-Syntactic Structure of Revelation

UL5	The Whole Text as a Narrative (1:1—22:21)			
	UL4	Introduction (1:1-8) Body (1:9—22:5) Ending (22:6-21)		
		UL3	Introduction to the story (1:1-8) Setting of the story: The heavenly setting and the earthly setting (1:9—4:11) Complication: The judgment of the Lamb with seals and the two witnesses with prophecy and the avenge of the beast against the two witnesses (5:1—11:19) Resolution: The Lamb and His followers as the conquerors against the evil powers and their followers, and as the earthly subjects of resolution, and the God Almighty as the heavenly origin of resolution (12:1—16:21) Evaluation: The mental and emotional reaction of characters about God's judgment and salvation (17:1—22:5) Coda/Moral: Epilogue (22:6-21)	
			UL2	Prologue (1:1-3) Epistolary prescript (1:4-8) Transferring the setting from heaven to earth: Command of Jesus Christ to write (1:9-20) The earthly setting: Messages to the churches (2:1—3:22) The heavenly setting: God ruling all the events (4:1-11) The judgment of the Lamb against the unsealed with six seals (5:1—6:17) The protection for the 144,000 sealed on earth and the worship of a great multitude in heaven (7:1-17) Increasing judgment with the seventh seal and the six trumpets (8:1—9:21) Complication between the two witnesses and the beast from the bottomless pit (10:1—11:13) Advent of Kingdom of God and Messiah with seventh trumpet (11:14-19) The appearance of resolution character, Son of Man, and the Dragon's attack against Jesus and woman (12:1-17) The saints' needs of endurance and faith and wisdom under the attacks of two beasts as resolution factors (13:1-18)

Structure and the Holy Spirit in Revelation

				Resolution accomplished on earth: Judgment and harvest by the Lamb and the 144,000 with witness and prophecy (14:1–20)	
				Resolution accomplished from heaven with the seven bowls of God's wrath (15:1—16:21)	
				The responses about judgment against the beast (Babylon/Great whore) and the false prophet (17:1—19:21)	
				The judgment against the Dragon (Satan/Ancient serpent) and those whose names were not found in the Lamb's book of life (20:1–15)	
				The advent of the New Jerusalem from heaven on earth (21:1—22:5)	
				The authentication of the book of Revelation (22:6-7)	
				The commands of the angel (22:8-11)	
				The sayings of Jesus Christ (22:12-16)	
				Final sayings and Epistolary postscript (22:17-21)	
				UL1	Title (1:1a)
					The process of Revelation (1:1b-2)
					The beatitude for the reader and those who hear and keep the prophecy (1:3)
					Sender and receiver of the letter and the sources of grace and peace: God, the Seven Spirits, and Jesus (1:4-6)
					The proclamation of Jesus' return and the identity of God Almighty: Alpha and Omega (1:7-8)
					Epiphany in the Spirit and the appearance of the glorified Jesus (1:9-16)
					Response to epiphany and self-identity of the glorified Jesus (1:17-20)
					Message to the church in Ephesus (2:1-7)
					Message to the church in Smyrna (2:8-11)
					Message to the church in Pergamum (2:12-17)
					Message to the church in Thyatira (2:18-29)
					Message to the church in Sardis (3:1-6)
					Message to the church in Philadelphia (3:7-13)

					Message to the church in Laodicea (3:14–22)
					Transporting into heavenly court in the Spirit (4:1–2)
					The description of the heavenly ones (4:3–7)
					The worship of the heavenly beings to God Almighty (4:8–11)
					Sealed Scroll and the Lion of the tribe of Judah (5:1–5)
					Heavenly liturgy for opening the seven seals (5:6–14)
					The first seal: Conquest (6:1–2)
					The second seal: Take peace from the earth (6:3–4)
					The third seal: A bad harvest (6:5–6)
					The fourth seal: A fourth of the earth killed (6:7–8)
					The fifth seal: Cry of the martyrs (6:9–11)
					The sixth seal: The great day (6:12–17)
					Sealing the servants of God (7:1–8)
					Praising God and the Lamb in heaven (7:9–17)
					The seventh seal and heavenly liturgy for seven trumpets (8:1–6)
					The first trumpet: A third of earth burned up (8:7)
					The second trumpet: A third of sea harmed (8:8–9)
					The third trumpet: A third of the waters turned bitter (8:7)
					The fourth trumpet: A third of the heavenly bodies turned dark (8:12)
					The fifth trumpet: Locusts from the abyss (8:13–9:12a)
					The sixth trumpet: Massacre of one third mankind and no repentance by the rest of mankind (9:12b–21)
					The seventh trumpet: Prophecy of the angel about the fulfillment of God's mystery, that is, "no more delay" (10:1–7)

					The prophet to be commanded to eat the scroll and to prophesy again as a witness (10:8–11)
					The authority of the two witnesses and the killing power of the beast from the bottomless pit over the two witnesses (11:1–10)
					The resurrection and ascension of the two witnesses and the repentance of the rest (11:11–13)
					Proclamation of the heavenly voices about the kingdom of Messiah (11:14–15)
					Proclamation of 24 elders about God's judgment and reward in the Kingdom of God (11:16–18)
					Temple opened and the ark of God's covenant seen (11:19)
					The ascension of Resolution character, Jesus under the Dragon's attack (12:1–6)
					The withdrawal of the Dragon and his angels through the war in heaven between them and Michael and his angels (12:7–12)
					God's protection for the woman and her descendents under the Dragon's attack (12:13–17)
					The saints' needs of endurance and faith under the attack of a beast from the sea (13:1–10)
					The saints' needs of wisdom under the attack of a beast from the earth (13:11–18)
					The Lamb and 144,000 as subjects of heavenly triumph (14:1–5)
					The endurance and faith, even to the death, needed in proclaiming gospel and the prophecy about the judgments against Babylon and the worshipper of the beast (14:6–13)
					One like the Son of Man resolves the complication with harvest and judgment (14:14–20)

					Worship song of Moses and the Lamb for God Almighty (15:1–4)
					Tent of witness in heaven opened as an origin of the seven bowls with God's wrath (15:5–8)
					The inauguration of the seven bowls of God's wrath poured on earth (16:1)
					The first bowl: against the worshippers of the beast with its mark on the earth (16:2)
					The second bowl: against the sea and its inhabitants (16:3)
					The third bowl: against the rivers and the springs of water; the blood of the saints and prophets as the reason why God's judgment against them is true and just (16:4–7)
					The fourth bowl: against the people with the fierce heat of sun; their curse against the name of God and their refusal to repent (16:8–9)
					The fifth bowl: against the beast's throne and people; their curse against the God of heaven and their refusal to repent (16:10–11)
					The sixth bowl: against the river Euphrates; the demonic spirits coming from the Dragon, the beast, and the false prophet assemble the kings at Harmagedon for battle on the great day of God the Almighty (16:12–16)
					The seventh bowl: against the air; the completion of God's wrath with the voice of the throne and temple, "it's done" with the greatest earthquake and fearful hailstone; the great city, Babylon is split and the cities of the nations and every island and mountains disappear (16:17–21)
					The proclamation of the judgment of the great whore and explanation why she is punished (17:1–6)

					John's amazement both about woman and the inhabitants of the earth and about the beast with 7 heads and 10 horns (17:7–8)
					The defeat in war of the beast and the 7 heads as 7 kings and the 10 horns as 10 kings by the Lamb and His followers (17:9–14)
					The destruction of the whore by the beast and 10 horns with the intervention of God into their hearts (17:15–18)
					The announcement of the fall of Babylon and the reasons for it are given to the people of God so they will not make the same mistakes (18:1–8)
					The response of kings and merchants and shipmasters, seafarers, sailors, sea traders about the fall of Babylon (18:9–19)
					The judgment for the saints and apostles and prophets against Babylon, the whore because of their blood (18:20–24)
					The righteousness and eternity of the judgment of God (19:1–3)
					Heavenly worship to God for the marriage of the Lamb with the saints who hold the testimony of Jesus and the righteous deeds (19:4–10)
					The portrayal of the rider on a white horse as "Faithful and True," "The Word of God," "King of kings and Lord of lords" (19:11–16)
					The defeat in war and judgment of the beast and the false prophet into the lake of fire by the rider on the white horse and his army (19:17–21)
					The Dragon captured and sealed for a thousand years (20:1–3)
					The priests of God and Christ reign with Christ for a thousand years as the first resurrection group (20:4–6)

					The defeat in war and judgment of the Dragon into the lake of fire by heavenly fire (20:7–10)
					The judgment of those whose names were not found in the Lamb's book of life into the lake of fire and the rewards for the saints according to their works (20:11–15)
					The qualification to be the members of the New Jerusalem as new creation: Those who conquer (21:1–8)
					The New Jerusalem's glory and wall with 12 gates (the names of 12 tribes of Israelites) and 12 foundations (the names of 12 apostles of the Lamb) (21:9–14)
					The length and width and height of the New Jerusalem and its wall, the materials of the New Jerusalem (gold) and its wall (jasper) and foundations (12 jewels), gates (12 single pearls) (21:15–21)
					God and the Lamb as the temple and light of the New Jerusalem and the openness of the New Jerusalem to the nations and kings and people and the qualification to enter the New Jerusalem: Those written in the Lamb's book of life (21:22–27)
					The river and tree of life with its fruits and leaves and the life of the servants of the Lamb in the New Jerusalem (22:1–5)
					The trustworthiness of Revelation of Jesus Christ (22:6)
					The beatitude for those who keep the prophecy (22:7)
					Worship only God (22:8–9)
					Do not seal the prophecy (22:10)
					Choose righteousness or evil (22:11)
					Coming soon with His reward according to one's work (22:12)

Structure and the Holy Spirit in Revelation

					The identity of the one coming: Alpha and Omega, the first and the last, the beginning and the end (22:13)
					Blessing to those who wash their robes and warning to those who are outside of the New Jerusalem (22:14–15)
					Further identity of Jesus as a sender of Revelation: the root and the descendant of David, and the bright morning star (22:16)
					Calling of the Spirit and the bride for everyone to come (22:17)
					Finalization of the text of Revelation and warning against changing the prophecy of the book (22:18–19)
					Another Jesus' proclamation of coming again and the plea for His return (22:20)
					Concluding with benediction (22:21)

Given this narrative-syntactic structure of Revelation, how can the characterization of the Divine Spirit be drawn out? In the following section, I shall attempt to discover it along with the narrative-syntactic structure of Revelation.

CHARACTERIZATION OF THE DIVINE SPIRIT ACCORDING TO THE NARRATIVE-SYNTACTIC STRUCTURE OF REVELATION

The characterization of the Divine Spirit in UL4 will be discussed here since the characterization of the Divine Spirit in UL3 has already been explored along with the plot of Revelation in chapter 4.

Firstly, the Divine Spirit works both in heaven and on earth. In Rev 1:4, the Divine Spirit is portrayed as the Seven Spirits before God's throne. In 22:17, the Divine Spirit with the bride invites nonbelievers on earth, that is, the people of God, to come. The pattern is that the Divine Spirit is portrayed to work firstly in the heavenly realm and finally in the earthly realm.[49]

---

49. Even though John is "in the Spirit" in 1:10 and the Spirit speaks to the Churches in chapters 2–3, they belong to the body part, not the introduction part.

Secondly, the Divine Spirit is mainly mentioned in the body of UL4, whereas the Divine Spirit appears only once each in the introduction and conclusion.

Thirdly, the Divine Spirit works for the church community in the body part of UL4. In chapters 2–3, the Divine Spirit mediates the words of Jesus to the seven churches, challenging them to transform. In chapters 4–5, the Divine Spirit is sent from the heavenly throne to all the earth to witness to the work of the Lamb. In chapters 6–16, the Divine Spirit is involved in the messianic war in which the saints or the two witnesses are killed in 11:11 and 14:13. The Divine Spirit affirms that the dead in the Lord are blessed because they will rest from their labors (14:13). The Divine Spirit also raises the dead in 11:11. In 17:1—22:5, the Divine Spirit shows John how Babylon will be destroyed and also how the New Jerusalem will be established. The Divine Spirit witnesses both to the judgment of the saints' enemies (including the Dragon) and to the establishment of the New Jerusalem as the Lamb's bride and dwelling-place of God's people on earth.

Thus, the Divine Spirit is depicted as the heavenly one who is sent to witnesses to the Lamb of God on the earth, working with the earthly churches in the messianic war by inspiring and reviving them to bring the New Jerusalem to the earth.

Fundamental-Syntactic Structure of Revelation (Actantial Model) and the Characterization of the Divine Spirit

Fundamental-syntactic structure of Revelation (actantial model)

As mentioned above, Jang proposes the single fundamental-syntactic structure of Revelation by applying an actantial model to the whole narrative as follows[50]:

---

50. Jang, "Narratological Approach," 158.

Structure and the Holy Spirit in Revelation

Diagram 5.2 The Actant Model with Three Axes of Communication

Power, and Volition*

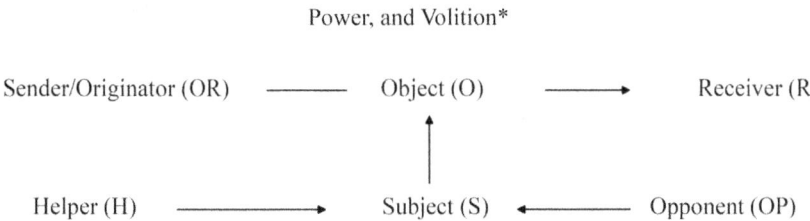

* Actant model is composed of the actants, object, and three axes. Axis of communication represents that sender or originator provides the object to the receiver with one way. Axis of power, however, represents that helpers and the subject confront the opposition of the opponents with two contradicting ways. Axis of volition represents that the subject has the volition to accomplish the object even in the conflict situation.

Diagram 5.3 Jang's Actant Model applied to Revelation

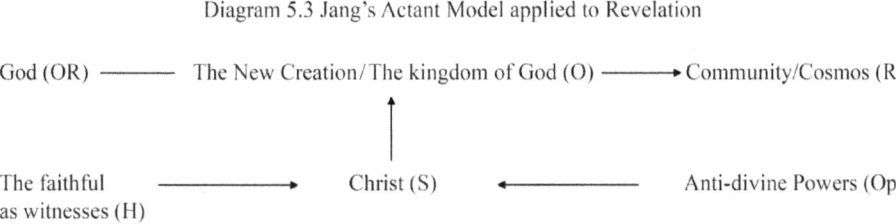

Jang asserts that "the deep structure for the whole narrative can be expressed by one actantial model."[51] However, I think that the fundamental-syntactic structure of Revelation is better analyzed by using more than one actantial model. Moreover, the actants in the whole narrative could easily be changed to reveal another fundamental-syntactic structure of Revelation.

THE WHOLE FUNDAMENTAL-SYNTACTIC STRUCTURE OF REVELATION

Firstly, the Divine Spirit needs to be added as an actant. Further, the community/cosmos as a receiver needs to be changed to the community on earth since the New Jerusalem will be established on earth, not in the cosmos or in heaven.

51. Jang, "Narratological Approach," 159.

A Dynamic Reading of the Holy Spirit in Revelation

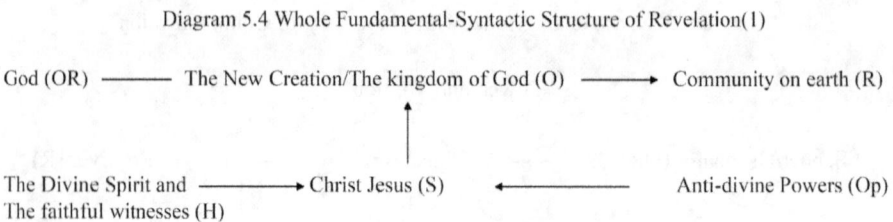

Diagram 5.4 Whole Fundamental-Syntactic Structure of Revelation(1)

Secondly, the Divine Spirit is a subject sent by God and works together with Jesus Christ. The following actantial model can be presented:

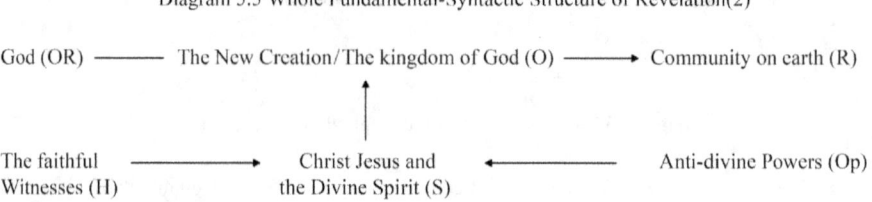

Diagram 5.5 Whole Fundamental-Syntactic Structure of Revelation(2)

The Partial Fundamental-Syntactic Structure of Revelation

As Stibbe suggests, "The actantial model works very well in the context of smaller and simpler narrative units."[52] Thus it is worth identifying a partial fundamental-syntactic structure within Revelation. I shall seek the partial fundamental-syntactic structure of unit level three which represents the whole plot of Revelation. This attempt can help us discern how this partial fundamental-syntactic structure conforms to, or differs from, the whole fundamental-syntactic structure of Revelation.

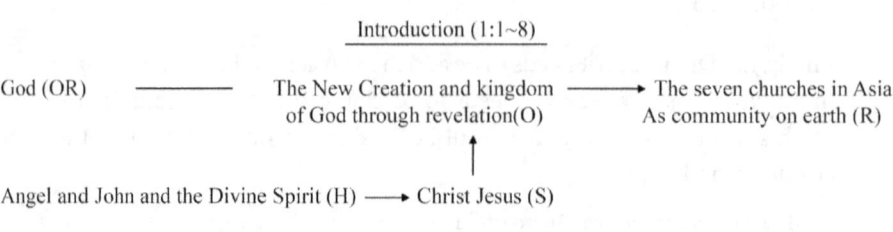

Diagram 5.6 Partial Fundamental-Syntactic Structure

---

52. Stibbe, *John as Storyteller*, 45.

Structure and the Holy Spirit in Revelation

Diagram 5.7 Partial Fundamental-Syntactic Structure

Setting (1:9~4:11)

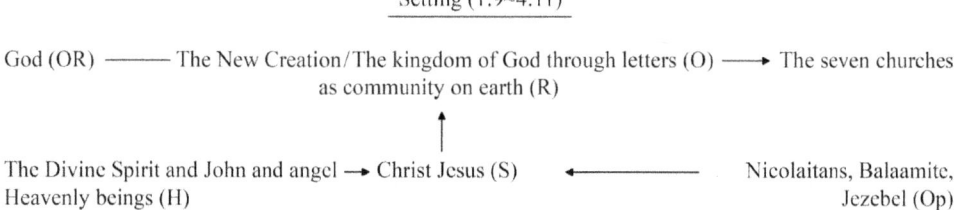

Diagram 5.8 Partial Fundamental-Syntactic Structure

Complication (5:1~11:19)

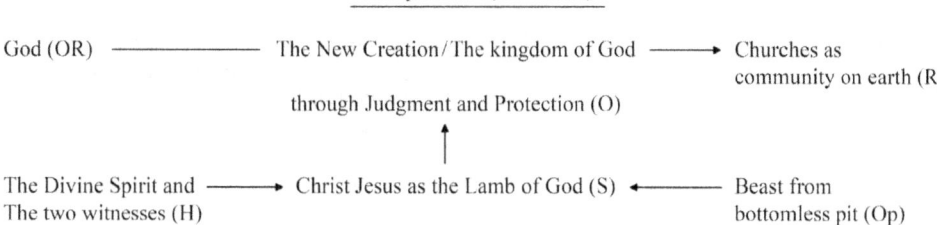

Diagram 5.9 Partial Fundamental-Syntactic Structure

Resolution (12:1~16:21)

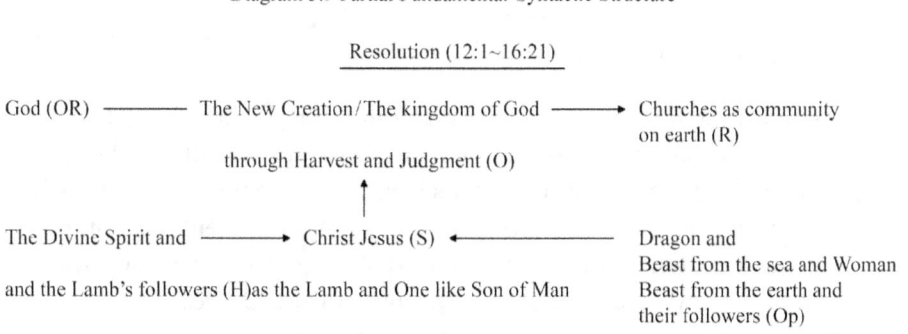

A Dynamic Reading of the Holy Spirit in Revelation

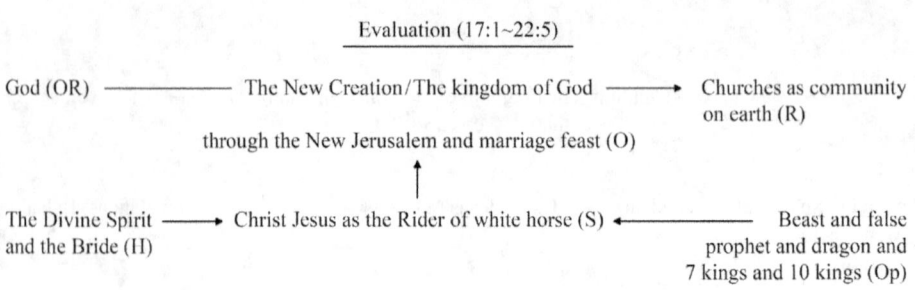

Diagram 5.10 Partial Fundamental-Syntactic Structure Evaluation (17:1~22:5)

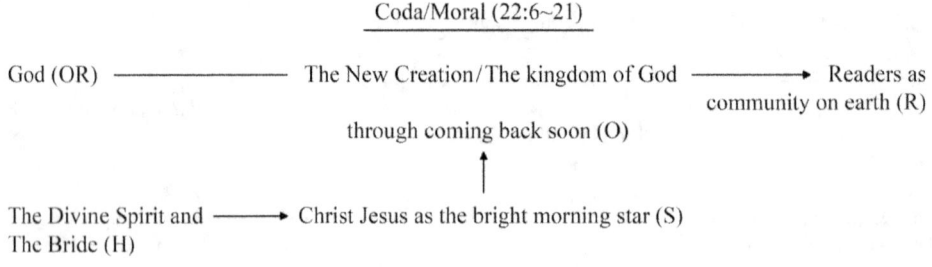

Diagram 5.11 Partial Fundamental-Syntactic Structure Coda/Moral (22:6~21)

Characteristics of Fundamental-Syntactic Structure of Revelation

As shown above, some characteristics can be explored. Firstly, there seems to be only a little difference between the fundamental-syntactic structure and the partial fundamental-syntactic structure. God acts as the sender throughout the narrative. Jesus similarly is a central agent in the whole narrative. The object of the whole narrative is the inauguration of the new creation and the kingdom of God. The receiver is the community on earth. Secondly, nevertheless, there are some differences among the actants in the fundamental-syntactic structure. Some changes can be identified with the opponents. As shown above, the introduction and the coda/moral have no opponents. Helpers are varied with the angel and John; John, the angel and heavenly beings; the two witnesses; the

Structure and the Holy Spirit in Revelation

woman and the Lamb's followers; and the bride of the Lamb. Opponents also change, with Nicolaitans, Satan, the Balaamites, Jezebel; the beast from the bottomless pit; the Dragon and the beast from the sea, and the beast from the earth and their followers; and the beast and 7 kings and 10 kings, and the false prophet and the Dragon. Thirdly, the Divine Spirit is throughout a helper even though there are other helpers. Thus, the partial fundamental-syntactic structure is varied with differing actants at different stages of the plot. However, the whole fundamental-syntactic structure of Revelation is consistently related to the partial fundamental-syntactic structure—with some variations. It should be noted that the opponent does not appear either in the introduction or the coda/moral. The opponents cannot play the main role in the Revelation narrative. The narrative originally is stable without any threat from the opponents. However, the appearance of opponents destabilizes the narrative. Finally after all conflicts have been solved, the unstable state will return to stability.

Characterization of the Divine Spirit according to fundamental-syntactic structure of Revelation (actantial model)

The key point in the fundamental-syntactic structure of Revelation is that the Divine Spirit plays a consistent role in every plot stage. Thus we can characterize the Divine Spirit according to the fundamental-syntactic structure. Firstly, the Divine Spirit is a helper who supports the subject, Jesus Christ, in establishing the kingdom of God on earth as in heaven. Secondly, sometimes the Divine Spirit is not only a helper, but also a co-worker of the subject, Jesus Christ. The Divine Spirit is sent to the earth to mediate the word of Jesus to the seven churches. Thirdly, the Divine Spirit is not only one of the actants, but also an omnipresent divine worker. The Divine Spirit is not limited to this role. The Divine Spirit explicitly works with every actant except the opponents. The Divine Spirit is before the throne of God and is sent to earth. The Divine Spirit speaks to the seven churches in Asia. The Divine Spirit helps and works with other helpers such as John, the angel, the heavenly beings, the two witnesses, and the followers of the Lamb. The Divine Spirit also focuses on establishing the kingdom of God on earth as in heaven with other actants such as God, Jesus Christ, the prophet John, angels, heavenly beings, the two witnesses, and the followers of the Lamb of God. We can suppose that the

Divine Spirit implicitly works against opponents such as the Dragon, the beasts, and their followers. Thus, the object of the narrative to establish the kingdom of God is consistently advanced by the Divine Spirit. However, nowhere does the Divine Spirit explicitly fight the opponents.

The Divine Spirit can also be characterized as using three axes in the actantial model: the communication axis, the volition axis, and the power axis. Along the communication axis, the Divine Spirit communicates with both God and the community on earth and takes a role as a communicator of the will of the sender, God, to the receiver, the community on earth, that is, the seven churches in Asia. In the communication axis, the Divine Spirit communicates the object of the narrative, that is, the kingdom of God and the new creation, to the earthly community. Along the volitional axis, the Divine Spirit desires to bring the kingdom of God to earth with Jesus. The Divine Spirit seeks those who keep the word of prophecy and follow the Lamb for the kingdom of God for the new creation will be experienced in them. The Divine Spirit desires to keep God's people on earth blameless and pure. That is why the Divine Spirit invites people to join the messianic feast. Finally, along the power axis, the Divine Spirit reinforces the people of God by giving them faith, endurance, and wisdom by which they conquer the anti-divine powers. Thus, the Divine Spirit is throughout a supporter or helper in the messianic war.

In short, the Divine Spirit can be called to play a role as a ubiquitous networking coordinator in the whole cosmos in terms of fundamental-semantic structure.

Narrative-Semantic Structure (Chiastic Structure) of Revelation and the Characterization of the Divine Spirit

CHIASTIC STRUCTURE AS A NARRATIVE-SEMANTIC STRUCTURE

The concentric structure can be accepted as a narrative-semantic structure of Revelation since the Jewish apocalyptic literature usually has a chiastic structure. Jang suggests that the narrative-semantic structure of Revelation is a chiastic structure superimposed upon the forward-moving plot.[53]

---

53. Jang, "Narratological Approach," 162–64. Jang seems to be the first Revelation scholar who connects the chiastic structure to the narrative-semantic structure of Revelation. Actually, Jang proposes not only a concentric structure, but also a

A Introduction (1:1-8)
  B Setting (1:9—4:11)
    C Complication (5:1—11:19)
    C' Resolution (12:1—16:21)
  B' Evaluation (17:1—22:5)
A' Conclusion (22:6-21)

Other Proposed Chiastic (Concentric) Structures

Since Fiorenza proposed a sevenfold chiastic structure, Revelation scholars have offered many kinds of concentric structures.[54] Two of the most plausible are as follows.

G. K. Beale

In Beale's, *The Book of Revelation*, he proposes a chiastic structure but not in the context of offering a semantic narrative analysis.[55] Thus:

A Prologue: imminence of the faithful witness's coming, with covenant sanctions (1:1–8)
  B Vision: imperfect church in the world promised salvation for perseverance (1:9—3:21)
    C Seven Seals: already and not-yet judgments on the world (4:1—8:1)
    Prelude: the conquering lamb-lion on heaven's throne (4:1—5:14)
    Vision: opening of the book, judgments initiated by the conquering
    horsemen and completed directly (6:1–17; 8:1)

---

macronarrative as the narrative-semantic structure of Revelation. However, I do not consider it valid since macronarrative structure looks to the macrostructure as a fundamental semantic structure.

54. Fiorenza, *Book of Revelation*, 159-80.

A 1:1-8 Prologue and Epistolary greeting
  B 1:9—3:22 Rhetorical situation in the cities of Asia
    C 4:1—9:21; 11:15-19 Opening the sealed scroll: Exodus plagues
      D 10:1—15:4 The bitter-sweet scroll: War against the community
    C' 15:1, 5—19:10 Exodus from the oppression of Babylon/Rome
  B' 19:11—22:9 Liberation from evil and God's world-city
A' 22:10-21 Epilogue and Epistolary frame

55. Beale, *Book of Revelation*, 130-31.

Interlude: saints protected, receiving final salvation from the lamb, clothed in white (ch. 7)

D Seven Trumpets: judgment on the ungodly world and the great city (8:2—11:18)
Prelude: heavenly commissioning of seven angels (8:2–6)
Vision: sounding of the trumpets of judgment (8:7—9:21; 11:14–18)
Interlude: witnessing church versus persecuting world (10:1—11:13)

E War of the Ages (11:19—14:20)
Prelude: ark of the covenant in heaven (11:19)
Vision: Dragon and beasts versus the heavenly woman, her child, and the saints (12:1—13:18)
Interlude: covenant sanctions involving judgment, though blessing is included (ch. 14)

D' Seven Bowls: judgments on the world and the great city (15:1—19:10)
Prelude: heavenly commissioning of seven angels (ch. 15)
Vision: bowls of judgment poured out (ch. 16)
Interlude: the world as an ungodly prostitute versus the church as a faithful bride (17:1—19:10)

C' The world's final judgment portrayed from various perspectives (19:11—21:8)
Prelude: the conquering Messiah and his army (19:11–16)
Vision: the messianic horseman judges the ungodly horsemen led by the false prophet, the judgment of Satan and his hordes, the opening of books for judgment (19:17—20:15)
Interlude: the lamb's bride adorned for her divine husband (21:1–8)

B' Vision: the perfect church in glory having received the promised salvation (21:9—22:5)

A' Epilogue: the imminence of Christ's coming attested by the faithful witness (22:6-21)

M. V. Lee

Lee proposed a chiastic structure in her article, "A Call to Martyrdom: Function as Method and Message in Revelation."[56] Like Beale, she does not use the concept of a narrative-semantic structure.

---

56. Michelle V. Lee, "Call to Martyrdom," 164–94.

A 1:1–20 Prologue
  B 2:1—3:22 Present situation
    C 4:1—5:14 The fundamental paradigm
      D 6:1–17 Judgment and defeat of God's enemies (first pair)
        E 7:1–17 The faithful believers
          F 8:1—10:11 Judgment and defeat of God's enemies (second pair)
            G 11:1–19 The false power of the beast
              H 12:1–6 Two women
                I 12:7–18 Judgment and defeat of God's enemies (third pair)
                  J 13:1–18 Moment of Decision
                    J' 14:1–20 Moment of Decision
                I' 15:1—16:21 Judgment and defeat of God's enemies (third pair)
              H' 17:1–6 Two women
            G' 17:7–18 The false power of the beast
          F' 18:1–24 Judgment and defeat of God's enemies (second pair)
        E' 19:1–10 The faithful believers
      D' 19:11–21 Judgment and defeat of God's enemies (first pair)
    C' 20:1–10 The fundamental paradigm
  B' 20:11—22:5 Future situation
A' 22:6–21 Epilogue

EVALUATION OF THE CHIASTIC STRUCTURES OF REVELATION

CRITERIA FOR EVALUATING THE CHIASTIC STRUCTURE

Robert W. Klund introduces Blomberg's nine criteria to evaluate the chiastic structure in his doctoral thesis, "The Plot of Rev 4–22." Suggesting that "it is important to have some type of method for the evaluation of any chiastic structure," Klund appeals to Blomberg's nine criteria for this purpose.[57] To help us evaluate some chiastic structures, let us look at Blomberg's nine criteria[58]:

1. Conventional outlines fail to resolve the structure of the text in question.

---

57. Klund, "Plot of Revelation 4–22," 51.
58. Blomberg, "Structure of 2 Corinthians," 4–7.

2. Most readers observe the clear parallelism irrespective of their overall synthesis.

3. Verbal (or grammatical) parallelism as well as conceptual (or structural) parallelism should characterize most if not all of the corresponding pairs of subdivisions.

4. The verbal parallelism should involve central or dominant imagery or terminology, not peripheral or trivial language.

5. Both verbal and conceptual parallelism should involve words and ideas not regularly found elsewhere within the proposed chiasmus.

6. Multiple sets of correspondences between passages opposite each other in the chiasmus as well as multiple members of the chiasmus itself are desirable.

7. The outline should divide the text at natural breaks which would be agreed upon even by those proposing very different structures to account for the whole.

8. The center of the chiasmus, which forms its climax, should be a passage worthy of that position in light of its theological or ethical significance. If its theme were in some way repeated in the first and last passages, the proposal would become that much more plausible.

9. Ruptures in the outline should be avoided if at all possible.

I adopt Blomberg's nine criteria since they seem to be comprehensive in evaluating the chiastic structures.

Evaluation of Each Chiastic Structure of Revelation

I shall apply Blomberg's stringent criteria to each suggested chiastic structure, noting Klund's comment that "the more any proposed chiastic structure fails to meet the various criteria, the more suspicion is cast on its legitimacy."[59] Then I shall offer my own evaluation.

---

59. Klund, "Plot of Revelation 4–22," 52.

A. Jang's Model

Jang analyzes the chiastic structure of Revelation in terms of its narrative-semantic structure. However, some weaknesses emerge. Firstly, he does not differentiate between the semantic structure and the syntactic structure since he uses the narrative-syntactic structure of Revelation to describe its narrative-semantic structure. Jang seems to confuse the plot and the chiastic structure.[60] Thus, the chiastic structure needs to be distinguished from the plot of Revelation. Otherwise, numbers 3 and 9 of Blomberg's criteria are transgressed.[61]

Secondly, the parallel between C (5:1—11:19) and C' (12:1—16:21) is not a contrast, but just a part of plot: complication and resolution. It does not show clear parallels and correspondence between the two, even though both describe the judgment of God with the seven seals, trumpets, and bowls. This violates numbers 2 and 6 of Blomberg's criteria.

Thirdly, a core content cannot be identified by the parallel ABCC'B'A'. CC' is too broad to be a climax. This violates number 8 of Blomberg's criteria.

Thus, it seems to be hard to accept Jang's model as the chiastic structure of Revelation since it violates numbers 2, 3, 6, 8, and 9 of Blomberg's criteria. These violations mean it is not a sound chiastic structure of Revelation.

---

60. As the definition is discussed in chapter 3, the plot is the narrative orderly flow with causality to impact the readers, whereas the chiastic structure finds the symmetric corresponding part from the central or climatic part of the structure.

61. Jang's chiastic model loses any parallels since he adopts the plot as a chiastic structure. That is why his model violates numbers 3 and 9 of Blomberg's nine criteria.

B. Beale's Model

Beale criticizes Snyder's concentric structure,[62] offering his own concentric model—which has some valid features.[63] Firstly, AA', the imminence of Christ's Parousia, and BB', the imperfect and perfect church, illuminate valid parallels in the chiastic structure. Secondly, he is creative in identifying the same structure of three elements, that is, prelude, vision, and interlude in each of CDED'C'. Thirdly, he identifies that the main theme in the chiastic structure of Revelation is the war of the ages. In this he broadly agrees with the chiastic analyses of Fiorenza, Snyder, Jang, and Beale, but not Michelle Lee in identifying this war as the climax of Revelation.

However, there are weaknesses in his model. Fundamentally, it seems too artificial to make three elements a parallelism. To make a pair in the prelude of CC', Beale omits the essential part, that is, the one who sits on the heavenly throne in 4:1—5:14. He also omits the fifth seal and the sixth seal to make an artificial pair in the vision of CC'. Additionally, he tries to make a pair in the prelude of DD' by including the peripheral issue of the heavenly commissioning of angels and by omitting the more essential issue of prayer in 8:2–6. Furthermore he omits the more important heavenly vision of the heavenly worship for the same reason—by

---

62. Snyder, "Combat Myth," 159–207. She proposes her own concentric structure of Revelation as follows:

   A Introduction: apocalypse, epistle, prophecy (1:1–3, 4–8, 9–20)
     B Vision: the saints on earth (ch. 2–3)
        C The Heavenly Sanhedrin Convened for Judgment and Enthronement (ch. 4–5)
           D Seven Seals (6:1—8:1)
              E Seven Trumpets (8:2—9:21)
                 F Theophany: the Lord's messenger descending to sea and land (ch. 10)
                    G War against the Saints on Earth (ch. 11)
                    G' War against the Dragon in Heaven (ch. 12)
                 F' Counter-Theophany: Yamm(Sea)'s two messengers ascending from sea and land (ch. 13)
              E' Unnumbered Series of Seven Proclamations (ch. 14)
           D' Seven Bowls (ch. 15–16)
        C' The Heavenly Sanhedrin Convened for Judgment and the Messianic Reign (ch. 17–20; cf. 20:4–15)
     B' Vision: the saints in heaven (21:1—22:5)
   A' Conclusion: apocalypse, epistle, prophecy (22:6–9, 10–20, 21)

63. Beale, *Book of Revelation*, 108–51.

Structure and the Holy Spirit in Revelation

trying to make a pair in the prelude of DD'—in chapter 15. This violates numbers 3, 4, and 7 of Blomberg's criteria. Thus, it is hard to accept Beale's model as a sound chiastic structure of Revelation.

C. M. Lee's Model

Klund commends Michelle Lee's chiastic structure based on three points. He asserts, "Michelle Lee structures the entire book through a chiasmus understanding of Revelation to combine method and message as the essential part of its function which is for the readers to respond to the call for the endurance and faith of the saints. There is much to commend in this chiastic structure, as Lee notes cohesion within most sections through inclusions and keyword repetitions. She also makes lexical connections between the proposed parallel sections."[64] However, Klund criticizes and rejects her model for two reasons. Firstly, "The central foci (J, J') neither forms the climax to the book, nor are they central to the message and thus violates Blomberg's criterion 8."[65] Secondly, "The third pair of judgment and defeat of God's enemies (I, I') are not truly parallel.... Also there is not connection with the song of Moses contained in the second section with anything in the first section. This aspect violates Blomberg's criteria 2 and 3."[66]

I suggest there are more weaknesses in her model. The "fundamental paradigm" of CC' does not represent its content. The "two women" of HH' does not match the content of its parts. Actually both parts describe only one woman, not two women, which violates numbers 3 and 4 of Blomberg's criteria. Thus, her model is not a useful chiastic structure of Revelation.

NEWLY PROPOSED CHIASTIC STRUCTURE OF REVELATION AS A NARRATIVE-SEMANTIC STRUCTURE OF REVELATION

Blomberg admits that his criteria "might be too rigid since even well-established chiastic structures seldom meet all the criteria" so that the perfect chiastic structure of Revelation will not be found.[67] However, I

---

64. Klund, "Plot of Revelation 4–22," 52.
65. Ibid.
66. Ibid., 54.
67. Blomberg, "Structure of 2 Corinthians," 7.

dare to propose the following narrative-semantic structure of Revelation while using Blomberg's criteria to help analyze other models.

> A 1:1–8 Introduction: apocalypse, epistle, prophecy, the imminence of the coming of Jesus
>   B 1:9—3:22 The bride of Christ on earth: the seven churches
>   C 4:1—5:14 God and the Lamb in heaven as the source of victory and judgment in heaven
>   D 6:1—11:19 The judgment over the earth with the opportunity of repentance through the witnessing protected churches
>   E 12:1—15:4 Spiritual warfare on earth between the messianic armies and the evil powers
>   D' 15:5—16:21 The last judgment over the evil ones without the opportunity of repentance
>   C' 17:1—20:15 God and the Lamb as the source of victory and judgment on earth
>   B' 21:1—22:5 The bride of Christ from heaven: the New Jerusalem
> A' 22:6–21 Conclusion: apocalypse, epistle, prophecy, the imminence of the coming of Jesus

This model seems to meet almost all of Blomberg's criteria. The conventional chiastic structure of Revelation may be resolved. Verbal and conceptual parallelism is clear with the unique ideas. Central or dominant images or terminologies are employed. Opposite sets of correspondence are used. The text is divided at natural breaks. The center of the chiasmus, E, represents the theological significance of the messianic war and feast, which can be considered as the main theme. Every effort has been made to avoid ruptures in the outline.[68]

Characteristics of the Newly Proposed Chiastic Structure of Revelation

What are the characteristics of the new model? Firstly, it is not so complicated and artificial, but simple and natural in identifying the flow of the narrative. Secondly, AA' represents the various genres of Revelation while emphasizing Jesus' Parousia. These two facts become keystones for interpreting the whole narrative tower of Revelation. BB' represents the church of the bride of Christ as another steppingstone for the narrative tower. With the imminence of the Parousia, BB' explores how the earthly

---

68. See number 9 of Blomberg's criteria.

church should be changed into the New Jerusalem that comes down from heaven. BB' emphasizes the significance of the church's role in the whole the narrative. CC' represents the sovereignty of God and the Lion-Lamb in the judgments. They are not only the source of the judgment over the evil powers and their followers, but also the executioners of these judgments. DD' represents the judgments, salvation history, and the participation of the church in salvation by means of the witnesses who make people repent. However, there is no chance for a deferred repentance at the last judgment. E represents the climax or core of the narrative.

This newly proposed chiastic structure of Revelation thus emphasizes the messianic war on earth. In this messianic war, the Messiah, the Warrior, shows his authority to conquer all opposition. Further, Revelation focuses on the participation of the saints as his messianic armies who follow the Warrior, the Messiah. However, in reaching this final triumph, the saints, just like their Master, are sometimes allowed to be defeated or killed by evil powers (13:7). That is why endurance and faith are called for in the saints in E (13:10; 14:12) after which "they will rest from their labors" (14:13b). The messianic war itself relates both to salvation and the judgment (14:14–20).

Summary: Significance of the Narrative-Semantic Structure of Revelation

From the narrative-semantic structure of Revelation, the following points can be made. Firstly, the core theme of the narrative is the messianic war on earth. Endurance and faith are needed. Wise discernment is called for to recognize the works of Satan, the beast, and the false prophet. Secondly, the saints' role in the messianic war is to testify to Jesus with His words so that all people groups are converted. The duration of this mission, though, will be interrupted by the last judgment. Thirdly, the will of God and the Lamb is not only to punish the evil powers, but also to prepare the earthly church as a bride from heaven. Fourthly, the saints in the earthly church need to live in expectation of Jesus' coming. This expectation leads them to the eschatological lifestyles in the here and now.

A Dynamic Reading of the Holy Spirit in Revelation

Characterization of the Divine Spirit according to the Narrative-Semantic Structure

According to the newly proposed chiastic analysis of Revelation, the Divine Spirit can thus be characterized:

1. The characterization of the Divine Spirit in the plane of AA'

In this plane of AA', the Divine Spirit appears explicitly twice, in 1:4 and 22:17. The first is before the heavenly throne, the other is on earth. The first instance gives grace and peace to the earthly churches, as the Divine Spirit cooperates with God and Jesus. In the second instance, the Divine Spirit works together with the bride to invite people to drink the water of life, and announces this with the bride, that is, the church. In other words, the Divine Spirit is involved not only in the churches' spiritual growth, but also in its mission to nonbelievers. Thus, the Divine Spirit works not only in heaven, but also on earth.

2. The characterization of the Divine Spirit in the plane of BB'

In the plane of BB', the Divine Spirit appears explicitly nine times. Twice, the Divine Spirit appears in the phrase "in the Spirit," in 1:10 and 21:10. Seven times, the Divine Spirit appears in the phrase "what the Spirit is saying to the churches," in 2:7, 11, 17, 29; 3:6, 13, 22. The two usages of the phrase "in the Spirit" are concerned with John himself. The seven usages of "what the Spirit is saying to the churches" are concerned with the seven earthly churches. In other words, the Divine Spirit in BB' works not only for individual people, but also for the church communities. The Divine Spirit in BB' also inspires the personal saint or the prophet, John, so that he sees the vision and hears the heavenly voice. While in the Spirit, in 1:10 John is inspired to see and hear the glorified Jesus. In 21:10, John is inspired to see "the holy city Jerusalem coming down out of heaven from God." The Divine Spirit in BB' also speaks to the churches with the words of Jesus. In chapters 2 and 3, the Divine Spirit mediates the words of the risen Jesus to the churches.

3. The characterization of the Divine Spirit in the plane of CC'

In the plane of CC', the Divine Spirit appears explicitly four times. Twice the Divine Spirit appears in the phrase "in the Spirit" (4:2; 17:3). On the other two occasions the Divine Spirit appears as "the Seven Spirits of

Structure and the Holy Spirit in Revelation

God" in 5:6 and "the Spirit of prophecy" in 19:10. The Divine Spirit inspires John to enter God's throne room in 4:2 and to move to a wilderness in 17:3. The Seven Spirits of God in 5:6 are depicted as the "seven horns and seven eyes" sent out into all the earth, indicating the Divine Spirit's universal terrestrial work. The Divine Spirit also witnesses to Jesus as "the Spirit of prophecy." Thus, the Divine Spirit in the plane of CC' is characterized as coming from heaven to witness to Jesus powerfully and to observe all deeds on earth. In other words, the Divine Spirit is portrayed as responsible for the church's worldwide mission.

4. The characterization of the Divine Spirit in the plane of DD'

In the plane of DD', the Divine Spirit appears just once, in 11:11. The Divine Spirit resurrects the two dead witnesses, which represent the persecuted church communities. The Divine Spirit also leads nonbelievers to repent and glorify God. In other words, the Divine Spirit reverses the saints' condition from death to life. The Divine Spirit not only inspires and strengthens the persecuted churches, but directs the mission to nonbelievers. Notably, the narrator does not associate the Divine Spirit with the last judgment in D' (15:5—16:21).

5. The characterization of the Divine Spirit in the plane of E

In the plane of E, the Divine Spirit appears just once in 14:13. The Divine Spirit talks with a voice from heaven. The Divine Spirit also knows that the martyred saints will rest and be blessed on the other side of death. The Divine Spirit also knows that the saints will be rewarded according to their deeds. In other words, the Divine Spirit encourages the saints with eschatological hope so that they willingly participate in the messianic war.

Fundamental-Semantic Structure (Macrostructure) of Revelation: The Functional Role of the Divine Spirit in the Messianic War and Feast[69]

The fundamental-semantic structure explores the main theme of the narrative. In our study, we have examined the centrality of the messianic

---

69. The messianic war has been a more common theme rather than the messianic feast. However, I insist that both need to be considered since they are presented

war and feast theme in the Revelation narrative.[70] If it is indeed the main theme, what is the functional role of the Divine Spirit in the messianic war and feast? We shall explore this topic in the narrative of Revelation.

The Divine Spirit, together with God and Jesus, is the subject of the messianic war and feast in Revelation. The blessings shall be given to the messianic armies by the Divine Spirit in Rev 1:4. However, the narrator seems reluctant to describe the Divine Spirit as pronouncing judgment against the evil ones. The Divine Spirit functions as the Spirit of prophecy to guide John's visions and his heavenly journey, and to inspire him to write Revelation itself. In other words, the Divine Spirit equips John as a prophetic soldier. Further, the Spirit is depicted as a Commander in the messianic war who communicates to the seven churches. The Divine Spirit works with the Messianic Warrior Jesus in directing the churches how to conquer. The Divine Spirit is also described as an Executer of God's power on earth. The Divine Spirit is characterized as a Warrior sent from the heavenly throne to intervene in the earthly churches, that is, the messianic armies. The Divine Spirit supports the messianic armies of the two witnesses who testify to the prophecy of the word of God for all peoples and rulers. The Divine Spirit empowers the two witnesses with power and authority in their ministry, just as Moses and Elijah were empowered in their ministries. When the two witnesses are killed by the beast, the Divine Spirit resurrects them on earth. The Divine Spirit thus plays a crucial role in turning the messianic war from defeat to victory. The resurrection of the two witnesses terrifies the world's people so that they glorify God. The Divine Spirit proclaims that even being killed will not defeat the messianic armies since they will rest and be rewarded for their deeds on earth. The Divine Spirit shows John the future end of the messianic war, that is, the destruction of Babylon and the coming of the New Jerusalem. The Divine Spirit is the Divine Witness to Jesus who supports the servants who keep the testimony of Jesus. The Divine Spirit is the Divine Mission Warrior who works with the saints on earth and invites all people to drink the water of life. The Divine Spirit plays

---

through the narrative. The latter is supported by the words and the episodes in Revelation: "conquer" (ch. 2 and 3), heavenly throne and the Lamb (ch. 4 and 5), the victorious followers of the Lamb (ch. 7 and 14), triumphal ministry of the two witnesses (ch. 11), the victory of the Lamb (ch. 15 and 19), and the ultimate triumph in New Jerusalem (ch. 21 and 22). The Divine Spirit works not only in the messianic war, but also for the messianic feast.

70. This chiastic structure of Revelation explores the theme of the messianic war and feast as a main theme of the Revelation narrative.

a significant role in bringing the kingdom of God from heaven to earth and the realization of the New Jerusalem on earth. Thus, the Divine Spirit guides the churches' mission and ministries on earth.

Thus, the Divine Spirit is an enigmatic character in Revelation. The Divine Spirit seems to be the omni-competent, omnipotent, and omniscient God the Warrior among the heavenly beings and the earthly peoples in the past, present, and the future. But the Divine Spirit also seems to be a human-friendly warrior—an encourager and advisor to the saints in the messianic war. As a heavenly being, the Divine Spirit functions like a supreme angel with a heavenly voice. The table below lists these points.

Table 5.3 Bible Verses Representing the Divine Spirit as a Divine Warrior Along the Fundamental Semantic Structure

1:1–8	1:9—4:11	5:1—11:19	12:1—16:21	17:1—22:5	22:6–21
From the Seven Spirits who are before his throne (1:4)	I was in the spirit on the Lord's day (1:10), Let anyone who has an ear listen to what the Spirit is saying to the churches (2:7, 11, 17, 28; 3:6, 13, 22), These are the words of him who has the Seven Spirits of God and the seven stars (3:1), At once I was in the spirit, and there in heaven	Then I saw between the throne and the four living creatures and among the elders a Lamb standing as if it had been slaughtered, having seven horns and seven eyes, which are the Seven Spirits of God sent out into all the earth (5:6), But after the three and a half days, the breath (spirit) of life from God entered	And I heard a voice from heaven saying, "Write this: Blessed are the dead who from now on die in the Lord." "Yes," says the Spirit, "they will rest from their labors, for their deeds follow them" (14:13)	So he carried me away in the spirit into a wilderness, and I saw a woman sitting on a scarlet beast that was full of blasphemous names, and it had seven heads and ten horns (17:3), Then I fell down at his feet to worship him, but he said to me, "You must not do that! I am a fellow servant with you	The Spirit and the bride say, "Come." And let everyone who hears say, "Come." And let everyone who is thirsty come. Let anyone who wishes take the water of life as a gift (22:17)

A Dynamic Reading of the Holy Spirit in Revelation

1:1–8	1:9—4:11	5:1—11:19	12:1—16:21	17:1—22:5	22:6–21
	stood a throne, with one seated on the throne (4:2), in front of the throne burn the seven flaming torches, which are the Seven Spirits of God (4:5)	them, and they stood on their feet, and those who saw them were terrified (11:11)		and your comrades who hold the testimony of Jesus. Worship God!" For the testimony of Jesus is the spirit of prophecy (19:10), And in the spirit he carried me away to a great, high mountain and showed me the holy city Jerusalem coming down out of heaven from God (21:10)	

Functional roles of the Divine Spirit as a Divine Warrior					
1:1–8	1:9—4:11	5:1—11:19	12:1—16:21	17:1—22:5	22:6–21
1) One of the Trinity as a Source of power and authority in the messianic war 2) Origin of the blessing from the messianic feast	1) Equipper, Mobilizer of the prophet in the messianic war 2) Commander to the messianic warriors of Churches with Jesus 3) Co-Commander with Jesus as God's Seven Spirits in the messianic war 4) Inspirer of the messianic warriors, prophet to experience spiritual journey 5) Heavenly burning torches for empowering the messianic war	1) Empower and Watcher in the messianic warfield 2) Ambassador sent by the Lamb 3) Revival Inspirer of persecuted churches, that is, two dead witnesses	1) Comforter for the persecuted saints 2) Reward-Giver for the witnesses according to their deeds	1) Prophetic Commander to show eschatological happenings of both the Harlot and the New Jerusalem to the prophet John 2) Encourager of the messianic armies to equip with true worship to God as a spiritual weapon in the messianic war	1) Co-worker with the Churches 2) A Warrior to win the people by invitation

A Dynamic Reading of the Holy Spirit in Revelation

Pragmatic-Structure of Revelation and the Characterization of the Divine Spirit

Pragmatic-Structure of Revelation

The pragmatic-structure of Revelation deals with how the narrative of Revelation is designed to change the perspective of the audience. Jang, using the literary theories of Patte and Lowry, suggests that Revelation transforms its audience by using the reversal strategy, representing that things described in the introductory parts are reversed in the last parts.[71] Jang also borrows insights about the external context from Fiorenza, Collins, Gager, and Barr so as to more accurately plot the change in Revelation's audience.[72] He thereby integrates the reversal strategy with historical approaches in presenting his proposal of the pragmatic-structure of Revelation. The diagram below illustrates these points.[73]

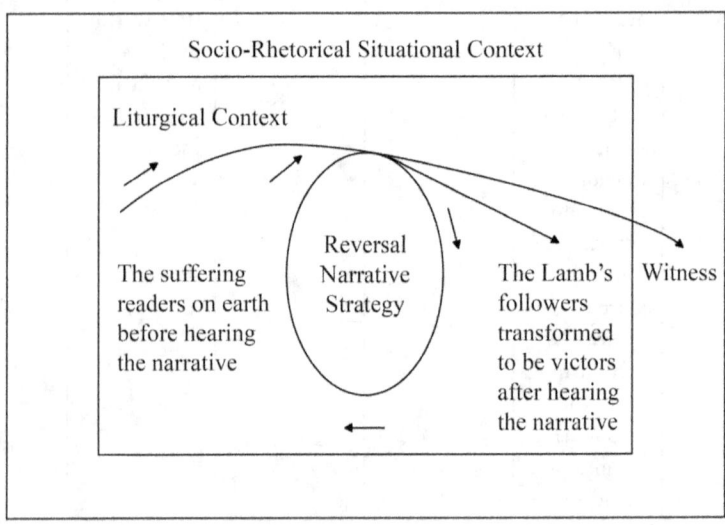

Diagram 5.12 Jang's Pragmatic Structure of Revelation

---

71. See Jang, "Narratological Approach," 207–15.

72. Ibid., 217–22.

73. This diagram shows how the participants in the liturgy are transformed by hearing the text. In the first step, they hear the text and then feel confliction through the story. Through this conflict, they are ready to be transformed to be witnesses in society or in the world.

Structure and the Holy Spirit in Revelation

I propose that this diagram needs to be revised to show the whole description of pragmatic-structure. I find certain details that need to be corrected to represent the whole pragmatic-structure of Revelation. These include three kinds of context: the literary, the liturgical, and the socio-rhetorical situational. That is why one more rectangle needs to be added to represent the literary context. The diagram should also include the reversal narrative strategy. However, two more lines need to be added for the literary and socio-rhetorical context since the participants in the liturgy also experience their socio-rhetorical context and literary context before the narrative of Revelation is read. One more line needs to be added after the reversal strategy since the literary context is also impacted. The diagram below illustrates these points.

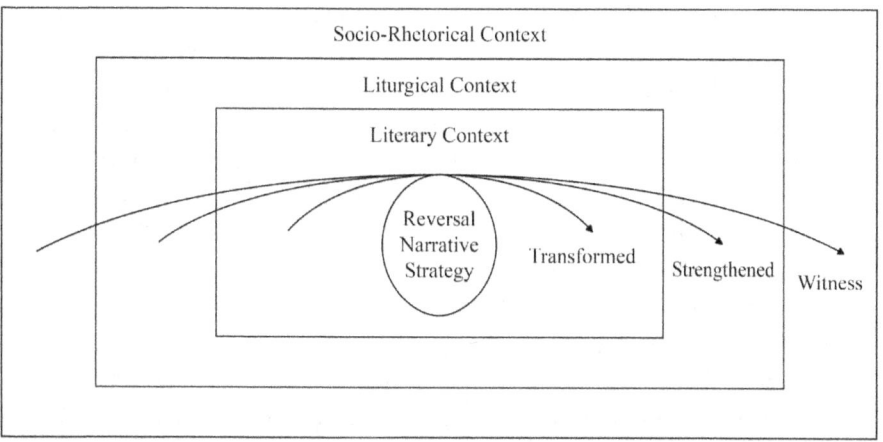

Diagram 5.13 Pragmatic-Structure of Revelation

To change the perspective of the audience, we find that at least three kinds of transformations are designed to happen in three different horizontal contexts—the literary, liturgical, and socio-rhetorical—through the reversal narrative strategy. In the first place, through the literary context the audiences are transformed from sufferers to conquerors as followers of the Lamb and members of the New Jerusalem who join in the messianic feast. Secondly, in the liturgical context the audiences are strengthened in their faith, endurance, and wisdom to be victors in the messianic war. Thirdly, in the socio-rhetorical context the audiences (as represented by the two witnesses) are encouraged to be sincere testifiers to Christ even in the face of death.

How can these transformations happen when the narrative is read before the audience? The reversal narrative strategy helps the audience experience transformation. Things that are described in the introductory part are reversed in the last part. In the first stage, the discrepancy between what happens on earth and what is hoped for in heaven is portrayed. The realized reign of God in chapter 4 is compared with the unaccomplished reign of God in the seven earthly churches in chapters 2 and 3. The difference is reinforced in the seven letters in chapters 2 and 3 by the description of the risen Jesus who rules with God in chapter 5. The suffering social situation of both John who writes the letter and the recipients in Rev 1:9–11 indicates another sort of discrepancy. The audience must be introduced to these discrepancies in the liturgical context at the first stage. These discrepancies draw the audience into the narrative world.

In the second stage, the tension of the narrative increases the suspense and uncertainty, which causes the audience to further attend to the narrative. John himself weeps "bitterly because no one was found worthy to open the scroll and its seven seals" (Rev 5:4). The opening of the seven seals also surprises the audience because of what happens next. The people are even more surprised by the seven trumpets and the series of harmful events that follow in chapters 8–11. On the other hand, a more positive surprise is induced by the protection both of the sealed ones in chapter 7 and those who worship in the temple in 11:1–2. Another positive surprise is elicited by the triumph of the two witnesses in chapter 11. However, this pleasing triumph is reversed by their martyrdom by the beast from the bottomless pit in 11:7–10. Thus, the suspense and surprise at this stage enlivens the narrative. The audience then anticipates a resolution of these discrepancies.

In the third stage, Jesus' birth and ascension in chapter 12 provide the missing link with which to resolve these discrepancies. Despite the threat of evil powers, such as the Dragon, the beast, and the false prophet in chapters 12 and 13, Jesus' birth and ascension as the Lamb of God offer hope to solve these problems in chapter 14. The Lamb and His followers may be victorious in the messianic war against the evil powers through God's support with the judgment in chapters 15 and 16.

In the fourth stage, in the messianic war, both the evil powers and their religious and politico-economic followers are destroyed completely by the word of God and His followers, in chapters 17–20. The New

Jerusalem motif as the bride of the Lamb brings hope of the new creation as the new heaven and new earth where God's reign is accomplished. The people's perspective about the earthly power system is changed in this stage. Their fear of both the Roman powers and the spiritually evil powers turns into hope for the new creation as the new community, that is, the New Jerusalem.

In the last stage, the audience is ready to choose the new way of life, as members of the New Jerusalem, that is, the new community of the people of God. The audience is persuaded to trust the godly prophet's words in 22:6 and not to add or take away from the words of the book of this prophecy in 22:18–19. Readers are commanded to keep these words in 22:7, and are summoned to worship God exclusively in 22:8–9. They are called to witness and live the words of the prophecy in 22:10–11, and the doing of good works is reinforced by the promise of reward in 22:12. They are warned not to be sorcerers, fornicators, murderers, idolaters, and practitioners of falsehood in 22:15. Those who do not yet follow Jesus are invited to freely drink the water of life in 22:17. The audience is encouraged to desire Jesus' return in 22:20. In short, the audience is persuaded not only by the literary context, but also by the liturgical and socio-rhetorical contexts.

Characterization of the Divine Spirit according to the Pragmatic-Structure of Revelation

How is the Divine Spirit characterized by the pragmatic-structure of Revelation? Briefly, the three contextual dimensions characterize the Divine Spirit. The characterization of the Divine Spirit by the literary context in the pragmatic-structure of Revelation has already been examined in chapter 4.

However, the characterization of the Divine Spirit by the liturgical context is not so explicit in the narrative. Nonetheless, some characterization of the Divine Spirit can be traced. Firstly, the "Seven Spirits" is portrayed as one of the members of the Trinity who receive worship in the churches' liturgy. The divinity of the spirits is confirmed by their position before God's throne in 1:4. Secondly, the Divine Spirit inspires John when he is worshipping in the liturgical context. This context is supported by the description of the time, that is, "on the Lord's day." Thirdly, the narrator employs the sevenfold phrase in the seven letters, "Let anyone who has an ear listen to what the Spirit is saying to the churches," to characterize the Divine Spirit as the one who speaks to the churches during their liturgical services. All of God's people are called to listen to the Spirit in the liturgical context. Fourthly, the Seven Spirits, as the seven flaming torches before the throne, are also worshipped in the heavenly liturgical context in 4:5. Fifthly, the Divine Spirit is presented as a sort of channel between the two liturgical contexts, that is, the earthly liturgy and the heavenly liturgy, by the phrase, "the Seven Spirits of God sent out into all the earth" in 5:6. Sixthly, the Divine Spirit testifies to Jesus by the word of prophecy in the liturgy in 19:10. In summary, the Divine Spirit speaks, connects, and inspires within the liturgical context of both heaven and earth. The Divine Spirit is also worshipped in the liturgical context as a part of the Divine Trinity.

In the socio-rhetorical context, the Divine Spirit is also characterized as the Seven Spirits who are before God's throne in 1:4 and 4:5 and are sent into the earthly social context in 5:6. In other words, the Divine Spirit not only works through John and among the churches, but also is involved with other communities on earth. This wider context is suggested by the Spirit's invitation to anyone who wishes to drink the water of life (22:17).

The Divine Spirit also intervenes in the messianic war by raising the two dead witnesses in 11:11. In doing so, the Divine Spirit expands the socio-rhetorical context to include a socio-cosmic context.

Is the Divine Spirit involved in the reversal strategy of the narrative? Indeed, the Divine Spirit is involved at each stage of the reversal strategy. In the first stage, the Divine Spirit not only guides John on his journey, but is also involved in guiding him to write the seven letters according to the command of the risen Jesus. Thus, the Divine Spirit implicitly causes the audience to realize the discrepancy between the earthly and heavenly realms. This role is confirmed by the fact that the Divine Spirit is placed before God's throne in 1:4 and 4:5. In the second stage, the Divine Spirit can be understood as the measure of this discrepancy between heaven and the earth by being sent from the heavenly throne into all the earth in 5:6. The Divine Spirit watches the reinforced suspense in the narrative: the judgments of the Lamb through the seven seals and trumpets in chapters 6, 8, and 9, the protection of the sealed in chapter 7, the prophetic acts of the two witnesses in chapters 10 and 11, the death and resurrection of the two witnesses in chapter 11, and the resurrection of the two witnesses in 11:11. The Divine Spirit strengthens the audience's belief and hope that the dead saints will be resurrected. In the third stage, the Divine Spirit transforms the audience's perspective about the death of the saints. The Divine Spirit transforms the audience's fearfulness about martyrdom by giving the promise of rewards in eternal life. In the fourth stage, the Divine Spirit guides the vision of both the judgment of Babylon in 17:3 and the emergence of the New Jerusalem in 21:10. In the last stage, the Divine Spirit invites the people to participate in life so that they may be good witnesses on earth in 22:17. In short, the Divine Spirit is involved in all stages of the reversal strategy in the narrative of Revelation.

Summary: The Whole Characterization of the Divine Spirit According to the Structure of Revelation

Up to now, I have discussed the characterization of the Divine Sprit along the five types of the structure in Revelation. Each characterization is summarized in the table that follows.

Table 5.4 Characterization of the Divine Spirit According to the Structure of Revelation

Narrative-Syntactic Structure	Fundamental-Syntactic Structure	Narrative-Semantic Structure	Fundamental-Semantic Structure	Pragmatic Structure
God-like heavenly provider in the introduction turns into person-like mission worker in conclusion	Angel-like helper for the subject, Jesus Christ, to establish the kingdom of God on earth as in heaven	God-like source of spiritual growth of the churches	God-like Warrior as a Subject in the messianic war and feast	One of Trinity
Presented mostly in the body part of the Revelation narrative	God-like co-worker of the subject, Jesus Christ, in speaking with Jesus' words	Person-like mission worker for the nonbelievers	God-like blessing Provider for the messianic armies	Angel-like inspirer in worshipping through both earthly liturgy and heavenly liturgy

A Dynamic Reading of the Holy Spirit in Revelation

Narrative-Syntactic Structure	Fundamental-Syntactic Structure	Narrative-Semantic Structure	Fundamental-Semantic Structure	Pragmatic Structure
Angel-like worker to support the church community	Omnipresent worker among all actants (God, the seven churches, John, the angel, heavenly beings, witnessing churches, followers of the Lamb, Jesus), except opponents.	Angel-like inspirer for the individual believer to see the vision and to hear the voice	Angel-like revelation Provider and Inspirer of the book of Revelation to John	Angel-like communicator to preach in the worship service of the local churches through the earthly liturgical context
	Angel-like communicator between the sender, God and the receiver, community on earth along the communication axis	Angel-like communicator to speak to the church communities	Angel-like heavenly Guardian and Guide in John's heavenly journey	God-like subject to be worshipped by the heavenly beings in the heavenly liturgical context
	Angel-like supporter with the desire to accomplish the kingdom of God along the volition axis	Person-like missionary to be sent from heaven to the earth	Messiah-like Commander to speak to the messianic armies in the messianic war	Angel-like channel between the earthly liturgy and the heavenly liturgy
	Angel-like reinforcer with the desire to purify the people of God and to keep God's word	Angel-like messenger to prophecy to witness to Jesus	Angel-like Divine Source of power in heaven	Angel-like witness to Jesus in the earthly liturgy

Structure and the Holy Spirit in Revelation

Narrative -Syntactic Structure	Fundamental -Syntactic Structure	Narrative -Semantic Structure	Fundamental -Semantic Structure	Pragmatic Structure
	Angel-like equipper to encourage the people of God to have the faith, the endurance and the wisdom in the face of the attacks from anti-divine powers.	Person-like inspirer and equipper for the persecuted saints with resurrecting power	Angel-like Divine Intervener in the earthly messianic war to empower the witnesses	Angel-like cross-cultural communicator between the heavenly context and the earthly social context
	Angel-like helper or supporter for the churches in the messianic war	Person-like converter for the nonbelievers to give glory to God	Person-like Encourager for the martyrs and the suffering messianic armies	Angel-like communicator in both spiritual community and secular society
		Omniscient to know the eternal reward and eternal life of the saints	Prophet-like Visionary to show what shall happen in the future	Angel-like worker in both socio-rhetorical context and socio-cosmic context
		Person-like encourager for the persecuted saints with eschatological hope to cope with the messianic war	Person-like Divine Witness to Jesus	Angel-like helper to make the readers realize the discrepancy between the earthly reality and the expected heavenly reality

A Dynamic Reading of the Holy Spirit in Revelation

Narrative-Syntactic Structure	Fundamental-Syntactic Structure	Narrative-Semantic Structure	Fundamental-Semantic Structure	Pragmatic Structure
			Person-like Missionary and Evangelist as Divine Warrior	Angel-like transformer for the persecuted saints to change their perspective of death
			God-like Creator of the New Jerusalem and new creation	Angel-like encourager for the saints to be good witnesses

6

Concluding Remarks

THIS STUDY HAS BEEN aimed to explore the Holy Spirit in Revelation through a new perspective: "a dynamic narrative approach." In view of this approach, I read the text of Revelation as "a final and unified form of ancient and canonical narrative" in which the Holy Spirit is rhetorically presented as a "divine character" and a "divine frame of reference." The dynamic interaction among the implied author or the narrator, the text, and the implied reader has been considered. I have also examined the characterization of the Holy Spirit along the plot and within the structure of Revelation.

Now in this last chapter, I summarize my several earlier analyses of the Holy Spirit and concisely draw out implications from the outcomes of this study as a whole: (1) the identity and role of the Holy Spirit, (2) the placement of the Holy Spirit, and (3) the theological significance of the Holy Spirit in Revelation. Then I offer some methodological remarks as well as the limitation of this book.

Summary

In chapter 1 I reviewed the past and present issues in the study of the Holy Spirit in Revelation by focusing on six scholars by means of their representative methodologies: F. F. Bruce, D. E. Aune, R. J. Bauckham, R. L. Jeske, J. C. de Smidt, and K. de Smidt. I observed that their research was mainly done with the "historical-critical approach" and without much resulting agreement. I also noted that the research employing the partial "narrative approach" to investigate the Holy Spirit in Revelation by scholars such as Du Rand, Desrosiers, Garrow, Barr, and Resseguie, were not so successful and even failed to identify the Holy Spirit in Revelation. To discover *a new and holistic* picture of the Holy Spirit in Revelation, I adopted *a dynamic narratological reading across the whole book of Revelation.*

To achieve this goal, in chapters 2, 3, 4, and 5 I explored the Holy Spirit in Revelation from several perspectives. The relationship between the narrator and his point of view and the Holy Spirit were discussed in chapter 2. Of note, the Holy Spirit plays a role to increase the reliability of the character, John, up to the level of that of the narrator. In other words, the Holy Spirit guides John to join in generating the narrator's viewpoint. Chapter 2 also elucidates how the Holy Spirit provides a special reference to the narrator's viewpoint. Firstly, the Holy Spirit significantly plays a literary role in expanding John's spatial-temporal viewpoint so that John shares the divine perception, that is, the *omnipresent* and *retrospective* viewpoint (perceptual facet) with the narrator. Secondly, the Holy Spirit also supports John by empowering him to share the *omniscient, reliable,* and *authoritative* viewpoint (psychological facet) with the narrator. Thirdly, the Holy Spirit also places a special role in molding the narrator's ideological viewpoint. The narrator is positively associated with the divine frame of reference through the Holy Spirit. "The Spirit" as a divine frame of reference provides a direct reference to the Spirit's ideological viewpoint, whereas the rhetorical expression of "in the Spirit" gives an indirect one through visions, heavenly voices, and heavenly beings. Thus, the narrator's viewpoint focuses not only on God and Jesus, but also on the Holy Spirit who also provides support to contour the cosmological and apocalyptic perspective of the narrator.

In chapter 3 the Holy Spirit is explicated as "a literary character" by means of narrative theories of "character" and "characterization." Chapter 3 shows that there are some characterizations that are common and repeated in each character-presentation: direct definition; indirect presentation; and analogy, which includes repetition, similarity, comparison, and contrast.[1] They can be highlighted with three points: (1) the Divine Spirit in Revelation is characterized as the "holy" Spirit;

---

1. Each character-presentation has its own identification for the Divine Spirit in the characterization. Some of them are overlapped and repeated.

Concluding Remarks

(2) this "holy" Spirit is frequently presented in close link with God, Jesus, and His witnesses, and is also separated from heavenly beings including angel(s); and (3) the Divine Spirit is presented mostly as the prophetic Spirit who witnesses to Jesus.

In addition, the roles of the Divine Spirit can also be summarized with thirteen points: (1) the omnipotent Spirit who coordinates all creatures both in heaven and on earth, offering salvation and natural grace as the powerful watcher over the whole world; (2) the Spirit of revelation who is involved in the whole process of revelation transmission; (3) the omniscient Spirit of communication who is speaking to the churches through preachers and prophets, by keeping eyes on the churches; (4) the Spirit of revival who is sent to revive the churches spiritually expressed through the giving of resurrection to the two witnesses; (5) the Spirit who guides the worship on the basis of the word of God; (6) the Spirit who engages in spiritual warfare; (7) the reliable witness to eternal blessings for the sincere saints; (8) the wonderful counselor to strengthen the faith of the saints; (9) the spiritual guide to direct the personal spiritual journey; (10) the evangelistic witness; (11) the mobilizer for the mission; (12) the omnipresent Spirit who presents in both the heavenly realm and the earthly realm; (13) and as the Spirit who has the same identity among all descriptions of the Divine Spirit with different characteristics.

Chapter 3 establishes that the narrative approach works effectively in defining five different forms of the Divine Spirit: The Seven Spirits, in the Spirit, the Spirit, the Spirit of prophecy, and the Spirit of life from God. Each of these is to be identified with the "holy" Spirit with the different cases and roles in view of literary perspective. The Divine Spirit is presented as an enigmatic divine character with two dialectic paradigms: person-likeness and person-unlikeness. Person-likeness is mainly related to the Spirit and the Spirit of prophecy, whereas person-unlikeness to the Seven Spirits, in the spirit, and the Spirit of life from God. In addition, the Seven Spirits are usually located in the heavenly realm, whereas the Spirit and the Spirit of prophecy in the earthly realm.

After the retrospection of past discussions of the plot of Revelation, in chapter 4 we showed that the plot of Revelation can be defined as a "sixfold and four-level scheme plot." According to this plot definition, I attempted to explore how the Divine Spirit can be characterized along the six stages: introduction, setting, complication, resolution, evaluation, and moral. The plot-based characterizations of the Divine Spirit can be classified into three main groups: God-likeness, person-likeness, and angel-likeness.

In each stage, its own specific characterizations can be found even though some overlap or are repeated. About thirty-two characterizations of the Divine Spirit appear in the whole narrative of Revelation. In the introduction stage, the Divine Spirit is characterized with five different characteristics, including God-like provider of divine blessing, God-like guide in the revelation process, God-like co-worker with Jesus in freeing people of God from sins and in making them priests and a kingdom, angel-like encourager for the saints to keep the Word, and person-like mission equipper for the servants of God to testify to the word of God. In the setting stage, the characterizations of the Divine Spirit are shown with seven different characters, such as God-like inspirer of the servants of God with fullness, angel-like guide to heavenly journey, angel-like equipper of the prophet for seeing the heavenly vision and hearing the heavenly voice, God-like orator to the earthly churches, God-like omniscient one of the earthly churches, God-like encourager for the saints to participate in the messianic war, and God-like heavenly flaming torches (fires). The complication stage embraces eight different characterizations: God-like co-worker with Jesus, the Lamb of God, in opening the scroll; God-like almighty and omniscient divine messenger descending from heaven; God-like prophetic participant in the history of church and the world; God-like equipper of the earthly churches; God-like rescuer of the persecuted churches—imaged as two dead witnesses; God-like helper of the two witnesses in ascension; person-like mission agent to encourage the earthly people to glorify God; and angel-like illuminator of the significance of the Scroll for the prophets and churches. Four different characterizations appear in the resolution stage: God-like witness of the visions of John, God-like comforter in the labor of the saints with the hope of the rest, angel-like guide in the spiritual warfare, and angel-like communicator with the heavenly voice. The evaluation stage shows another four characterizations: angel-like guide in heavenly journey, person-like prophetic messenger, God-like inspirer for the testimony of Jesus to the prophets, and God-like guide to the messianic war and the messianic feast. The moral stage also shows four characterizations: God-like inviter for the messianic feast to anyone who wants to join; God-like co-worker with Jesus; person-like mission worker who is working on earth with the bride, that is, the church; and angel-like co-worker with the angels.

Concluding Remarks

In chapter 4 some characteristics of the characterization of the Divine Spirit in relation to the plot are explained. Firstly, the Divine Spirit is characterized as being 63 percent God-like, whereas 28 percent of the characteristics are angel-likeness, and 9 percent are person-likeness. Secondly, the usage of God-likeness is focused on the first half, whereas it decreases in the last half. In other words, angel-likeness and person-likeness increase in their usage in the second half. Thirdly, the Divine Spirit is characterized as having profound concern for the eternal life of the people of God and as working hard for the conversion of all nations. Fourthly, the Divine Spirit is also characterized as employing the word of God, that is, the Scroll, as a tool. In another words, the Divine Spirit is characterized as a prophetic Spirit. Fifthly, the movement of the Divine Spirit from the heavenly realm to the earthly realm is clear; the Divine Spirit is characterized as a missionary sent by God to the earth just as Jesus was.

Chapter 5 brought further exploration of the characterizations of the Divine Spirit according to the structure of Revelation. After I attempted to review the discussions of how to define the structure of Revelation, I proposed five aspects of the whole structure of Revelation: (1) narrative-syntactic structure, (2) fundamental-syntactic structure (actantial model), (3) narrative-semantic structure (chiastic model), (4) fundamental-semantic structure, and (5) pragmatic structure. The characterizations of the Divine Spirit are also explored in relation to each aspect of the whole structure. In each aspect of structure, its own specific characterizations can be found, even if some overlap or are repeated. The whole picture of the characterization of the Divine Spirit can be drawn out by combining all the characterizations of the Divine Spirit from these five aspects of the structure of Revelation.

Two significant characterizations of the Divine Spirit could be discovered in the narrative-syntactic structure by focusing on unit level 4. Firstly, the Divine Spirit is depicted as working mainly in the heavenly realm in the introduction, whereas the Divine Spirit works mainly in the earthly realm in the conclusion. Secondly, almost all of the descriptions of the Divine Spirit could be found in the Body. Here, the Divine Spirit is mostly portrayed to work for the churches or the people of God on earth. The Divine Spirit is sent to speak to the seven churches. The Divine Spirit takes a significant role in the messianic war by empowering, equipping, encouraging, consoling, and reviving the churches. The conquest of the messianic war depends on the testimony given through the Scroll, which is inspired by the Divine Spirit. In short, the Divine Spirit is characterized in the Body (1:9—22:5) as being a coach who guides the churches about how to conquer in the messianic war.

As fundamental-syntactic structure, I proposed two types of the actantial model: the whole narrative actantial model and the partial narrative actantial model. All actants such as God (Sender/Originator: OR), church community on earth (Receiver: R), the faithful witnesses (Helper: H), Jesus Christ (Subject: S), and anti-divine powers (Opponent: OP), participate in building the new creation of the kingdom of God in the whole narrative of Revelation. Amongst all actants, the Divine Spirit is characterized as acting not only as a helper of Jesus, but also a subject with Jesus.

However, the actants who are helpers and opponents in the partial narrative are varied from section to section: angels and John (H), and no opponent (OP) in the introduction; heavenly beings, angels and John (H), and Nicolaitans, Satan, Balaamite and Jezebel (OP) in the setting; the two witnesses (H), and the beast from the bottomless pit (OP) in the complication; woman and the Lamb's followers (H), and the dragon, beast from the sea, beast from the earth, and their followers (OP) in the resolution; the bride (H), and the beast, seven and ten kings, false prophet, and the Dragon (OP) in the evaluation; and the bride (H), and no opponents (OP) in the moral.

The Divine Spirit is characterized mostly as a helper who supports Jesus in His messianic war against the anti-divine powers. It is notable that the Divine Spirit inspires Jesus spiritually as the Lamb of God who is One like the Son of Man: the Rider of the white horse, sent to conquer in the messianic war. In other words, the Divine Spirit is portrayed as one who participates in building the kingdom of God through the messianic war in relation to the fundamental-syntactic structure of Revelation. In the introduction, the Divine Spirit, along with angels and John, helps Jesus in establishing the kingdom of God without any opponents. In the setting, the Divine Spirit helps Jesus to set up the kingdom of God through purifying the seven churches from the challenge of the Nicolaitans, Balaamites, and Jezebel with the messages to the churches. In the complication, the Divine Spirit helps Jesus to expand the kingdom of God through reviving the two witnesses who were killed by the beast from the bottomless pit. In the resolution, under strengthened attacks from the

Concluding Remarks

Dragon, the beast from the sea and the earth and their followers, the Divine Spirit helps Jesus, the Lamb of God, with His followers to expand the kingdom of God through harvesting the people of God and judging the evil ones. In the evaluation, the Divine Spirit helps Jesus, the rider of the white horse, to accomplish the final task of building the kingdom of God even in the midst of wholehearted attacks by the evil assemblies. In the moral, without the existence of evil powers, the Divine Spirit helps Jesus, the bright morning star, with the bride to bring the kingdom of God as the new creation of the New Jerusalem on earth. The Divine Spirit can also be characterized as a ubiquitous networking coordinator among all the actants along the axes of communication, power, and volition in terms of fundamental-semantic structure.

As narrative semantic structure, I proposed a chiastic structure after discussing some prior chiastic models. The characterization of the Divine Spirit can be traced along each chiastic plane: AA' (two times), BB' (ten times), CC' (five times), DD' (one time), and E (one time). The Divine Spirit is characterized as being involved not only in the spiritual growth of the saints and churches, but also in joining the mission work to the nonbelievers in AA'. In BB', the Divine Spirit is characterized as mainly focusing on the life of saints and churches by pouring himself upon them and by speaking the prophetic words of Jesus. In CC', the Divine Spirit is characterized as the heavenly omnipotent and omniscient One who guides the ministry of testimony to Jesus. In DD', the Divine Spirit is pictured as one who revives the two witnesses, and as the one inspiring the churches and the nonbelievers. As the core part of the narrative, E characterizes the Divine Spirit as encouraging the saints and the churches to participate in the messianic war, even in the face of death.

As fundamental-semantic structure, I proposed the messianic war and feast as the main theme of the narrative. The characterization of the Divine Spirit can be traced through the descriptions about the messianic war and feast in the narrative. Above all, the Divine Spirit is characterized as the subject of the messianic war and feast, who bestows the blessing to the messianic armies, whereas the narrator is reluctant to describe Him as a judge. The Divine Spirit is characterized as the Spirit of prophecy to equip John as a prophetic soldier who is inspired to write Revelation and to have visions in his heavenly journey. The Divine Spirit is also characterized as a Commander in the messianic war who directs the seven churches about how to conquer as the messianic armies. The

Divine Spirit is characterized as a heavenly warrior who executes God's power on earth. The Divine Spirit is characterized as intervening deeply into the messianic war by supporting, empowering, and resurrecting the messianic armies imaged in the two witnesses. Furthermore, the Divine Spirit is portrayed as playing a crucial role in reversing the result of the messianic war from being defeated to conquering. The Divine Spirit is depicted as one ensuring the final triumph of the saints and the churches even in their death. In other words, the Divine Spirit is involved in destroying Babylon and in establishing the New Jerusalem. The mission of the Divine Spirit in the messianic war and feast is related to the conversion of all nations through his role as a missionary Warrior. Thus, the characterizations of the Divine Spirit can be summarized as one who is an enigmatic character in the narrative with two different faces: heavenly omni-competent Warrior and human-friendly Warrior.

Finally, I attempted to discover the pragmatic structure so as to discern how the narrative changes the perspectives of the audience through the reversal narrative strategy. I explored how the discrepancy is inaugurated, developed, and resolved through the five stages of the narrative. Then the characterization of the Divine Spirit was surveyed along five stages of reversal strategy as well as the literary, liturgical, and socio-rhetorical contexts in the pragmatic structure.

In the reversal narrative strategy, the Divine Spirit is characterized as helping the audience realize how much discrepancy exists between the heavenly realm and the earthly realm, by communicating Jesus' words to the churches in their liturgical and socio-rhetorical contexts. In the intensified discrepancy of the narrative, and through the liturgical context, the Divine Spirit encourages the audience to have stronger faith in the resurrection even in the face of death. Finally the Divine Spirit is successful in reversing the perspective of the saints about death by announcing the promised rewards after their death. Furthermore, the Divine Spirit is characterized as being successful in changing their perspective on earthly life such as respecting, obeying, and witnessing God's Word, by opening the visions of the destruction of Babylon and the coming of the New Jerusalem. Thus the Divine Spirit is characterized as intervening deeply in the reversal narrative strategy that employs the discrepancy.

In the liturgical context, the Divine Spirit is characterized as one of the Trinity who bestows all blessings to the saints by inspiring John, the spiritual leader, to preach what he experienced, what he saw and heard,

Concluding Remarks

to the audience in the worship service. The Divine Spirit is characterized, in the liturgical context, as coming down from heaven upon the audience on earth while they worship. Further, the Divine Spirit is characterized as a channel to connect the earthly worship service to the heavenly worship. The Divine Spirit is also characterized as a witness to testify to the truth of Jesus with the word of prophecy in worship services. Thus the Divine Spirit is mainly depicted as the "Holy Spirit" who inspires preachers and testifies to the truth of Jesus in the earthly worship service, binding it with the heavenly one.

In the socio-rhetorical context, the Divine Spirit is characterized not only as working for the church communities, but also in the social context as serving the nonbelievers in communities that are thirsty for the water of life. By intervening in the messianic war, the Divine Spirit is characterized as expanding His context from the socio-rhetorical context to the socio-cosmic context. In the end, chapter 5 summarizes the whole characterizations of the Divine Spirit according to the five modes of structure in Revelation. Then the characterizations of the Divine Spirit along the five aspects of the structure of Revelation are summarized within a table.

Implications

So far, I summarized what was discussed in previous chapters. On the basis of the summary, I will now attempt to draft some implications of the identity and role, the placement, and the theological significance of the Holy Spirit.

Identity and Role of the Holy Spirit[2]

In that there is no usage in Revelation of the specific term "Holy Spirit," establishing whether the Divine Spirit can be identified with "The Holy Spirit" of early Christianity is crucial. This question was affirmatively answered in chapter 3. Indeed, Revelation, using this terminology, presents a particularly rich interpretation of the Holy Spirit, characterized as *the Holy, Divine, Complete (Perfect), Powerful, Watching, Life-giving,*

---

2. It is not easy to separate the role from the identity since the identity of who the Holy Spirit is closely relates to the role of what the Holy Spirit does. That is why I put both the identity and the role together in this section.

A Dynamic Reading of the Holy Spirit in Revelation

and Prophetic Spirit, who works with both God and Jesus in both heaven and earth. In other words, the Divine Spirit is portrayed as a manifold character in Revelation, characterized by God-likeness, angel-likeness, and person-likeness, which each embrace the role of the Holy Spirit as explored in chapters 2, 3, 4, and 5.[3]

God-likeness

The divinity of the Holy Spirit is clearly presented in the narrative of Revelation, yet as a character distinct from God, *who is and who was and who is to come*, and the Lamb. He has His own identity embracing His own ministries and concerns for the narrative, even though the Holy Spirit is closely related to God and the Lamb. Thus the Holy Spirit can be identified as a God-like character who owns three group identities. Firstly, the Holy Spirit works as the divine frame of reference in the whole narrative of Revelation. The Holy Spirit plays a God-like role as he shapes the ideology of the narrator as well as measures the reliability of the characters. Secondly, the Holy Spirit is depicted as one member of the Trinity. He provides the blessing for the faithful saints together with God and Jesus. He takes part in forgiving the sins of the people of God and making them priests and a kingdom with Jesus. He works together with Jesus in opening the seals of the scroll. He is also praised with Jesus and God by the heavenly beings in the heavenly worship context. He works as a Creator of a new creation. He networks with all other characters such as God, Jesus, angels, heavenly beings, heavenly voice, and earthly peoples, just like the ubiquitous organizer. He also works anywhere, like the omnipresent God who works in the heavenly realm as well as the earthly realm. He rules all creatures both in heaven and on earth with salvation and natural grace. Thirdly, the Holy Spirit participates in the messianic war as a Messianic Warrior with Jesus. He coordinates the whole process of the messianic war. He recruits messianic armies, training and equipping them to witness to Jesus with faith, endurance, and wisdom. He commands them as a Commander in the war-field on earth. He also practices the recovering treatments for the bruised armies by preaching the word of God. He

---

3. Three categories are not absolute, but rather relative in that they can overlap or repeat. Among all of the characterizations of the Divine Spirit presented in chapters 2, 3, 4, and 5, I grouped them as God-like when their identities seem to be more similar to God, and person-like when their identities are more similar to persons. The middle group is categorized as angel-like.

Concluding Remarks

is responsible for the spiritual growth of the saints and the churches. He strengthens even the dead witnesses to experience the spiritual revival by offering His life-giving Spirit. He watches over all the churches as well as all the earth. He also provides rewards for the labor of the faithful armies on earth, that is, the churches. He helps the ascension of the saints as a confirmation of their conquest. He is also responsible for the messianic feast by giving heavenly blessing and rewards. He prepares the messianic feast in the kingdom of God by new creation through the advent of the New Jerusalem. Thus, as a God-like being, the Divine Spirit, the Holy Spirit plays manifold roles in the narrative of Revelation. Besides this, the Holy Spirit works in the narrative of Revelation just like an angel.

ANGEL-LIKENESS

As Bauckham insists, the Holy Spirit is quite distinct from angels in Revelation. However, the Holy Spirit works with angels in Revelation, and further plays seven group roles just like the angels. Firstly, the Holy Spirit guides John, the prophet, to experience a heavenly journey, like a guardian spirit. The Holy Spirit helps him prepare for the spiritual journey by filling him with Spirit. The Holy Spirit guides him to see heavenly visions and to hear the heavenly voices. The Holy Spirit is a witness to John's heavenly journey so that John's writings are certified to be reliable. Secondly, the Holy Spirit works as a connector in the socio-rhetorical context. He connects the heavenly realm to the earthly realm by communicating with the Word. Furthermore, he mediates the earthly worship to the heavenly worship in order to generate the true worship of God. The Holy Spirit plays a role as a cross-cultural communicator between heavenly God and the earthly churches as well as between the nonbelieving and believing communities on earth. Thirdly, the Holy Spirit is involved in the transformation of the personal life of the saint or the readers (audience). The Holy Spirit helps the audience or readers to recognize the discrepancy between the reality of heaven and that of earth so that they may be transformed in their faith and value system and change their perspective on death. The Holy Spirit inspires them in His fullness to receive the vision and the voice in their spiritual journey. The Holy Spirit communicates with them to continue to be pure by keeping the word of God. Fourthly, the Holy Spirit takes care of not only the personal saints, but also the church community. The Holy Spirit speaks to the churches through inspiring the preachers and the prophets. He reminds the churches of the significance of the word of God. Fifthly, the Holy Spirit participates in the messianic war like an angelic guardian. He encourages and empowers the saints to participate in the messianic war on earth with faith, endurance, and eschatological hope and wisdom as faithful witnesses. He strengthens and consoles the persecuted churches by showing the vision of the messianic feast that will offer rewards to the messianic armies. Sixthly, the Holy Spirit is responsible for the whole process of revelation, whereas an angel is responsible for only a process of revelation. He inspires John to write the book of Revelation. He illuminates the word of Jesus so that the churches understand it. Seventhly, as an angel instructed John to worship God, the Holy Spirit is also concerned about the worship of the churches. He communicates to them through the worship service. He participates in the Scripture-based worship services and illuminates the will of Jesus among audiences. He connects the earthly worship services to the heavenly worship.

Person-likeness

The Holy Spirit works just like a human does on earth. He evangelizes the nonbelievers with the churches by inviting them to drink the water of life, like a cross-cultural missionary. He witnesses to Jesus as a human evangelist. Like a human coach, he equips the preachers or the leaders of the churches so that they are prepared for their ministry. He counsels the saints about the problems in their lives like a human counselor. He restores them from their weaknesses like a human doctor. He helps Jesus establish the kingdom of God on earth. He provides a prophetic vision of the future to the churches like a human prophet. He inspires the nonbelievers to glorify the name of God through the revival of the persecuted churches.

Thus, the implications of the characterization of the Holy Spirit in relation to the whole narrative of Revelation indicate that the Holy Spirit is an enigmatic character who has multi-faces as well as ubiquitous relations with multiple functions.

Concluding Remarks

Placement of the Holy Spirit in Revelation

The Holy Spirit in Revelation is depicted as located in multi-places such as heaven and earth. However, Revelation is not explicit whether he is located in hades and the lake of fire. In heaven, the Holy Spirit is portrayed as being before the throne of God (1:4; 4:5) as the seven flaming torches (4:5). He is placed in heaven as part of the Holy Trinity as well as among the heavenly beings: four animals, twenty-four elders, angels, and heavenly voices. Uniquely, the narrator of Revelation places the Holy Spirit in heaven whereas almost all descriptions of the New Testament writings about the Holy Spirit are focused on what the Holy Spirit does on earth. In other words, Revelation reveals the heavenly substance of the Holy Spirit, not just his role on earth. The Holy Spirit does not work alone, but also works together with the heavenly ones.

Notably, Revelation presents the placement of the Holy Spirit as moving from heaven to the earth. The Holy Spirit is sent to the earth as a representative of the heavenly ones, including God and Jesus. The descending Spirit we read about in Acts 2:2–3, where "suddenly from heaven there came a sound like the rush of a violent wind, and it filled the entire house where they were sitting. Divided tongues, as of fire, appeared," might be seen as the seven flaming torches came down to the earth in Rev. 4:5.

We have seen that the Holy Spirit is placed on earth not only among the churches and the saints, but also among many nonbelievers who have refused to give glory to God. The Holy Spirit guides believers to take part in the messianic war on earth as witnesses to the saving grace of Jesus until all nations shall be converted. The Holy Spirit helps and supports the believers' community in many ways so that they will receive eternal rewards in the messianic feast.

Theological Significance of the Holy Spirit in Revelation

The narrator or implied author of Revelation presents the Holy Spirit in terms of being with God in the first chapter as Yahweh's holy Spirit as in the Jewish Bible. However, the characterization of the Holy Spirit in Revelation is developed by employing various expressions, such as the Seven Spirits, the Spirit of life from God, the Spirit of prophecy and in the Spirit, the Spirit witnessing to Jesus, the Spirit working with Jesus, and even the independent Spirit working alone.

In Revelation, only the gifts of prophecy and witness, rather than all of the charismatic gifts of the Holy Spirit are described. Even though special descriptions of spiritual gifts are not given directly in Revelation, it is easy to recognize in the narrative that all kinds of spiritual gifts are provided to the churches to give witness to Jesus since all powers and gifts given to Moses and Elijah are given to the two witnesses. Revelation is unique in that it opens the gifts of vision as an important gift given by the Holy Spirit who guides John to take the spiritual journey to see the heavenly realm. Revelation also opens the gifts of communication so that believers can hear the voice of Jesus.

In Revelation, the general description of the fruit of the Holy Spirit is not given. However, the faith, the endurance, and the wisdom are required for the conquering life of the saints. As for the fullness of the Holy Spirit, Revelation does not give a general description. However, that this possibility is open to the individual saints is seen from the presentation of John as in the Spirit. Another possibility of the fullness of the Holy Spirit is open to all the churches by presenting the Seven Spirits as sent to the earth. It is not clear whether Jesus poured the Holy Spirit onto John or the churches, even though this possibility cannot be denied. It is clear that the purpose of the fullness of the Holy Spirit is related to the witness to Jesus until all nations are converted. The fullness of the Holy Spirit is also related to making a character in the narrative a reliable character.

How are the results of this study about the Holy Spirit relevant to the modern reader? The responses of the readers are various and different according to their theological perspectives of the Holy Spirit. However, this new approach to the study of the Holy Spirit in Revelation may expand the present understanding of the Holy Spirit.[4] Modern readers and theologians may choose what they want to find out from this study of the Holy Spirit.

Methodological Remarks

This study offers *a* reading of the Holy Spirit in Revelation by means of *a* new perspective. A character, John, who was in the Spirit, is considered as a reliable character. However, in the literary framework, John's visions and actions are controlled by the implied author or the narrator with

---

4. Until now, the theological studies of the Holy Spirit have been focused on other books of the New Testament but not Revelation.

a view to shaping his entire narrative as reliable and authoritative. We can accept that the narrator is characterized as an "off-stage" character. The narrator may have a close relation to the Holy Spirit in that he narrates the inspired character, John, and adopts the Holy Spirit as his divine frame of reference. If the narrator is a character closely related to the Holy Spirit, the text of Revelation, organized or narrated by him, can be considered as a Spirit-inspired narrative. Furthermore, the narrator of Revelation emphasizes the protection of the Revelation text as a reliable and authoritative text in 22:18–19.

This approach focuses just on the final text, not on the historical dimension of the text. Nevertheless, we must note that this dynamic reading may help readers find out the multi-functional aspects of the Holy Spirit. This reading methodology differentiates itself from our earlier approaches—the historical-critical and narrative approach—in discovering the Holy Spirit in Revelation. This approach may be applied not just to the Holy Spirit, but also to the other characters such as Jesus, God, and the angels.

Limitations of This Book

This book is limited to using just the final text, not its historical background. I hope in a further study to expand this approach to use the historical-critical analysis. By doing that, we may understand what the early Christians understood about the Holy Spirit more in detail.

"Amen. Come, Lord Jesus!" (Rev 22:20b)

Appendix

Tables for the Divine Frame of Reference in Revelation

Table A.1 Divine Frame of Reference of the Narrator in Revelation: Small Visions (I saw: εἰδῶ)[1]

Seer	Related characters or visions	Related verse(s)	Words used
John	Someone like the Son of Man	1:12–16	I saw: εἰδῶ 1
John	A door and a throne in heaven; someone on the throne; seven lamps, that is, the Seven Spirits of God; a sea of glass; four living creatures; twenty-four elders	4:1–11	I looked: εἰδῶ
John	A scroll with the seven seals; a mighty angel; a Lamb; seven horns and seven eyes, that is, the Seven Spirits of God; many angels	5:1–11	I saw: εἰδῶ
John	The Lamb's opening of the seven seals; four horses; the slain souls; a great earthquake; sun, moon, and stars; kings; princes; generals; the rich; the mighty, every slave, and every free man in the cave	6:1–17	I saw: εἰδῶ
John	Four angels standing on the four corners of the earth; another angel coming from the east; a great multitude from every nation, tribe, people, and language; all the angels around the throne	7:1–17	I saw: εἰδῶ

1. Revelation narrator seems to attempt to differentiate the usage of word "I saw" in the original text between εἰδῶ and βλεπω. For the usage of the divine frame of reference in vision, εἰδῶ is used to describe when the seer, John, experiences each vision. βλεπω is employed to summarize what John saw in the visions as a whole in Rev 1:12 and 22:8, or to look at the scroll in Rev 5:3–4, or just see in Rev 9:20.

Appendix

Seer	Related characters or visions	Related verse(s)	Words used
John	Seven angels with seven trumpets; another angel with a golden censer of prayers; four angels blowing trumpets and disasters such as hail and fire with blood; something like a great mountain burning with fire; a great star, Wormwood, blazing like a torch; an eagle proclaiming the three woes; a star that opened the shaft of the bottomless pit; the appearance of locusts like scorpions and their king, an angel, Abaddon or Apollyon; two hundred million troops of cavalry; horses and their riders	8:2—9:21	I saw: εἰδῶ
John	Angel to hold the open scroll, throne vision (without "I saw" format—seventh angel to trumpet): twenty-four elders worship; God's temple in heaven and the ark of God's covenant; a pregnant woman; a great red Dragon; the ascension of the Son to God's throne; the woman fleeing; the heavenly war between Michael and the Dragon and their angels; the Dragon thrown down; the beast from the sea; the beast from the earth	10:1—13:18	I saw (looked): εἰδῶ
John	The Lamb on Mount Zion with the 144,000; the angel flying in midheaven with an eternal gospel; one like the Son of Man seated on the cloud; the seven angels with the seven bowls; those who had conquered the beast and sea of glass mixed with fire; the temple of the tent of witness in heaven; the three foul spirits like frogs coming from the mouth of the Dragon, from the mouth of the beast, and from the mouth of the false prophet; the seventh angel and the last plagues	14:1—16:21	I saw (looked): εἰδῶ
John	The woman sitting on a scarlet beast and drunken with the blood of the saints and witnesses to Jesus; angel coming down from heaven; having great authority with splendor; white horse and its rider and heavenly armies; angel standing in the sun to call the birds; the beast and the kings of the earth with their armies to fight against the rider on the horse	17:1—19:21	I saw: εἰδῶ

Tables for the Divine Frame of Reference in Revelation

Seer	Related characters or visions	Related verse(s)	Words used
John	Angel coming down from heaven, holding in his hand the key to the bottomless pit and a great chain to seize the Dragon; those seated on thrones to judge and the souls of those who had been beheaded for their testimony to Jesus and for the word of God; the one who sat on a great white throne; the dead standing before the throne; the book of life; a new heaven and a new earth; the new Jerusalem; no temple in the city but the Lord God the Almighty and the Lamb; the river of the water of life	20:1–22:7	I saw: εἰδῶ, The angel showed me (22:1): δείκνυω

Table A.2 Divine Frame of Reference of the Narrator in Revelation: Heavenly Voice(s)

Type of voice	Voice sent to	Voice received by	Related verse(s)	Contents
A voice	Heaven	John	10:4	Seal up what the seven thunders have said, and do not write it down
A voice	Heaven	John	10:8	Go, take the scroll that is open in the hand of the angel
A loud voice	Heaven	The two witnesses	11:12	Come up here!
Loud voices	Heaven		11:15	The kingdom of the world has become the kingdom of our Lord and of His Messiah, and he will reign forever and ever
A loud voice	Heaven	John heard	12:10–12	Now have come the salvation and the power and the kingdom of our God and the authority of his Messiah, for the accuser of our comrades has been thrown down, who accuses them day and night before our God. But they have conquered him by the blood of the Lamb and by the word of their testimony, for they did not cling to life even in the face of death. Rejoice then, you heavens and those who dwell in them! But woe to the earth and the sea, for the devil has come down to you with great wrath, because he knows that his time is short!

APPENDIX

Type of voice	Voice sent to	Voice received by	Related verse(s)	Contents
A loud voice	Temple	Seven angels	16:1	Go and pour out on to the earth the seven bowls of the wrath of God
A loud voice	Temple, Throne		16:17	It is done
A voice	Heaven	John heard	18:4	Come out of her, my people, so that you do not take part in her sins, and so that you do not share in her plagues
The loud voice of a great multitude	Heaven	John heard	19:1–2	Hallelujah! Salvation and glory and power to our God, for his judgments are true and just; he has judged the great whore who corrupted the earth with her fornication, and he has avenged on her the blood of his servants.
A voice	Throne		19:5	Praise our God, all you his servants, and all who fear him, small and great
The voice of a great multitude		John heard	19:6–8	Hallelujah! For the Lord our God the Almighty reigns. Let us rejoice and exult and give him the glory, for the marriage of the Lamb has come, and his bride has made herself ready; to her it has been granted to be clothed with fine linen, bright and pure
A loud voice	Throne	John heard	21:3–4	See, the home of God is among mortals. He will dwell with them; they will be his peoples, and God himself will be with them; he will wipe every tear from their eyes. Death will be no more; mourning and crying and pain will be no more, for the first things have passed away

Tables for the Divine Frame of Reference in Revelation

Table A.3 Divine Frame of Reference of the Narrator in Revelation: Angel(s)

Speaker/ Seer	Related characters Identity of angel(s)	Related verses Receiver	Content of messages	
John	A mighty angel	(John)	5:2	Who is worthy to open the scroll and break its seals?
John	Another angel having the seal of God	(John)	7:3	Do not damage the earth or the sea or the trees, until we have marked the servants of our God with a seal on their foreheads.
The narrator	All the angels around the throne		7:11–12	Fell on their faces before the throne and worshiped God, singing, "Amen! Blessing and glory and wisdom and thanksgiving and honor and power and might be to our God forever and ever! Amen."
John	A mighty angel		10:1–2, 5–7	And I saw another mighty angel coming down from heaven, wrapped in a cloud, with a rainbow over his head; his face was like the sun, and his legs like pillars of fire. He held a little scroll open in his hand. Setting his right foot on the sea and his left foot on the land, raised his right hand to heaven. 5 Then the angel whom I saw standing on the sea and the land raised his right hand to heaven and swore by him who lives forever and ever, who created heaven and what is in it, the earth and what is in it, and the sea and what is in it: "There will be no more delay, but in the days when the seventh angel is to blow his trumpet, the mystery of God will be fulfilled, as he announced to his servants the prophets."

Appendix

Speaker/ Seer	Related characters Identity of angel(s)	Related verses Receiver	Content of messages	
John	Mighty angel	John	10:9	Take it, and eat; it will be bitter to your stomach, but sweet as honey in your mouth.
John	Another angel		14:6, 7	Flying in midheaven, with an eternal gospel to proclaim to those who live on the earth—to every nation and tribe and language and people. "Fear God and give him glory, for the hour of his judgment has come; and worship him who made heaven and earth, the sea and the springs of water."
The narrator	Another, second angel		14:8	Fallen, fallen is Babylon the great! She has made all nations drink of the wine of the wrath of her fornication.
The narrator	Another, third angel		14:9–11	Those who worship the beast and its image, and receive a mark on their foreheads or on their hands, they will also drink the wine of God's wrath, poured unmixed into the cup of his anger, and they will be tormented with fire and sulfur in the presence of the holy angels and in the presence of the Lamb. And the smoke of their torment goes up forever and ever. There is no rest day or night for those who worship the beast and its image and for anyone who receives the mark of its name.

Tables for the Divine Frame of Reference in Revelation

Speaker/ Seer	Related characters Identity of angel(s)	Related verses Receiver	Content of messages	
The narrator	Another angel from the temple		14:15–16	Calling with a loud voice to the one who sat on the cloud (like the Son of Man), "Use your sickle and reap, for the hour to reap has come, because the harvest of the earth is fully ripe." So the one who sat on the cloud swung his sickle over the earth, and the earth was reaped.
The narrator	Another angel from the altar		14:18–19	The angel who has authority over fire (from the altar) called with a loud voice to another angel who had the sharp sickle (from the temple), "Use your sharp sickle and gather the clusters of the vine of the earth, for its grapes are ripe." Another angel from the temple swung his sharp sickle over the earth and gathered the vintage of the earth, and he threw it into the great wine press of the wrath of God.
John	Angel of waters		16:5–6	You are just, O Holy One, who are and were, for you have judged these things; because they shed the blood of saints and prophets, you have given them blood to drink. It is what they deserve!
John	One of seven angels with seven bowls	John	17:1–2	Come, I will show you the judgment of the great whore who is seated on many waters, with whom the kings of the earth have committed fornication, and with the wine of whose fornication the inhabitants of the earth have become drunk.
John	One of seven angels with seven bowls	John	17:7	Why are you so amazed? I will tell you the mystery of the woman, and of the beast with seven heads and ten horns that carries her.

APPENDIX

Speaker/ Seer	Identity of angel(s) [Related characters]	Receiver [Related verses]	Content of messages
John	Another angel from heaven	18:1–3	Fallen, fallen is Babylon the great! It has become a dwelling place of demons, a haunt of every foul spirit, a haunt of every foul bird, a haunt of every foul and hateful beast. For all the nations have drunk of the wine of the wrath of her fornication, and the kings of the earth have committed fornication with her, and the merchants of the earth have grown rich from the power of her luxury.
The narrator	A mighty angel	18:21–24	With such violence Babylon the great city will be thrown down, and will be found no more; and the sound of harpists and minstrels and of flutists and trumpeters will be heard in you no more; and an artisan of any trade will be found in you no more; and the sound of the millstone will be heard in you no more; and the light of a lamp will shine in you no more; and the voice of the bridegroom and the bride will be heard in you no more; for your merchants were the magnates of the earth, and all nations were deceived by your sorcery. And in you was found the blood of prophets and of saints, and of all who have been slaughtered on earth.
John	The angel	John	19:9	"Write this: Blessed are those who are invited to the marriage supper of the Lamb." "These are true words of God."

Tables for the Divine Frame of Reference in Revelation

Speaker/ Seer	Related characters / Identity of angel(s)	Related verses / Receiver	Content of messages
John	An angel standing in the sun		19:17–18	Called to all the birds that fly in mid-heaven, "Come, gather for the great supper of God, to eat the flesh of kings, the flesh of captains, the flesh of the mighty, the flesh of horses and their riders—flesh of all, both free and slave, both small and great."
John	An angel coming down from heaven		20:1–3	Holding in his hand the key to the bottomless pit and a great chain. He seized the Dragon, that ancient serpent, who is the Devil and Satan, and bound him for a thousand years, and threw him into the pit, and locked and sealed it over him, so that he would deceive the nations no more, until the thousand years were ended. After that he must be let out for a little while.
John	One of seven angels with seven bowls	John	21:9	Come, I will show you the bride, the wife of the Lamb.
John	The angel from heaven	John	22:1	Showed me the river of the water of life, bright as crystal, flowing from the throne of God and of the Lamb …
John	The angel from heaven	John	22:6	These words are trustworthy and true, for the Lord, the God of the spirits of the prophets, has sent his angel to show his servants what must soon take place.

APPENDIX

Table A.4 Divine Frame of Reference of the Narrator in Revelation: Heavenly Being(s)

Speaker and seer	Related Characters / Heavenly beings	Receiver	Related verse(s)	Content of messages
The narrator	Twenty-four elders		4:4	Seated on the twenty-four thrones, dressed in white robes, with golden crowns on their heads
The narrator	Twenty-four elders		4:10–11	Fall before the one who is seated on the throne and worship the one who lives forever and ever; they cast their crowns before the throne, singing, "You are worthy, our Lord and God, to receive glory and honor and power, for you created all things, and by your will they existed and were created."
The narrator	One of twenty-four elders	John	5:5	Do not weep. See, the Lion of the tribe of Judah, the Root of David, has conquered, so that he can open the scroll and its seven seals.
The narrator	Twenty-four elders		5:8–10	Fell before the Lamb, each holding a harp and golden bowls full of incense, which are the prayers of the saints.... "You are worthy to take the scroll and to open its seals, for you were slaughtered and by your blood you ransomed for God saints from every tribe and language and people and nation; you have made them to be a kingdom and priests serving our God, and they will reign on earth."
The narrator	Elders		5:14	Fell down and worshiped to God and the Lamb.
The narrator	One of elders	John	7:13	Who are these, robed in white, and where have they come from?

Tables for the Divine Frame of Reference in Revelation

Speaker and seer	Related Characters / Heavenly beings	Related verse(s) / Receiver	Content of messages
The narrator	Twenty-four elders	11:16–18	Fell on their faces and worshiped God, singing, "We give you thanks, The Lord God Almighty, who are and who were, for you have taken your great power and begun to reign. The nations raged, but your wrath has come, and the time for judging the dead, for rewarding your servants, the prophets and saints and all who fear your name, both small and great, and for destroying those who destroy the earth.
The narrator	Twenty-four elders	19:4	Fell down and worshiped God who is seated on the throne, saying, "Amen. Hallelujah!"
The narrator	Four living creatures	4:6	Full of eyes in front and behind
The narrator	Four living creatures	4:8	Each of them with six wings, are full of eyes all around and inside. Day and night without ceasing they sing, "Holy, holy, holy, the Lord God the Almighty, who was and is and is to come."
The narrator	Four living creatures	5:8–10	Fell before the Lamb, each holding a harp and golden bowls full of incense, which are the prayers of the saints. They sing a new song: "You are worthy to take the scroll and to open its seals, for you were slaughtered and by your blood you ransomed for God saints from every tribe and language and people and nation; you have made them to be a kingdom and priests serving our God, and they will reign on earth."
The narrator	Four living creatures	5:14	Amen!

Appendix

Speaker and seer	Related Characters Heavenly beings	Related verse(s) Receiver	Content of messages	
John	One of four living creatures		6:1	Come!
The narrator	One of four living creatures		15:7–8	Gave the seven angels seven golden bowls full of the wrath of God, who lives forever and ever; and the temple was filled with smoke from the glory of God and from his power, and no one could enter the temple until the seven plagues of the seven angels were ended.
The narrator	Four living creatures		19:4	fell down and worshiped God who is seated on the throne, saying, "Amen. Hallelujah!"
John	The souls of those who had been slaughtered		6:9–10	Slaughtered for the word of God and their testimony. "Sovereign Lord, holy and true, how long will it be before you judge and avenge our blood on the inhabitants of the earth?"
John	The souls of those who had been beheaded		20:4	Beheaded for their testimony to Jesus and for the word of God. They had not worshiped the beast or its image and had not received its mark on their foreheads or their hands. They came to life and reigned with Christ a thousand years.
The narrator	The altar		16:7	Yes, O The Lord God, the Almighty, your judgments are true and just!

Afterword

WE RECOMMEND TO STUDENTS of the book of Revelation, which of course includes scholars, the new and fresh book *A Dynamic Reading of the Holy Spirit in Revelation* by Hee Youl Lee. For centuries, and especially during the last one hundred fifty years, both lay and scholarly Christians have wrestled with the Apocalypse of John almost exclusively from an eschatological viewpoint, seeking to overlay past, present, and future historical events into the map of the twenty-two chapters of Revelation. Many have urged a preterit interpretation, placing the events of chapters 6–19 entirely into the first century AD, with emperors Nero and Domitian filling the major interpretational roles. Then came the historicists, who saw chapters 6–19 as mapping out the world's future from Nero in the first century on to the French Revolution, World War I, and beyond.

The futurists, in contrast, saw most of the events of these chapters as portraying the happenings of the final seven years pivoting on Daniel 9:27 and Matthew 24:15's eschatological chronology. Actually, I lean toward this view. Still others see the book of Revelation as a book in code for the "Gnostics" of today in-the-know (i.e., it was either viewed as a secret book of philosophy, or even of love).

Now we are presented with Dr. Lee's entirely new way to examine and study this wondrous book, focusing on its portrayal of the dynamic work of the Holy Spirit, the divine author and instrumentality of the working of the book in this world. It is as if we were examining a complex object from the outside and surmising its purpose, when suddenly we are offered to view it through an x-ray machine. We at last view different aspects of it that we had never before seen or even considered.

I recommend this work to the reader for a fresh view of the Apocalypse, and for the blessed insights that will be gained thereby. Dr. Lee

Afterword by Gary G. Cohen

not only gives us these insights, but using his background in studying Muslim culture in Indonesia, he is a guide who points out new vistas to us. Is this book the last word of the book of Revelation? No, no book is until the consummation of all things becomes a reality. Nevertheless it is recommended to the Christian readership for offering a fresh aspect, one not often noticed of the Apocalypse, which when studied piously should surely bring the reader into a deeper Christian spiritual experience.

Gary G. Cohen, ThD

Bibliography

Abrams, M. H. *A Glossary of Literary Terms*. Fort Worth: Harcourt Brace Jovanovich College Publishers, 1993.
Alter, R. *The Art of Biblical Narrative*. New York: Basic Books, 1981.
Aristotle. *Poetics. Aristotle in 23 Volumes*. Vol. 23. Translated by W. H. Fyfe. London: William Heinemann, 1932.
Ashbaugh, K. *Studies in Daniel and Revelation*. Brushton, NY: TEACH Services, 2004.
Aune, D. E. *Revelation 1-5*. Dallas, TX: Word Books, 1997.
———. *Revelation 6-16*. Dallas, TX: Word Books, 1998.
———. *Revelation 17-22*. Dallas, TX: Word Books, 1998.
Bal, M. *Narratologie: Essais sur la signification narrative dans quatre romans modernes*. Paris: Klincksieck, 1977.
Barnett, P. "Polemical Parallelism: Some Further Reflections on the Apocalypse." *JSNT* 35 (1989) 111-20.
Barr, D. L. "The Apocalypse as a Symbolic Transformation of the World: A Literary Analysis." *Int* 38 (1984) 39-50.
———. *Reading the Book of Revelation: A Resource for Students*. Leiden: Brill, 2003.
———. *The Reality of Apocalypse: Rhetoric and Politics in the Book of Revelation*. Leiden: Brill, 2006.
———. *Tales of the End: A Narrative Commentary on the Book of Revelation*. Santa Rosa, CA: Polebridge, 1998.
———. "Using Plot to Discern Structure in John's Apocalypse." *Proceedings of the Eastern Great Lakes and Mid-West Biblical Societies* 15 (1995) 23-33.
Bauckham, R. J. *The Climax of Prophecy: Studies on the Book of Revelation*. Edinburgh: T. & T. Clark, 1993.
———. *Holy War in the Book of Revelation*. Nottingham: Shaftesbury Project, 1987.
———. *The Theology of the Book of Revelation*. Cambridge: Cambridge University Press, 1993.
Beale, G. K. *The Book of Revelation: A Commentary on the Greek Text*. Grand Rapids: Eerdmans, 1998.
———. *John's Use of the Old Testament in Revelation*. Sheffield: Sheffield Academic, 1998.
———. *The Use of Daniel in Jewish Apocalyptic Literature and in the Revelation of St. John*. London: University Press of America, 1984.
Beasley-Murray, G. R. *The Book of Revelation*. London: Oliphants, 1974.
Bell J. S. *Plot and Structure: Techniques and Exercises for Crafting a Plot that Grips Readers from Start to Finish*. Cincinnati, OH: Writer's Digest, 2004.

Bibliography

Ben-Daniel, J., and G. Ben-Daniel. *The Apocalypse in the Light of the Temple: A New Approach to the Book of Revelation.* Jerusalem: Beit Yochanan, 2003.
Best, E. *Mark: The Gospel as Story.* Edinburgh: T. & T. Clark, 1983.
Bewes, R. *The Lamb Wins!: A Guided Tour Through the Book of Revelation.* Fearn, Scotland, UK: Christian Focus, 2000.
Blomberg, Craig. "The Structure of 2 Corinthians 1–7." *Criswell Theological Review* 4 (1989) 3–20.
Bodson, G. R. *Cracking the Apocalypse Code: The Shocking Secrets of the Book of Revelation Decoded.* Shaftesbury: Element, 2000.
Booth, W. C. *The Rhetoric of Fiction.* Harmondsworth: Penguin, 1983.
Boring, M. E. "Narrative Christology in the Apocalypse." *CBQ* 54 (1992) 701–23.
———. "The Theology of Revelation: 'The Lord our God the Almighty Reigns.'" *Int* 40 (1986) 257–69.
Bowman, J. W. *The Drama of the Book of Revelation.* Philadelphia: Westminter, 1955.
Brooks, P. *Reading for the Plot: Design and Intention in Narrative.* Cambridge, MA: Harvard University Press, 1984.
Bruce, F. F., ed. *The Spirit in the Apocalypse: Christ and Spirit in the New Testament.* Cambridge: Cambridge University Press, 1973.
Campbell, W. *The Book of the Revelation of Jesus Christ.* Tresta: Open Bible Trust; Winona, MN: Bible Search Publications, 2000.
Carey, G. *Elusive Apocalypse: Reading Authority in the Revelation to John.* Macon, GA: Mercer, 1999.
Carrell, P. R. *Jesus and the Angels: Angelology and the Christology of the Apocalypse of John.* Cambridge: Cambridge University Press, 1997.
Charles, R. H. *The Apocrypha and Pseudepigrapha of the Old Testament in English with Introductions and Critical and Explanatory Notes to the Several Books.* Oxford: Clarendon, 1913.
———. *A Critical and Exegetical Commentary on the Revelation of St. John.* Edinburgh: T. & T. Clark, 1920.
Chatman, S. B. "On the Formalist-Structuralist Theory of Character." *JLS* 1 (1972) 57–79.
———. *Story and Discourse: Narrative Structure in Fiction and Film.* Ithaca, NY: Cornell University Press, 1978.
Collins, A. Yabro. *The Combat Myth in the Book of Revelation.* Missoula, MT: Scholars Press, 1976.
———. *Cosmology and Eschatology in Jewish and Christian Apocalypticism.* Leiden: Brill, 2000.
———. *Crisis and Catharsis: The Power of the Apocalypse.* Philadelphia: Westminster, 1984.
Collins, J. J. "Introduction: Towards the Morphology of a Genre." *Semeia* 14 (1979) 1–20.
———, ed. "The Jewish Apocalypses." *Semeia* 14 (1979) 21–65.
———, ed. *Semeia 14: Apocalypse: The Morphology of a Genre.* Atlanta: Society of Biblical Literature, 1979.
Court, J. M. *The Book of Revelation and the Johannine Apocalyptic Tradition.* Sheffield: Sheffield Academic, 2000.
———. *Myth and History in the Book of Revelation.* London: SPCK, 1979.

Culpepper, R. A. *Anatomy of the Fourth Gospel: A Study in Literary Design.* Philadelphia: Fortress, 1983.
Darr, J. A. *On Character Building: The Reader and the Rhetoric of Characterization in Luke-Acts.* Louisville, KY: Westminster/John Knox, 1992.
De Smidt, J. C. "The Holy Spirit in the Book of Revelation–Nomenclature." *Neotestamentica* 28 no. 1 (1994) 229–44.
De Smidt, K. "Hermeneutical Perspectives on the Spirit in the Book of Revelation." *Journal of Pentecostal Theology* 7 (1999) 27–47.
Desrosiers, G. *An Introduction to Revelation.* London: Continuum, 2000.
Du Preez, J. "Die Koms van die koninkryk volgens die boek openbaring." *Annale University van Stellenbosch*, vol. 2, serie B, no. 1. Cape Town: Nasionale, 1979.
———. "The Holy Spirit and the Church in the Book of Revelation." *Kerugma* 11 no. 39 (1971) 48–54.
———. "The Holy Spirit in the Book of Revelation." *RES Theological Bulletin* 2 no. 3 (1974) 1–10.
Du Rand, J. A. *Johannine Perspective.* Midrand: Orion, 1991.
———. "'. . . Let Him Hear What the Spirit Says . . .': The Functional Role and Theological Meaning of the Spirit in the Book of Revelation." *Ex Auditu* 12 (1997) 43–58.
———. "A Socio-Psychological View of the Effect of the Language (Parole) of the Apocalypse of John." *Neotestamentica* 24 (1990) 351–65.
———. "'. . . Your Kingdom Come . . . on Earth as it is in Heaven': The Theological Motif of the Apocalypse of John." *Neotestamentica* 31 (1997) 75–91.
Duff, P. B. *Who Rides the Beast?: Prophetic Rivalry and the Rhetoric of Crisis in the Churches of the Apocalypse.* Oxford: Oxford University Press, 2001.
Egan, K. "What is the Plot?" *NLH* 9 (1978) 455–73.
Ewen, J. *Character in Narrative.* Tel Aviv: Sifriat Poalim, 1980.
———. "The Theory of Character in Narrative Fiction." *Hasifrut* 3 (1971) 1–30.
Farrer, A. M. *A Rebirth of Images: The Making of St. John's Apocalypse.* Boston: Beacon, 1949.
———. *The Revelation of St. John the Divine.* Oxford: Clarendon, 1964.
Fiorenza, E. S. *The Book of Revelation: Justice and Judgment.* Philadelphia: Fortress, 1985.
———. "Composition and Structure of the Book of Revelation." *CBQ* 30 (1977) 537–69.
———. *Revelation: Vision of a Just World.* Minneapolis, MN: Fortress, 1991.
Fish, S. E. *Is There a Text in this Classic?* Cambridge, MA: Harvard University Press, 1980.
Ford, J. Massyngberde. "For The Testimony of Jesus in the Spirit of Prophecy." *Irish Theological Quarterly* 42 (1975) 284–91.
Frye, Northrop. *The Great Code: The Bible and Literature.* New York: Mariner, 2002.
Gager, J. *Kingdom and Community: The Social World of Early Christianity.* Englewood Cliffs: Prentice Hall, 1975.
Garrow, A. J. P. *Revelation.* London: Routledge, 1997.
Genette, G. *Narrative Discourse.* Ithaca, NY: Cornell University Press, 1980.
Giblin, C. H. *The Book of Revelation: The Open Book of Prophecy.* Collegeville, MN: Liturgical, 1991.
———. "Recapitulation and the Literary Coherence of John's Apocalypse." *CBQ* 56 (1994) 81–95.

Glasson, T. F. *The Revelation of John*. Cambridge: Cambridge University Press, 1965.
Greimas, A. J. *Structural Semantics: An Attempt at a Method*. Lincoln: University of Nebraska Press, 1991.
Hartman, L. "An Attempt at a Text-Centered Exegesis of John 21." *Studia Theologia* 38 (1984) 29–45.
———. "Survey of the Problem of Apocalyptic Genre." In *Apocalypticism in the Mediteranean World and the Near East*, edited by D. Hellholms, 12–17. Tubingen: Mohr [Siebeck], 1983.
Herms, R. *An Apocalypse for the Church and for the World: A Literary-Narrative and Tradition-Historical Reading of the Book of Revelation*. Durham: University of Durham, 1984.
Hill, D. "Prophecy and Prophets in the Revelation of John." *NTS* 18 (1971) 401–18.
Hellholm, D. *Das Visionenbuch des Hermas als Apokalypse: Formgeschichtliche und texttheoretische Studien zu einer literarischen Gattung*. Lund, Sweden: Gleerup, 1980.
———. "The Problem of Apocalyptic Genre and the Apocalypse of John." *Semeia* 36 (1986) 13–64.
Hosier, J. *The Lamb, the Beast and the Devil: Making Sense of the Book of Revelation*. London: Monarch, 2002.
Hur, J. *A Dynamic Reading of the Holy Spirit in Luke-Acts. Journal for the Study of the New Testament*. Supplement series 211. Sheffield: Sheffield Academic, 2001.
Iser, W. *The Act of Reading: A Theory of Aesthetic Response*. Baltimore: Johns Hopkins University Press, 1978.
———. *The Implied Reader: Patterns of Communication in Prose Fiction from Bunyan to Beckett*. Baltimore: Johns Hopkins University Press, 1974.
Jang Y. "A Narratological Approach to the Structure of the Apocalypse of John." PhD diss., University of Stellenbosch, South Africa, 2001.
Jauhiainen, M. *The Use of Zechariah in Revelation*. Tübingen: Mohr Siebeck, 2005.
Jeske, R. L. "Spirit and Community in the Johannine Apocalypse." *NTS* 31 no. 3 (1985) 452–66.
Johns, L. L. "The Origins and Rhetorical Force of the Lamb Christology of the Apocalypse of John." Phd diss., Princeton Theological Seminary, 1998.
Keller, C. *Apocalypse Now and Then: A Feminist Guide to the End of the World*. Boston: Beacon, 1996.
Kempson, W. R. "Theology in The Revelation of John." PhD diss., Southern Baptist Theological Seminary, Louisville, KY, 1982.
Kingsbury, J. D. *Matthew as Story*. Philadelphia: Fortress, 1986.
Klund, R. W. "The Plot of Revelation 4–22." PhD diss., Dallas Theological Seminary, 2002.
Knight, J. *Revelation*. Sheffield: Sheffield Academic, 1999.
Krieg, R. A. *Story-Shaped Christology: The Role of Narrative in Identifying Jesus Christ*. New York: Paulist, 1988.
Lambrecht, J. *L'Apocalypse Johannique et L'Apocalyptique Dans Le Nouveau Testament*. Leuven: Leuven Universitiy Press, 1980.
Lee, D. *The Narrative Asides in the Book of Revelation*. Oxford: University Press of America, 2002.
Lee, P. *The New Jerusalem in the Book of Revelation: A Study of Revelation 21–22 in the Light of Its Background in Jewish Tradition*. Tübingen: Mohr Siebeck, 2001.

Lee, H. Y. "The Concept of the Messianic War and the Role of Christians in the Messianic War in Revelation." MA Thesis, University of Bristol and Trinity College, Bristol, UK, 2000.
Lee, Michelle V. "A Call to Martyrdom: Function as Method and Message in Revelation." *Novum Testamentum* 40 (1998) 164–94.
Lindsey, H. *The Late Great Planet Earth*. Grand Rapids: Eerdmans, 1970.
Lundin, R. *Disciplining Hermeneutics: Interpretation in Christian Perspective*. Leicester, England: Eerdmans, 1997.
Malbon, E. S. *Narrative Space and Mythic Meaning in Mark*. Sheffield: JSOT, 1991.
Malbon, E. S., and E. V. McKnight. *The New Literary Criticism and the New Testament*. Sheffield: Sheffield Academic, 1994).
Malina, B. J. *On the Genre and Message of Revelation: Star Visions and Sky Journeys*. Peabody, MA: Hendrickson, 1995.
Malina, B. J., and J. J. Pilch. *Social-Science Commentary on the Book of Revelation*. Minneapolis, MN: Fortress, 2000.
———. *Social Scientific Models for Interpreting the Bible: Essays by the Context Group in Honor of Bruce J. Malina*. Leiden: Brill, 2001.
Martin, W. *Recent Theories of Narrative*. New York: Cornell University Press, 1986.
Matera, F. J. "The Plot of Mathew's Gospel." *CBQ* 49 (1987) 233–53.
Mazzaferri, F. D. *The Genre of the Book of Revelation from a Source-Critical Perspective*. Aberdeen: University of Aberdeen, 1986.
McCormack, P. J. "The Nature of Judgment in the Book of the Revelation." Phd diss., Queen's University of Belfast, 2001.
McKenzie, S. L., and S. R. Haynes. *To Each Its Own Meaning: An Introduction to Biblical Criticisms and Their Application*. Westminster: John Knox, 1993.
Michaels, J. R. "Revelation 1:19 and The Narrative Voices of the Apocalypse." *NTS* 37 (1991) 604–20.
Miller, J. *Apocalypse 2000: The Book of Revelation*. Berkeley, CA: Seastone, 1998.
Moor, J. C. de, ed. *Synchronic or Diachronic?: A Debate on Method in Old Testament Exegesis*. Leiden: Brill, 1995.
Morris, S. L. *The Drama of Christianity: An Interpretation of the Book of Revelation*. London: Wakeman Trust, 2002.
Mounce, R. H. *The Book of Revelation*. Cambridge: Eerdmans, 1998.
Moyise, S. *Studies in the Book of Revelation*. Edinburgh: T. &T. Clark, 2001.
Munger, M. A. *The Rhetoric and Function of Angels in the Book of Revelation*. Deerfield, IL: Trinity International University, 1998.
Murphy, F. J. *Fallen is Babylon: The Revelation to John*. Harrisburg: Trinity Press International, 1998.
Newport, K. G. C. *Apocalypse and Millennium: Studies in Biblical Eisegesis*. Cambridge: Cambridge University Press, 2000.
Patte, D. *The Religious Dimensions of Biblical Texts: Greimas's Structural Semiotics and Biblical Exegesis*. Atlanta, GA: Scholars Press, 1990.
———. *Structural Exegesis for New Testament Critics*. Minneapolis: Fortress, 1990.
———. *What is Structural Exegesis?* Philadelphia: Fortress, 1976.
Pattemore, S. W. *The People of God in the Apocalypse: Discourse, Structure, and Exegesis*. Cambridge: Cambridge University Press, 2004.
Peters, O. K. *The Mandate of the Church in the Apocalypse of John*. New York: Peter Lang, 2004.

Bibliography

Pippin, T. *Apocalyptic Bodies: The Biblical End of the World in Text and Image.* London: Routledge, 1999.
Powell, M. A. *What is Narrative Criticism?* London: SPCK, 1993.
Resseguie, J. L. *Revelation Unsealed: A Narrative Critical Approach to John's Apocalypse.* Leiden: Brill, 1998.
Rhoads, D. M., and D. Michie. *Mark as Story: An Introduction to the Narrative of a Gospel.* Philadelphia: Fortress, 1982.
Rhoads, D. M., et al. *Mark as Story: A Introduction to the Narrative of a Gospel.* Minneapolis, MN: Fortress, 1999.
Rhoads, D. M., and K. Syreeni. *Characterization in the Gospels: Reconceiving Narrative Criticism.* Sheffield: Sheffield Academic, 1999.
Rimmon-Kenan, S. *A Glance Beyond Doubt: Narration, Representation, Subjectivity.* Columbus: Ohio State University Press, 1996.
———. *Narrative Fiction: Contemporary Poetics.* London: Methuen, 1983.
———. *Narrative Fiction: Contemporary Poetics.* 2nd ed. London: Routledge, 2002.
Rogers, A. *Unveiling the End Times in Our Time: The Triumph of the Lamb in Revelation.* Nashville, TN: Broadman & Holman, 2004.
Roloff, J. *The Revelation of John.* Minneapolis, MN: Fortress, 1993.
Rossing, B. R. *The Rapture Exposed: The Message of Hope in the Book of Revelation.* Oxford: Westview, 2004.
Schooling, S. J. *The Structure of the Book of Revelation: A Discourse Analysis Perspective.* Bristol: University of Bristol, 2004.
Shannon, F. H., and R. Elliot. *The Scroll With Seven Seals: What the Book of Revelation Really Says.* Alhambra, CA: Green Leaf, 2004.
Sheeley, S. M. *Narrative Asides in Luke–Acts.* Bloomington, IN: JSOT, 1992.
Shepherd, M. *The Paschal Liturgy and the Apocalypse.* Richmond, VA: John Knox, 1960.
Shepherd, W. H., Jr. *The Narrative Function of the Holy Spirit as a Character in Luke-Acts.* Atlanta: Scholars Press, 1994.
Siew, T. *The War Between the Two Beasts and the Two Witnesses: A Chiastic Reading of Revelation 11:1—14:5.* London: T. & T. International, 2005.
Smith, C. R. "The Structure of the Book of Revelation in the Light of Apocalypse Literary Conventions." *NovT* 36 (1994) 373–93.
Snyder, B. W. "Combat Myth in the Apocalypse: The Liturgy of the Day of the Lord and the Dedication of the Heavenly Temple." PhD Diss., Graduate Theological Union and University of California, Berkeley, 1991.
Stauffer, E. *Christ and the Caesars: Historical Sketches.* London: SCM, 1955.
Stevenson, G. *Power and Place: Temple and Identity in the Book of Revelation.* New York: Walter de Gruyter, 2001.
Stibbe, W. G. *John as Storyteller: Narrative Criticism and the Fourth Gospel.* Cambridge: Cambridge University Press, 1994.
Stuckenbruck, L. C. *Angel Veneration and Christology: A Study in Early Judaism and in the Christology of the Apocalypse of John.* Tubingen: J. C. B. Mohr, 1995.
Sweet, C. *Hell and Judgment in the Book of Revelation.* Reading, UK: Open Bible Trust, 1992.
Swete, H. B. *Commentary on Revelation.* Grand Rapids: Kregel, 1977.
Talbert, C. H. *The Apocalypse: A Reading of the Revelation of John.* Westminster: John Knox, 1994.
Tannehill, R. C. *The Narrative Unity of Luke-Acts.* Philadelphia: Fortress, 1986.

Bibliography

Tate, W. R. *Biblical Interpretation: An Integrated Approach*. Peabody, MA: Hendrickson, 1991.
Tenney, M. C. *Interpreting Revelation*. Grand Rapids: Eerdmans, 1957.
Thompson, L. L. *The Book of Revelation: Apocalypse and Empire*. New York: Oxford University Press, 1990.
Thomson, R. *The Book of Revelation*. London: Bloomsbury, 1999.
Tompkins, J. P. *Reader-Response Criticism: From Formalism to Post-Structuralism*. Baltimore: Johns Hopkins University Press, 1980.
Trafton, J. L. *Reading Revelation: A Literary and Theological Commentary*. Macon, GA: Smyth & Helwys, 2005.
Turner, E. *The Triumph of the Lamb: A Guide to the Book of Revelation*. Moseley, Birmingham, UK: Power of Truth, 2002.
Ulfgard, H. *Feast and Future: Revelation 7:9-17 and the Feast of Tabernacles*. Lund: Wallin & Dalholm, 1989.
Uspensky, B. A., et al. *A Poetics of Composition: The Structure of the Artistic Text and Typology of a Compositional Form*. Translated by Valentina Zavarin and Susan Wittig. Berkeley: University of California Press, 1973.
Van Dijk, T. A. *Macrostructures: An Interdisciplinary Study of Global Structure in Discourse, Interaction, and Cognition*. Hillsdale, MI: Lawrence Erlbaum, 1980.
———. *Text and Context: Explorations in the Semantics and Pragmatics of Discourse*. London: Longman, 1977.
Viduya, J. T. *The Book of Revelation, the Mystery Finally Unveiled (Volume One): The Seven Churches*. Burbank, CA: Fiesta Manila, 2004.
Wall, R. W. *Revelation*. Peabody, MA: Hendrickson, 1991.
Walvoord, J. F. *The Revelation of Jesus Christ*. Chicago: Moody, 1966.

www.ingramcontent.com/pod-product-compliance
Lightning Source LLC
Chambersburg PA
CBHW071239230426
43668CB00011B/1502